PENGUIN
COMPASS

THE RELUCTANT SAINT

Donald Spoto, who earned his Ph.D. degree in theology at Fordham University, taught religious studies, Biblical literature, and
Christian mysticism on the university level for more than twenty
years. His other eighteen books include internationally bestselling
biographies of Alfred Hitchcock, Laurence Olivier, Tennessee
Williams, and Ingrid Bergman. He lives in Los Angeles, California.

DONALD SPOTO

Reluctant Saint

The Life of
Francis of Assisi

PENGUIN COMPASS

PENGUIN COMPASS
Published by the Penguin Group
Penguin Group (USA) Inc., 375 Hudson Street,
New York, New York 10014, U.S.A.
Penguin Books Ltd, 80 Strand,
London WC2R 0RL, England
Penguin Books Australia Ltd, 250 Camberwell Road, Camberwell,
Victoria 3124, Australia
Penguin Books Canada Ltd, 10 Alcorn Avenue,
Toronto, Ontario, Canada M4V 3B2
Penguin Books India (P) Ltd, 11 Community Centre, Panchsheel Park,
New Delhi - 110 017, India
Penguin Books (N.Z.) Ltd, Cnr Rosedale and Airborne Roads, Albany,
Auckland, New Zealand
Penguin Books (South Africa) (Pty) Ltd, 24 Sturdee Avenue,
Rosebank, Johannesburg 2196, South Africa

Penguin Books Ltd, Registered Offices:
80 Strand, London WC2R 0RL, England

First published in the United States of America by Viking Compass,
a member of Penguin Putnam Inc., 2002
Published in Penguin Compass 2003

1   3   5   7   9   10   8   6   4   2

Frontispiece: Giotto di Bondone (1266–1336). *Saint Francis Receives the Stigmata*, from
The Story of Saint Francis cycle. Cappella Bardi, Sta. Croce, Florence, Italy.
Scala/Art Resource, New York.

ISBN 0-670-03128-3 (hc.)
ISBN 0 14 21.9625 8 (pbk.)
CIP data available

Printed in the United States of America
Set in Fournier
Designed by Francesca Belanger

for Frederica von Stade—

great artist and cherished friend

"To sing is to pray twice."
—SAINT AUGUSTINE

Acknowledgments

My litany of saints includes many generous people and good friends whose practical assistance and support accompanied me at every stage in the preparation of this book.

Alice Gallin, O.S.U., facilitated my introduction to the Franciscan Institute of St. Bonaventure University, one of the world's great repositories of Franciscana. I must thank Margaret Carney, O.S.F., who is the Institute's director and the Dean of the School of Franciscan Studies, and Noel H. Riggs, the Executive Administrative Assistant.

At the Walters Art Museum, Baltimore, I received important assistance from Cathleen A. Fleck and Teresa Nevins in the Department of Manuscripts and Rare Books and from Kate Lau, the coordinator of photographic services.

The expertise of several gifted physicians was invaluable: in this regard, I am grateful to Graham Waring, M.D., who discussed epidemiology, tropical diseases and intestinal illnesses relative to the life of Francis of Assisi; and to John Hofbauer, M.D., and Laura Fox, M.D., who provided critical information on the etiology and history of trachoma.

For assistance with special problems in medieval Italian history, John Darretta as usual offered timely help—as did Irene Mahoney, O.S.U., whose wide-ranging scholarship includes fine points in the history of Western Christian spirituality.

In Rome and Assisi, my tasks were much facilitated by the guidance of two first-rate scholars, Lewis Falb and Gerald Pinciss. Also in Rome and Assisi, I was much helped by Stefano Bonimi, who seems to know how to get anywhere and find anything. In Paris, Matthieu Louanges made important and obscure sources available to me.

For 25 years, Elaine Markson has been my literary representative; she has guided my career with unfailingly astute counsel and faithful friendship. In her offices, I receive constant daily support and cheerful assistance from

Gary Johnson, Geri Thoma, Sara De Nobrega, Elizabeth Shenkman and Kirsten Neuhaus.

The idea for this book originated with George Stelzner, who thought it would also provide the basis for an important film documentary. That it has been doubly realized owes much to his encouragement—not to say his dedication as the producer of the motion picture.

Richard P. Kot, my editor at Viking, offered not only the benefits of his scholarship, his love of language and his passion for clarity in all its exactitude: Rick has also extended to me the long arm of his friendship. He guided this book at every step and contributed to it wisely. I am glad and grateful that we are even now committed to further collaboration.

On the dedication page appears a name well known to millions, for she is one of the great artists of our time.

The mezzo-soprano Frederica von Stade, who has appeared on the stage of every major opera house and concert hall in the world, continues to delight audiences as she has for over 30 years—just as an enormous company of admirers values her many recordings. Composers have created operas for her, conductors from all over the world have vied to work with her and singers, actors, writers and directors (both the experts and the novices) learn a great deal from her impeccable musicianship and unerring interpretations. It is universally acknowledged that, in both operatic roles and in recital, she has very few peers.

Flicka (as she is known to her friends) also spends her considerable energies on behalf of a wide range of important humanitarian and educational organizations; her profound dedication to people and their needs is inspiring. A woman of extraordinary generosity, warmth and spiritual wisdom, she enriches every life she touches.

I rejoice in the depth of her devoted friendship, her encouragement and her constancy. Francis of Assisi, who was a singer and a poet, would have applauded her artistry and admired her faith. Like him, Frederica von Stade makes the world a better place—and in ways past counting.

D.S.

Los Angeles
Easter 2002

Contents

Introduction

ALMOST 40 YEARS AGO, the translators of a biography of Francis of Assisi undertook a count of the books and articles the French author had consulted. Their final tally was 1,575 works in four languages. Up to and since that time, no saint has been the object of more attention from historians and biographers.

But even the last century's most important books on Francis—by Sabatier (1906), Jörgensen (1912), Fortini (1959) and Engelbert (1965)— were severely limited. Since their publications, discoveries made in a number of fields, and especially the results of Franciscan scholarship since 1990, have been extremely significant and directly affect our understanding of the times and events in Francis's life. Curiously, no writer (so far as I can tell) has taken these studies into account and pursued their implications for a thorough and up-to-date biography. Hence the book you are now reading.

At the outset of my research, I quickly surveyed about 350 articles in five languages, covering only the contributions of the past decade— archival work in the fields of medieval history, biography, medicine and education; the annals of art; and literary, linguistic and archaeological studies. As my investigation expanded to include the contributions of those who worked before 1990, I became ever more convinced of the need for a new life of Francis for the general reader who is not a specialist.

At first, the sheer weight of new material—and the data that continued to surface each month—seemed overwhelming. In fact, there were so many important books and articles by learned men and women that, in the early months of my research, I nearly despaired: there were resources, for example, on the fine points of assessing manuscripts from the Middle Ages; on medieval economics; on the history of the Crusades; on the chronicles of the commune of Assisi; on the early years of Francis; on his illnesses and the tradition of the stigmata; and on the problems inherent in studying commentaries that in some cases are almost 800 years old.

Today, the scholarship is being produced everywhere, by university professors and archivists in Italy, Germany, France and America, and from contributors in Spain, Holland and Brazil. In America, in 2001, a trio of editors—working with 16 translators, eight consultants and nine technical assistants—published the last of three volumes of medieval literature on Francis. Together, these hefty tomes contain 2,362 pages.

I continued only because, after this start, I was incurably intrigued. Concerning Francis's own writings and letters, for example, there have been major discoveries that are notably absent from recent books. Although he was no scholar and in fact had little formal education, Francis was a born poet and an irrepressible singer. He wrote in medieval Latin and in Umbrian Italian, and he composed (so far as we know) the first Italian song. That is but one area much neglected.

To begin to know Francis, we must try to view him as much as possible outside the framework of our modern preconceptions; we must try, in other words, to see him as a medieval Italian, a man with a specific understanding of reality that was in important ways different from, and even opposed to, our own. This approach presents many challenges, and not only because Francis died almost 800 years ago. For one thing, dates are very difficult to fix, for no standard method of measuring time existed until almost 1890. Only then did most (but not all) of the so-called developed world agree to mark the beginning of a day from the stroke of midnight, and to measure hours from points in Greenwich, England, and the arbitrarily created International Date Line.

The problem of time also presents a number of historical and literary dilemmas that take us all the way back to the 13th century. In that era, testimonies of individual lives were not chronologically but thematically ordered, and narratives of saints were written to edify, to authenticate holiness or to encourage devotion. Today we believe that biographical inquiry ought to be as objective as possible and concern itself only with empirical data, but there was no such restriction centuries ago. Then, exaggeration and embellishment were seen not as the license of fiction or as misrepresentation but rather as the basic tools of hagiography, or writing about the saints.

The phenomenon of Francis also bears the burden of some long-established legends, often based on romantic sentiment for the age of castles, knights, fair ladies and chivalric honor—motifs far more suited to the pages of illuminated manuscripts or to Hollywood films than ever they were in real life.

The vocabularies of the saints and those who wrote and write about them likewise often reflect eras in which certain presumptions were made about institutional supremacy, with an almost smug self-reference. This has been especially evident since 1234, when Pope Gregory IX decreed that only popes had the authority to canonize; before then, saints were chosen locally, by acclamation of the people and usually with the endorsement of their bishops. (It was Gregory, in fact, who canonized his old friend from Assisi in 1228, less than two years after Francis's death.)

We need not only a scholarly methodology but also a process of intuition and of discernment so that we can isolate some of the sure facts hidden beneath ancient styles. Since the 19th century, for example, it is axiomatic that the authors of the New Testament were writing for people who found themselves in critical situations decades after the time of Jesus of Nazareth—people seeking the meaning of faith, coping with political and legal ostracism, and grappling with divisions among themselves. The four gospels, in other words, were responses to community needs in light of faith in the ongoing presence of the Risen Christ.

The goal was similar for the writers about Francis of Assisi, who used contemporary literary forms to present the truth as they perceived it. Just as we must carefully study the Bible in order to determine what its writers intended in the context of their own language and within the constraints of their own time, so we must exercise the same caution in examining the early biographies of Francis.

More than a dozen accounts of Francis's life were circulated during the first century after his canonization, and anyone undertaking a biography today has to consider the uneven value of these sources, their credibility, the degree of their mutual interdependence and the motivation for their composition.

For the most part, a process of idealization set in as soon as Francis was canonized. The first widely known biography, for example—that of the Franciscan friar Thomas of Celano, who knew his subject personally and whose first life of Francis appeared in 1229 or 1230—clearly intended not only the celebration of a saint but also the promotion of the Order he supposedly intended to found.

That was even more the goal of Giovanni da Fidanza, a great philosopher, theologian and mystic otherwise known as Saint Bonaventure. His Franciscan colleagues commissioned him to glorify the Order by writing the official life of Francis. After reading other accounts and speaking with many people, he produced a remarkable work—a highly imaginative and pious book, to be sure, but one whose political agenda has to be considered very carefully indeed. As Octavian Schmucki, one of the great Franciscan scholars of the 20th century (and a devoted friar), has cautioned, we must be wary of "Bonaventure's general untrustworthiness in handling historical data." Beneath the surface of Bonaventure's work, one can discern the bitter struggles then raging not only within the Franciscan Order but also between factions within other Church groups.

After Bonaventure completed his work, some forty years after Francis's death, a command went forth from the Franciscans that everything previously written about the saint was to be destroyed—even the writings by the founder's closest friends. Fortunately, these orders were never completely carried out, for numerous accounts preceding Bonaventure's that are extremely valuable were spared. Studies of these manuscripts continue today, and I have tried to consider most of what has been done in this area up through the year 2001. The Notes section at the end of this book provides details on these sources.

As for Francis's own writings: about three dozen documents have also come down to us. These exhortations, letters to groups and to individuals, prayers and canticles often cannot be accurately dated, nor can the precise circumstances of their composition be fixed. Rather than belabor the fine points of scholarly debate on this matter, I hope I have not been unfaithful to his spirit in using these primary writings when they are relevant to a particular stage of his life. Again, the Notes try to guide the reader through this particular thicket of history.

But over and above such academic considerations, there is the matter that most defines this man, and that is most problematic for modern readers: he is not Signor Francesco Bernardone but Saint Francis of Assisi. If we treat him as if he were only a wandering preacher from the Middle Ages, an ecologist before his time, a friend to animals or a social rebel, we are missing the point. Just as it would be impossible to write a biography of Thomas Jefferson without considering his passion for 18th-century politics and history, a life of Francis must accept with absolute gravity the fact that he believed in a personal and loving God.

Francis was born in 1182 and died at the age of 44, in 1226. Today, we would count him a man cut off in his prime; at that time, he was considered fortunate to have survived so long. Two years after his death, he was proclaimed a saint. Canonization by decree can be a cunning way to appropriate, to tame and to isolate remarkable people and turn them into the property of official Catholicism. But Francis remains something of a wonderful embarrassment to the Church and the world. His life and example—and not, let it be stressed, anything specific he said or wrote—had an integrity that challenges our presumptions about what constitutes a good life, not to say a respectable approach to religion.

Because so few of the traditional categories of saintliness or holiness seem to have much to say to people today, I have in this book offered some preliminary and tentative ideas toward a fresh understanding of conversion and the nature of authentic holiness. Earlier concepts have with time become too rarefied, linked to an almost absurd idea of perfection and a denial of humanity. Francis, in contrast, seems to me one of the most obviously human and necessary among saints. He was also one of the most reluctant to undertake a spiritual journey—hence my title.

It is critical, I think, to try to shed light on the humanity of Francis, who had little interest in becoming (much less being called) a saint. In fact, his life bears witness to the fact that holiness is not by necessity a denial of one's humanity, or something added on to it. Holiness may in fact be the deepest achievement of what is authentically human. Here we are very close to the Christian mystery of the Incarnation.

Francis has left his mark on the art, literature and history of Western civilization—beginning with Dante, who was born 40 years after his death and who devoted to Francis almost an entire canto of the *Commedia*. It is no exaggeration to say that all subsequent Italian expressions of religious culture are indebted to Francis, from the frescoes of Cimabue and Giotto to the films of Vittorio de Sica and Federico Fellini, which are suffused with a deeply Franciscan sensibility.

Outside of Italy, the so-called Saint Francis Prayer ("Lord, make me an instrument of your peace . . .") lovingly captured the man's spirit in modern times and terms; its author, a French Catholic aristocrat who composed it during the First World War, clearly understood the relevance of Francis the peacemaker and defender of the outcast and the marginalized. And in 1983, the great French composer Olivier Messiaen completed his opera *Saint François d'Assise*, which received its American premiere at exactly the time of this book's publication.

In the American Southwest, and particularly in California, it is impossible to escape the influence of the original Franciscan missions—in art, architecture and in names directly linked to his life: Santa Clara and Santa Cruz, for example, and, obviously, San Francisco. The original name of the city I call home, Los Angeles, simply abbreviates the formal name bestowed by the original settlers: Nuestra Señora la Reyna de los Angeles de Porciúncula—Our Lady Queen of the Angels of the Portiuncula—which is the name of the place, just outside Assisi, that is most identified with Francis, and where he died.

Francis brought the world a life of radical simplicity, unmoored to possessions and therefore free to follow the promptings of grace and the path toward God, wherever and whenever God summoned him. His spirit was one of remarkable spontaneity: he leaped to the needs of others, just as he hurried to catch up with God, Who was always inviting him to a new adventure.

Francis was no theoretician of the spiritual life. He never spoke of God in any but experiential terms, because he was a witness to a living and acting God. He could speak only of what he saw, heard and felt. In this regard, he remains before us, across the centuries, as an example of what God can do—which is primarily to astonish, to alter radically the way we live and move. In the dramatic passages of his own life, and the remarkable ways in which a genial but rather shallow young playboy became a model of service to the world, he revealed that God is present in time and history. In other words, he has such credibility because he demonstrated that we are at our best when we dare to allow God into our lives.

The extremes of Francis's life, during which he passed from playboy to penitent to poor man to saint, reveal an individual who stood at the margin of the world. In his identification with those whom polite society rejects, Francis called into question the folly of relying on money, goods and material things for happiness. He is a figure who appeals to just about everyone, probably because (unlike most saints) he is not Roman Catholic property. The first great modern biography was written by a French Protestant; one of the most important historians of Franciscanism was an Anglican bishop; a powerful novel on his life was written by a Greek Orthodox; and when the Dalai Lama was photographed at a peace conference in Assisi, he chose to be seated at the place Francis most loved, and where he died.

Much in this man's life remains hidden and ambiguous, but one thing is clear beyond argument: for the second half of his life, he was haunted by the presence of God, even as he was suffering most from the ravages of serious disease, blindness and the dissolution of his most cherished hopes. In a way, his life sometimes seems (but only seems) a long struggle with futility; this, I think, is the key to understanding him.

Reluctant Saint has been written from the author's perspective that faith is primarily an attitude about reality. In the final analysis, this is what attracted me to Francis of Assisi—that he saw his journey to God as a process, a constant deepening and adjustment of his aspirations, a refinement of his presumptions about what God wanted and a winnowing of his own good intentions. In that regard, his conversion was not the event of a day but the work of a lifetime.

After all these centuries, that may be why so many people find his life both poignant and pertinent. Francis had a strong sense of self—and an even stronger sense of God.

Reluctant Saint

ONE

1181–1187

IN 1181, the harvest in southern Europe was exceptional—especially in Umbria, a fertile region in central Italy, roughly equidistant between Rome, to the south, and Florence, to the north. In the Spoleto valley, grapevines, olive and mulberry trees, stately cypresses and gnarled oaks shimmered alongside wheat and corn fields in the first light of the autumn days, when peasant families went out to work until dusk.

Men drove oxcarts, leaned makeshift ladders against the tallest trees and worked quickly before thieves and brigands threatened their progress and produce. Their wives and young children accompanied the men, picking and sorting and filling tubs with ripened fruit. In Umbria, as throughout Europe, 90 percent of the population was engaged in agriculture. Some procedures had not altered since the ancient Etruscan civilization, of which traces could still be found.

In the morning's misty coolness, workers could ignore the bees, which seemed almost as lazy and unthreatening as the wandering sheep grazing for breakfast. Occasionally a woman threw a scrap of brightly colored cloth over a vine to discourage the birds, but everyone knew this was mostly a futile gesture. The cloudless sky was usually ostrich-egg blue and the air clean. Breezes carried the scent of rosemary and oleander from neighboring fields.

Tucked onto the lower slope of Mount Subasio, just to the north of this sparkling valley, was the walled and gated commune of Assisi. One of the oldest villages of Italy, it had been nominally Christian since the second century, and had been conquered in 1160 by the Holy Roman Emperor Frederick Barbarossa, who ruled the areas we now call Germany, Austria, Switzerland, France (half of it), the Netherlands and Italy (except for the

Papal States). The people of Assisi did not submit willingly, however, and soon arose in open revolt, which was put down in 1174 by the German prince-bishop Christian of Mainz.

With Assisi uneasily in liege to the emperor, every man had to serve duty on the turrets of the fortress above the town, watching the road westward to Perugia, which was under papal control and so carefully monitored by imperial minions. When he visited Assisi, the emperor lived in the Rocca Maggiore, or fortress, but otherwise it was the residence of his legate. In 1181, that role was filled by Conrad of Urslingen, duke of Spoleto, whose primary responsibility was to ensure that the nobility supported the emperor in a society in which peace had no meaning and war was both a habit and a dominating passion.

§

But on those bright mornings at harvest time in Assisi, one could almost believe a day would pass without violence or threat of war. The red-tiled roofs and rose-colored stone houses reflected the early sunlight, and the narrow, crooked and steep streets echoed with the rattle of carts and with the clatter of shutters on the small windows of homes and shops.

Church bells marked the hours for work and prayer; town criers announced news and legal decisions; jugglers, acrobats and troubadours strolled and leaped in the squares to a cacophony of tambourines and wooden flutes. Everywhere could be heard the cries of geese and chickens, the braying of sheep and the honking of pigs and mules. Life in Assisi was very much an outdoor life, for the houses were cramped and dark.

In the larger squares of Assisi—the Piazza San Rufino, in front of the cathedral, and the Piazza del Comune, the site of the Roman temple of Minerva—women drew water from the fountains while merchants and notaries hurried to attend to the day's first business. Here and there, girls who would be punished when they returned at dawn from a night out shunned (or welcomed) the attentions of young men, themselves still bleary-eyed from carousing. Stopping to improvise a love lyric, the boys in their colorfully patched vests and pants were not as menacing to the girls as the pickpockets, beggars and rapists who seemed to lurk at the corners of every square and alley.

Assisi was frequently referred to as a new Babylon, a place of wild debauchery, where murder and street fights to the death were commonplace. Revenge was considered a right, vendetta almost a sacred duty.

In January 1182, the routines of Assisi were suddenly and roughly altered when a violent storm raged down from the north, striking humans and animals all over the countryside and ravaging crops down to their roots. So began a five-year famine that forced vast segments of the population to live on wild grasses. Chroniclers could not keep track of the casualties, and the rituals of death became a daily occurrence in almost every city and hamlet of the peninsula. Even the imperial and papal courts and the most powerful lords felt the effects of the national disaster.

§

In Assisi, one of the most ambitious and successful of these merchants was a fabric dealer named Peter Bernardone. He sold to the few who could afford them the colorful brocaded cloaks, vests, furred hats, gold collars and gray stocking caps that were sewn in his workshop from materials he obtained farther north. The men he employed in his shop were considered far more fortunate than those who chopped trees, pulled roots, hauled rocks or dug fields.

Commerce in cloth, carpets, silks, towels and muslins was a relatively new business in Europe. Turkish and Indian tribes had been skilled in the textile arts since the early Middle Ages, but they were not introduced into Europe until the Arab conquest of Sicily in the ninth century. Then, about 1130, skilled Greek weavers came to Palermo and began producing elaborate fabrics.

Fifty years later, those who traded successfully could become very rich indeed, and with money—now a dominating force in the economy—came power. The merchant class became more involved in local politics, and alongside Christian devotion (taken for granted, if not always seriously) came a new spirit of anticlericalism and aggressive capitalism.

§

In 1182, a citizen of Assisi was legally classified in one of three groups—the *maiores* (those of "greater" standing, essentially nobles), the *mediani* (of "middling" importance) and the *minores* (of "lesser" importance)—divisions that had been in place for almost two centuries. Because the economy was becoming more complex, however, the term *mediani* was rarely used, and so there was only one practical distinction—whether or not a person was considered significant. With this demarcation came the inevitable struggles, and the *maiores*—who indeed had more power—had to fight increasingly to maintain their social, political and religious dominance. With the rise of the merchant class and the new power of money, it was no longer simply a matter of commoners against lords or nobles: it was a question of social ascendancy.

The battle of the *minores* (now mostly merchants, who were socially if not always financially outcast) was not based on any declaration of what we now call human or civil rights, for such a concept was completely foreign to the Middle Ages. There was, at the time, little sense of what we would later call social justice or shared responsibility; only very rarely would someone make a cause of the welfare of others. On the contrary, the struggle of the *minores* for political power against the nobles was undertaken to separate them from the vast majority of the population, who were grindingly poor. Their goal was not to help anyone but themselves, and that meant dismantling the feudal system and introducing a more egalitarian structure called the commune, a city-state seeking economic independence from the aristocracy, the papacy and the empire.

Peter Bernardone, evidently a well-regarded businessman, had managed to dominate the Assisi market in decorative fabrics, damasks, velvets, furs and cloth of gold and silver for fine apparel. He lived with his wife, Pica, in a half-timbered stucco dwelling, five or six small rooms above his shop, which was probably located between the churches of San Nicolò and San Paolo, near the Piazza del Comune. No matter the economic status of the family, such homes contained only a few wooden chairs, benches and storage chests and a bed, perhaps canopied with dyed fabric. The fine art of decorating furniture had not yet extended to many private homes. Kitchens were primitive, with small fireplaces; outhouses were located in open courtyards between buildings, and no one expected much privacy. Because there were but a few small shuttered windows (mostly without glass, which was used sparingly until the fifteenth century) and because taller buildings flanked the house, daylight rarely penetrated the dark rooms.

But such accommodations were considered good living; the vast majority of families were miserably poor and lived in one or at most two small rooms in a hut, usually sharing their space with their few sheep, pigs or geese, the better to prevent nighttime thievery. The floor was pounded clay, the rafters made of branches, the beds piles of straw.

Peter's business, his and his wife's names and the location of his dwelling are virtually all that we know for certain of the Bernardones before 1182; no archives or documents provide details of their backgrounds or characters.

§

As soon as the fierce storms subsided in the spring of 1182, Peter joined one of the caravans departing for trade in France—a venture that normally occupied him several times a year, for the great cloth markets and textile fairs were flourishing in Toulouse, Montpellier, Burgundy and Flanders. Leaving behind his pregnant wife and her three-year-old son, Angelo (by a first husband who had died), Peter was still absent when, very likely in late September, she gave birth to a son. According to custom, a few days later the infant was taken to the Church of Santa Maria del Vescovado in Assisi, where he was christened. His mother chose the name John, in honor of the Baptist, a popular saint in medieval Italy; last of the prophets, he was the herald and reputed cousin of Jesus of Nazareth.

Some months later, Peter returned in a rage over his wife's choice of the child's forename. In medieval Europe as in the biblical world, enormous significance was attached to the assignment of a name; it was virtually a totem, the carrier of one's destiny as much as the emblem of one's spiritual roots. Peter would not have as his son's patron the ancient desert hermit who (like Elijah in the Old Testament) had dressed in camel's hair and lived on locusts and wild honey.

There was no revoking the baptismal name, but Bernardone insisted that his son henceforth be known as Franciscus, or in the Umbrian dialect then emerging out of late medieval Latin, Francesco—an uncommon but not unknown designation for someone meaning "Frenchman," or we might say, "Frenchy." Peter's boy was thus familiarly named after France, where his father was making his fortune and whence he brought the fashions and forms of social elegance he so admired. From infancy, the boy was addressed as Francesco—in English, Francis.

The destiny of Peter's son, it was understood, would be to assume the management of his father's business and to expand the family fortune by successful international commerce. Like most sons of merchants, young Francis occasionally accompanied his father on his working travels to France and the Netherlands. Thus, at home and abroad, the boy learned a dialect of French (most likely Provençal, the language of the troubadours) just as he did the new forms of the Umbrian idiom, which had not yet become what we know as Italian.

§

Young Francis was fortunate. Most newborns did not survive the first few months, and a majority of those who did never reached adolescence. In the absence of anything like antiseptics, and with little more than a few plants or herbs for medicine, children routinely succumbed to conditions that later became easily treatable, including fevers, influenza, diarrhea and minor infections, which quickly became gruesome and morbid.

Adults, too, were vulnerable to regular epidemics of pneumonia, typhoid, malaria, tuberculosis, smallpox, scarlet fever, leprosy, plague, anthrax, trachoma and a whole legion of other ailments—many of them brought back from the East by traders, soldiers and pilgrims. Syphilis, contracted venereally and passed along to partners and children, was virulent, and in its final stages it left even people in their 20s and 30s blind and mad, wandering the streets of every town in Europe. There was no pure water (even rain was tainted by public squares and wells), or hygienic waste and sewage disposal, and food was quickly subject to spoilage.

Living close to animals and livestock presented other health risks. Pasteurization, refrigeration and careful cooking methods were unknown; spoilage was sometimes retarded by boiling meat or fish or by the heavy application of fiery Moorish spices, but the result was often without nutritional value or flavor. People who survived to adulthood often lost limbs and teeth or were otherwise deformed due to poor diet, birth defects, war or assault.

Quarantine was the most effective tool against contagion. With their rotting limbs and oozing sores, lepers especially (and their number included those with all manner of disfiguring skin conditions) were forced to live in the wilderness, and they could enter villages for food or alms only by sounding a warning with a clapper or bell that sent almost everyone fleeing. Few people came close enough to toss them scraps of food or rags for comfort in wintertime.

Still, it would never have occurred to anyone living during the Middle Ages to ask why life was so wreathed in suffering, or to complain about his lot. Pain and early death were taken for granted, and there was a profound, universal resignation in the face of them. In this context, faith was paramount, for in medieval Europe, it alone provided a way of coping with the grimness of everyday reality.

§

The misery to which all were subject helps to explain the extraordinary double standard of the time regarding another aspect of physical life: sexual customs and behavior. While much that we take for normal was officially held to be sinful by both civil and Church authorities, the conduct of most people was astonishingly unrestrained. Sexual activity (much of it wild and dangerous) was the norm for boys, and although girls were expected to be chaste and eventually monogamous, these were mostly ideals. With so many men away at war, on Crusades or traveling for whatever reasons, their wives were often available to friends or strangers, and willingly so. Those who refused to comply were often raped, and for such assaults only noblewomen or those at the emperor's court had legal recourse.

Weddings were blessed, but adultery was expected—at least partly, perhaps, because the notion of marrying for love was virtually unknown. Unions were arranged for purposes of politics and property, and where there is marriage without love, there is almost certain to be love without marriage. Very often, parents contracted nuptials for their eight- and nine-year-old children, and the same parents then awaited (indeed, they often forced) the biological consummation as soon as it was possible. Contraceptive methods were primitive and for the most part ineffective, and so most fertile girls had already borne several children by the time they were 15 or 16—if indeed they even survived a first pregnancy.

As for the clergy, since early Christian times, ministerial celibacy had been an honored option but had not been required. It was mandated only a century before Francis, during the papacy of Gregory VII (1073–1085), who went so far as to urge the laity to revolt against married clergy and who called for priests' wives to be hunted down and banished (or worse). By the time of the Second Lateran Council, in 1139, the wives of priests were proclaimed to be disreputable concubines, and their children were kidnapped to become Church slaves. There was massive resistance against this ruling, but Rome prevailed, at least legally. As a tactic for restricting ecclesiastical power solely to the clergy and for disenfranchising the laity, it was brilliantly successful. But compulsory celibacy also severed the ministerial life from the people, who became completely subordinate to a priestly caste, themselves considered lower than the lordly pope.

By the end of the 12th century, many good men continued to chafe at the unreasonable demand that priestly service to God and humanity precluded a wifely companion, and in fact, the unfortunate results of this forced practice, with all the attendant moral crises, have endured from the Middle Ages to the present. The coarsest jokes of the medieval fabliaux concerned lecherous clerics who seduced housewives and maidservants.

Few people at the time of Francis did not know (or know of) at least one son or daughter of a clergyman, which did little to bolster anyone's confidence and respect. And because the medieval clergy were in a state of such disrepute, witches and astrologers often won the loyalty of ordinary citizens.

Uneducated, as poor as the laity and subject to the caprices of the bishops and local nobles, the medieval clergy were for the most part unhappy dependents. Bibles, missals (which contained the readings and rites for Mass) and Office books (containing daily monastic hymns, psalms and prayers) had to be hand-copied, and so were rare and expensive—and, in fact, little in demand, since so few people were literate.

The idea of providing a theological education to the clergy had not yet been widely accepted, and the idea of offering learning to the masses was regarded suspiciously by both Church and empire. Cathedral schools thrived in a few places, but advanced curricula were only beginning to appear. At Bologna, there had been a confederation of scholars since about the year 1000, but the form of the university was just taking shape at Paris and Oxford. Hence both priests and laity were virtually ignorant about anything other than rudimentary religion and superstition—a deficiency at least partly countered in the brilliant depiction of Bible stories in stone and stained glass, arts then being refined in splendid cathedrals like Chartres.

§

Christendom, or the religious and cultural world of medieval Europe, consisted of two spheres of influence—the authority of the Roman Catholic Church (*sacerdotium*) and the secular authority of the Holy Roman Emperor (*imperium*). In 1050, the realm of these spheres comprised all the territories we now call Western and Central Europe, Britain and Ireland, Scandinavia, Poland, Hungary and Russia, while the Islamic territories included most of Spain, Sicily, Africa, the Eastern Mediterranean and the Holy Land.

In theory, the Church and the empire worked together to minister to the spiritual and temporal needs of citizens; in practice, society was rent with divisions between popes and emperors, who were perpetually locked in a power struggle. Emperors wanted to control the appointment of bishops and the authority to decide doctrinal disputes, while popes anointed kings and emperors, owned armies and cities and fought for control of state affairs. The result was predictable: constant disputes, skirmishes, political maneuvering to the point of deception and murder—and the ceaseless outbreaks of war in one place or another. By Francis's time, the bishops of Rome were about to proclaim that their jurisdiction extended to the entire world, in every aspect of its sacred and secular reality.

At the pinnacle of Christendom, of course, was the bishop of Rome, the pope, who was then the representative of an institution in almost complete chaos. Orlando Bandinelli, who was a lawyer and priest but neither a bishop nor a cardinal, was named to the papacy in 1159 at a conclave that had stipulated that the election had to be unanimous. As it happened, a handful of cardinals voted for Cardinal Ottaviano, who was supported by the Holy Roman Emperor, Frederick Barbarossa. Violence broke out after Bandinelli's majority was announced, and Ottaviano's armed lackeys tore the papal garb from Bandinelli's shoulders and forced him from the room. In exile, he was consecrated bishop of Rome and named pope as Alexander III —while at the same time, Ottaviano was consecrated as Pope Victor IV.

But Victor IV was simply a false pretender, a jealous, bitter antipope, and it was Alexander III who was rightful heir to the throne of Peter. To complicate the matter still further, three more antipopes succeeded Victor IV between 1164 and 1180.

It should be stressed that the rules for papal elections have changed time and again (and were sometimes simply ignored)—hence it is occasionally difficult to determine which claimants were duly elected and which not. The first antipope (one who persisted in his rightful claim to the role even after he was rejected as invalid) was in fact later proclaimed, and remains to this day, canonized: Saint Hippolytus, who in vain asserted his primacy from 217 to 235. He was a major ecclesiastical writer and author of the *Apostolic Tradition,* a valuable record of the Roman Christian liturgies in the second and third centuries. From then to 1449, there were 40 more antipopes.

This remains a complex matter: the official list of popes (in the *Annuario Pontificio*) from time to time moves a name from one side of the list to the other, and to this day the Vatican is still undecided about at least four claimants. Those who insist on an unbroken line of consecrated Roman bishops stretching all the way back to Saint Peter are simply ignorant of the Vatican's own historical scholarship.

۞

The pope during Francis's first three years of life was Lucius III, who spent most of his four-year term arguing with Emperor Frederick about (among other issues) military assistance against those Roman citizens who were disloyal to the pope. Irascible and worldly, Lucius died in 1185, perhaps universally unmourned.

He was succeeded by the indifferent Urban III, who died after less than two years in office, during which he conducted even more bitter disputes with the emperor than his predecessor. Much of their discord concerned who would be appointed bishop to which area: a candidate sympathetic to the pope, or one beholden to the emperor.

In the autumn of 1187, just after Francis turned five, Urban died. His successor was an 87-year-old cardinal who took the name Gregory VIII. To his credit and to the astonishment of many bishops, Gregory tried to resolve the conflicts in papal-imperial relations; in addition, he was sincerely interested in clerical reform. Unfortunately, he also called for a campaign against the Muslims—who, under Saladin, sultan of Egypt and Syria, had captured Jerusalem three weeks before Gregory took the papal crown.

The news from the Holy Land shocked all Christendom, for the holiest of pilgrimage destinations had again been lost to them. Gregory sent ambassadors to raise the Third Crusade and, convinced that the infidels' capture of Jerusalem was divine punishment for Christian sin, commanded all Crusaders to wear penitential garb.

All this the pope managed to legislate in a reign that lasted less than two months. A week before Christmas 1187, Gregory was dead, succeeded by Clement III, who devoted himself to mustering the troops to take back Jerusalem, whose loss was both an affront and a threat to Christian sensibilities. The Muslim victory in the Holy Land meant that homes and farms all over Europe might soon, by a kind of domino effect, be imperiled.

1187–1196

*I*N ASSISI, the seizure of Jerusalem by Muslim forces was the occasion for widespread lamentation for much of the next three years. One or two days a week, almost everyone went about in the penitential covering of sackcloth and ashes, professing that sin was the cause of the divine scourge in the Holy Land. Minstrels sang of the faithless Muslims as frequently as they did of love and fair ladies, and painted drapes were suspended all over town, depicting Christ tortured by the enemy.

It is commonly accepted that the Crusades were defined by the worst kinds of venality and the infliction of cruel massacres and plunder on both sides. In Christendom, the movement had an expressly religious mission, and those who participated were promised spiritual rewards in this life and the next. But while the Crusades were the joint pious effort of pope and emperor, they were also a campaign to attain political power, in the form of control of trade with the East and a number of territorial imperatives. To achieve these ends, no brutality was spared.

Those Christians who recognized the profoundly unchristian nature of the Crusades—inflicting pain for pain and instigating battle for battle—quietly withdrew from them, thus contravening the orders of their emperors, popes and bishops, and risking excommunication and (it was firmly believed) eternal damnation. Perhaps only a few had the strength of conscience or theological intelligence for that step; their names are unknown to us. For the most part, the Crusades transformed peaceful pilgrims into armed invaders.

Earlier in the Church's history, the proclamation of God's drawing near to humanity—the only true aim of the apostolic Church—had nothing to do with power, domination or political control; indeed, it meant the abandonment of such worldly concerns. Until the early fourth century, in fact, the Church had been disenfranchised, illegal, a threat to the Roman Empire and a movement to be exterminated by persecution. All that changed with Constantine, and by the time of the birth of Francis, the legitimacy and power of the Church—a veritable monarchy with the pope at its apex—had become so politically entangled that its work had become largely war work.

At the beginning of the Crusades, responsibility for combat had been in the hands of knights committed to the chivalrous life—a glorious and glamorous destiny, at least until they were faced with actual warfare. The ordinary laity also sought to make concrete their faith by *doing* something, by seeking their salvation in the carrying out of heroic deeds. Heeding the popes and their legates, the people believed that the Crusades gave them an opportunity to make a pilgrimage to Jerusalem—and hence an opportunity for salvation (or even martyrdom), without having to take the drastic step of becoming priests or monks.

These realities of the time and place in which Francis came to maturity must be taken into account in order to appreciate fully his impact on his own era as well as on far different cultures centuries later. That Francis was an Umbrian Italian of the late 12th and early 13th centuries, a time of both great achievement and monstrous cruelty, is an important factor in assessing both his character and his message.

Ordinary or extraordinary, every life is simultaneously enriched and limited by historical circumstance; it is, therefore, impossible to comprehend the achievements, struggles, challenges and what we might consider the failings of any life without reference to the context of its immediate past. This is not to endorse mechanistic or biological determinism; it is simply to state what should be self-evident—namely, that if Francis had been completely dissociated from the world of his time, he could never have had so profound an influence on it.

The same must be said of the one to whom he ultimately committed himself, Jesus of Nazareth. We cannot begin to understand Jesus without serious reference to the particulars of his background and culture—that is, to his life as a Jew at a painful and poignant moment of his people's history, in a land dominated by unsympathetic foreign invaders.

These circumstances of Jewish history provided the Aramaic language, the Semitic tropes and the Jewish modes of communication through which Jesus thought and expressed himself, just as the New Testament writings about him used the Greek language, tropes and modes available to its authors and comprehensible to their specific audiences. The meaning and message of Jesus as expressed in the Scriptures will remain beyond our grasp unless we attempt to understand something of the culture that gave rise to them.

Similarly, the less we consider the particulars of our social, cultural and (at least in the broadest sense of the word) spiritual roots, the more easily do we fall into the trap of considering ourselves and everyone else as some kind of mythic "human standard issue." The particulars of time and place always matter; more to the point, faith in God means that God continues to disclose Himself in the particulars of our time, our life, our circumstances. In this regard, one of the glories of medieval Christian spirituality was its conviction that God was God *for them*—that is, the confidence that God had not fallen silent, had not ceased to play a role in history. A God Who is distant and uninvolved, or Who once spoke and acted but has ceased to do so, is not God but a fragment and figment of an impoverished imagination.

§

Despite the cruelties of war, the social injustices and the widespread decadence in the world and the Church of Francis's time, it is beyond dispute that this was also an era of unparalleled achievement.

There were, for example, remarkable improvements being made in farming and military implements; more and stronger castles were built; and the great cathedrals and their schools began to proliferate. The rise of cities and towns and the enrichment of artistic and intellectual life involved a concomitant increase in certain demands and specific markets—primarily, of course, in the buying, selling and bartering of food and clothing. The traditional trio of commercial traders (butchers, bakers and candlestick makers) suddenly thrived at the same time that the growing economy was making town and city traders in newer goods—like Peter Bernardone— wealthy. Those in rural areas, however, seldom benefited from this economic expansion, and, then as always, a few people were becoming very rich at the expense of many others.

At the same time, there was dramatic progress in art and architecture, poetry and philosophy—indeed, in almost every arena of human life and experience. And there was, it must be added, an astonishing leap forward in what might be called the life of the mind and the spirit. The long and successful efforts of Irish monks to keep literature alive contributed greatly to the formation of new intellectual syntheses—first in monastic schools, and then in the great universities of Bologna, Padua, Paris and Oxford.

And while artisans were perfecting the classic forms of Gothic architecture and sculpture in the cathedrals rising across Europe, so, too, were guilds, city councils, civic associations and monasteries establishing new measures of autonomy. Despite the primacy of emperors and popes, the concept of legal and government representation was also developing, and so local political assemblies were being formed that made decisions for their communities.

Even the fiercest opponent of ecclesiastical culture and politics had to acknowledge what centuries of historical studies have since confirmed: the only force capable of providing a basis for social unity in medieval Europe was, whatever its shortcomings, the Roman Catholic Church. Faith itself persisted, whatever barbarities were permitted by the institutional Church and the not always very Holy Roman Empire.

§

The late 12th century was also a time of experimentation in religious life, as many monks abandoned their monasteries to live individually as hermits or in smaller, isolated communities that rejected the wealth, land and feudal privileges accumulated by their abbots. Simultaneously, the rise of lay poverty movements and independent preachers summoning people to penance and a reformed life led to serious consideration of precisely how one could live the Christian faith in the midst of a swiftly changing and suffering society.

These new currents in religious thought and practice underscored the paradox of the Church. Rooted in the past that gave the sharpest impetus toward the future, the Church instituted first-rate schools and subsidized their use by the finest minds. However, by carefully preserving its primacy, prerogatives and territories, it also sowed the seeds of dissent among its ranks.

To mention only three of the most significant religious thinkers just prior to the appearance of Francis is to have some idea of the theological concerns at the time. Each of them had a singularly passionate personality that made him attractive to very many followers.

Born in Italy and trained in France, Anselm of Canterbury (1033–1109) was perhaps the first great Christian intellectual of the Middle Ages. Benedictine monk, theologian and later archbishop of Canterbury, he meditated and wrote on a variety of theological and religious issues, such as the problem of free will. "Faith seeking understanding" characterized his program of intellectual-spiritual pursuits and represented a significant step toward linking rational thought with mystic insight.

Peter Abelard (1079–1142), the French theologian and logician, published commentaries on Aristotle and led a rigorous academic life. His affair with Héloïse produced a son, and although the lovers married (and later led separate cloistered lives), Abelard was castrated on orders of her uncle, a severe old moralist who was canon of Notre-Dame Cathedral in Paris. Happily, this dreadful retribution did not put an end to Abelard's religious or scholarly pursuits, and during his last 25 years he was a prolific writer and teacher of philosophy, logic and piety, even behind monastic walls.

The Cistercian mystic, statesman and spiritual writer Bernard of Clairvaux (1090–1153) set down his inspiring, moving teachings in a rich series of sermons and treatises that are studied to this day. During 38 years as abbot, he oversaw the foundation of 68 Cistercian (that is, reformed Benedictine) monasteries and traveled in the service of philosophers and popes as well as ordinary people. "It is difficult to grasp how popular he was," according to one modern chronicler. "To many people, he was something like Mahatma Gandhi, the Dalai Lama and Mother Teresa rolled into one." He also accepted with remarkable grace, candor and penance the humiliation that came to him on the failure of the Second Crusade, which he had preached throughout northern Europe.

It should be noted, however, that this exemplary trio was schooled in and wrote from the viewpoint of an essentially monastic spirituality. By the time Francis was born—less than thirty years after the death of Bernard—the ordinary layman, by now almost completely alienated from the language and class of priests and monks, looked for a religious life that was neither clerical nor monastic in spirit and form.

The spirituality of pilgrimage answered some of this need. Pilgrimages were not a novelty, of course: the Irish monks had regarded missionary travel as a powerful symbol of life itself, as a pilgrimage to God. But by the end of the 12th century, pilgrimages provided the laity a focus for their religious aspirations. Every Christian hoped at some point to visit Jerusalem, Rome and Santiago de Compostela; by 1230, Assisi would be added to the list, simply because Francis lived and died there.

§

The mind, which by tradition was always to be focused on contemplation of God, was now being applied to more secular pursuits in the university. Almost suddenly, the dark ages were yielding to light, and areas of intellectual pursuit were being structured, organized by scholars and students. Ideas—not just concrete matters like deeds or crops—were more widely discussed; not surprisingly, emperor and pope were suspicious of this development, for criticism could begin to undermine their power base.

And so it would, commencing at Chartres between 1120 and 1140. It was there that teachers would be among the first to suggest that the world was not only infinitely mysterious but also a suitable subject for rational study and analysis. Young people and apprentice scholars journeyed from Chartres to Paris and back again, arguing and discussing every topic that had taken hold of their agile minds.

There was also a new group of students—those who wanted to learn crafts, history, philosophy, architecture and art itself. Some of these youths who thronged into the cities had been trained in monastic schools, which had left them with not only the sense of transcendence but also an appreciation for the past, of which the monasteries were the greatest repositories.

Here were the ancient texts and languages and ancient forms of worship; here, too, the writings from the Church and the world of the past were laboriously copied and preserved.

Since the end of the 11th century, the Church had championed the renewal of the schools, which had flourished during the Carolingian Empire. Only three years before Francis's birth, in 1179, the Third Lateran Council ordered that schools be opened at cathedrals wherever it was economically feasible; they were intended mostly for candidates to the priesthood who could afford a stipend. (Other aspiring clerics could be ordained despite illiteracy.) In small towns, schools opened for young children, but with very modest goals; they were nothing like the structured parish schools of later times.

§

Francis himself was sent to the *schola minor* at the Church of San Giorgio, a kind of primary school for young boys of Assisi. Set on a lovely spot commanding a wide view over the valley below, San Giorgio offered an education that was uneven and informal, under the tutelage of a resident priest. Classes, such as they were, were held according to no fixed daily schedule, in the portico of the church. Francis attended between the ages of about seven and ten, and usually from Eastertide to early autumn, and his entire formal education seems to have lasted no more than three years, from about 1189 to 1192.

During this time, he learned enough Latin to recite the Lord's Prayer and the Creed at Mass, and he memorized passages from the Latin translation of the Hebrew psalms. But Francis never mastered Latin, and his knowledge of it remained elementary; as is clear from the two existing manuscripts that have survived in his own hand, he could not even write it without the help of a secretary. Even then, he mostly managed only Italianized Latin. (His contemporary Thomas of Eccleston referred to a letter of Francis as "written in bad Latin.")

This does not imply that Francis lacked a lively native intelligence, for that is indeed evident in his later life. Rather, it reveals a truth about the lack of books and teaching materials and the state of contemporary pedagogy—as well as the typical reliance on memorization. In short, Francis was, as his contemporary Stephen of Bourbon wrote, "a man of very little education"—but more than most laypeople of his time.

§

The Bible was, of course, the basic medieval text for all education in the universities as well as in parish schools, where it was the tool for literacy; it was also thought to contain all scientific as well as religious knowledge. Because bound manuscripts were so rare and expensive and most people were illiterate, few people actually read the Bible; studying it was the task of the clergy, most of whom had never had access to the entire text.

His teacher's choice of the Book of Psalms, large portions of which were assigned for memorization, explains how Francis could later easily quote so many passages from it. But the main source of his biblical knowledge was the Mass, at which the Bible, though read in Latin, formed the basis for each Sunday's sermon in the vernacular.

As for other school subjects, there were occasional lessons in elementary arithmetic (with the aid of an abacus); in liturgical or choir singing; and in the basic teachings of the faith. This minimal formal education was sufficient to enable Francis to enter his father's trade. He was never anything like an intellectual, never a well-read man—indeed, reading and writing were always challenges. But in his adult life, even with these limitations, he demonstrated a consistently quick grasp of human character and experience.

§

The patron saint of San Giorgio was, of course, Saint George. Not long after his death, in about the year 307, George became one of the most universally popular figures of Christian piety, celebrated and invoked in England, Palestine, Egypt, Sweden, Portugal, Russia and Ethiopia. A fresco of the saint is still visible on a wall of San Giorgio, showing him on horseback, plunging his lance into a dragon's neck while a prayerful princess looks on in rapture. Precisely the same scene is depicted virtually all across Europe, and as far north as Stockholm.

According to the legend, George slew the monster of ungodly war, a symbol of pagan forces wherever Christians found them. The priests of

San Giorgio were among many throughout Christendom who used Saint George as a model as they taught the virtues of courage and faith to schoolchildren. They might soon be summoned to a Crusade, the boys were told, but were assured that they would proceed under the patronage and with the blessing of their very own saint.

But there was an important coda to the story. George was honored and praised for finally putting aside his weapons and serving the poor. This was more consistent with early Christian teaching, for military men who presented themselves for baptism were subsequently forbidden from carrying out an execution, however legally permissible. "A soldier who is in a position of authority is not to be allowed to put anyone to death; if he is ordered to, he is not to do it." So stated the *Apostolic Tradition* of Saint Hippolytus, the antipope who set down the standard articles of faith and practice of the ancient Church about the year 215, a century before Saint George. Unfortunately, this essential tenet of Christianity—the primacy of peace and the prohibition against either acting violently or seeking vengeance—was often more notable for its absence, especially in the bellicose Middle Ages.

Soon after George appeared Martin of Tours, an equally popular figure who was likewise revered as a saint throughout Europe. Martin's life was far more thoroughly documented than George's. He lived from about 336 to 397, and he had the posthumous advantage of having for his biographer his friend and contemporary the historian Sulpicius Severus. The life of this saint made an especially profound impression on young Francis.

Martin's parents were not Christian, and his father, a Roman military tribune in Italy, tried to check the boy's interest in Christianity by exploiting a law under which a son had to follow his father's profession. Forced into army life, Martin fought in the imperial guard north of Paris, where there occurred the incident with which history identifies him to this day. On a bitterly cold winter afternoon, Martin saw a half-naked beggar shivering with cold. Passersby ignored him, but Martin was touched with pity. With nothing but his armor and his cloak, he drew his sword, cut the cloak in two pieces and handed half to the beggar.

That night in a dream, Martin saw Jesus wearing the piece of cloak he had given away and saying, "Martin has covered me with this garment"—recalling the gospel teaching "I was naked and you gave me clothing." It also hearkened to the experience of Saul on the road to Damascus. "Saul, Saul, why are you persecuting me?" the Risen Jesus asked the future Saint Paul, who was persecuting the first Christians; hence what is done in cruelty or kindness to any individual is done to Christ himself.

Soon after the dream, Martin was baptized, despite the objections of his parents. Then about twenty and still in the army, he was summoned before the emperor to receive a war bounty, which he rejected: "Up to now, I have served you as a soldier. Give the money to others who will fight—I am now a soldier of Christ, and it is no longer lawful for me to do so." Discharged, he went to Poitiers, where Bishop Hilary welcomed the brave young man.

After a period of solitude, Martin formed what was the first monastic community in Gaul, and he went about preaching in the countryside. The clergy and people of Tours clamored for him to serve as their bishop, an honor he declined until their persistence won him over. A tireless preacher, defender of the poor and founder of monasteries, he always set aside time for periods of private contemplation, which he believed were the source of all his energy on behalf of others.

A lifelong pacifist who refused to dole out the usual harsh punishment to heretics, he died in a remote village and was buried in Tours. That city became a popular place of pilgrimage in his honor, and churches dedicated to him were built in France, Italy, Spain, Germany, the Netherlands and England (where the oldest extant church bears his name).

The boys at San Giorgio were also told about the early bishops of Assisi—the saints Rufino, Vittorino and Savino, all of whom died agonizingly at the order of savage Roman emperors. Martyrdom was proclaimed as the most glorious death a Christian could endure, a guarantee of Paradise and the closest one could come to achieving an imitation of Christ, and the patron bishops of Assisi were presented at the school and in Church sermons as the models for knights brave enough to risk their own martyrdom in the Crusades.

Such were the most powerful ideas and images presented to Christian children in Assisi. The dragon slayer and the saints of old were emblems of romance, chivalry, courage and generosity, and they were set before young Christians not only as models of conduct but also as their heavenly intercessors. Two elements in their lives seem particularly to have struck young Francis. Once the dragon of war was dispatched and the people converted, George left the realm—"but before leaving, he gave the horse on which he rode and his richly decorated armor to the poor, for the love of Christ." Similarly, Martin shared his cloak with the beggar who was then revealed to be Christ's surrogate. And the martyrs demonstrated the extreme to which fidelity could extend.

The examples set by George and Martin took concrete form in Assisi, for the priestly community of San Giorgio often accepted goods and alms from townsfolk for the benefit of those suffering in their *ospedale*. Ten very ill poor people could be accommodated within the church precinct's little hospital, where the boys sometimes stopped to speak or to share a scrap of midday meal with those who lay dying, some of them doubtless of the effects of the famine.

§

Although hunger ravaged rural Italy during the first five years of Francis's life, the Bernardones, as members of a fortunate, rising middle class, were able to escape its worst and lasting effects. For one thing, Peter benefited from the population explosion that was then spreading across Europe, despite the generally low state of public health. This led to a dramatic shift in population centers, as people were forced to look for new land to plow or to seek new kinds of employment in towns. The immediate effect of this phenomenon was to further enrich and empower the new merchants, who also began to travel more widely for trade and clients.

About 1294, as Francis was just reaching adolescence, Peter took him out of school and, like many other fathers who went abroad on business, brought his son along on the first of several expeditions—to teach him as early as possible the elements of his trade and to expose the boy to French mercantilism and Gallic culture. Pica remained at home to supervise the shop.

Over the next several years, Peter and his boy headed for France and Flanders two or three times annually on trips that lasted perhaps as long as two months. The roads from northern Italy through France and into the Low Countries were thronged with beggars and troubadours, merchants and minstrels, and Francis, like any child, picked up and mimicked the language of the people, their popular songs and poems, their tropes and figures of speech. He was particularly fascinated by the troubadours and loved to imitate their songs.

The image we have today of troubadours and wandering minstrels is one of handsome, brash young swains in colorfully tattered costumes, strumming lutes and singing their way through life. In fact, for the most part, they were a diverse group of drifters and seducers who improvised mediocre poetry and indifferent songs. A medieval boy would have found them beguiling for the same reasons youngsters of later periods would respond to circus clowns with ukuleles or to magicians. Listening to the troubadours also enabled Francis to perfect his French (perhaps in its northern dialect for trade and the southern for songs), which was the language in which he later sang and recited at times of great emotion.

The journey to and from the fairs exposed the boy to more than just the usual complement of troubadours, beggars, brigands, errant, disreputable clerics and forlorn prostitutes. On the roads and in the forest camps, it would have been impossible for him to avoid seeing the everyday signs of violence: fights to the death over a skin of wine, a loaf of bread or a handful of pearls; vicious killings for the sake of diversion; tortures inflicted for vengeance or sport or mere pastime. And then there was falconry: the sport of releasing hawks to kill wrens and sparrows, quail, geese, ducks and pheasants, which were then cooked for dinner or sold to hungry travelers. There was bigger quarry for the killing, too: wild boar and deer, for example. And of course, everywhere there were lepers, the blind and the lame, those wounded in foreign war or local battles.

When Peter and Francis finally reached the great fairs of the Champagne country and the Netherlands, they found even more exotic people and customs. Merchants came from every port in Europe, spoke every dialect and traded with different methods and expectations. The just and the kind mingled with scoundrels and brutes, polite men dealt with rude sycophants and everyone seemed to eat and drink excessively and to find time for all sorts of rude gratifications, even if they had to seize them violently.

Wealth and quality merchandise marked the pinnacle of success in such a commercial scramble, and the fairs glittered with fabrics embossed with gold and silver; there were also hoards of ivories and coffers full of gems and pearls. There were piles of tapestries and carpets, stacks of fur, rolls of velvet—and spices and wines, perfumes and incense. The fairs were crowded with notaries, brokers and caravan captains, and Peter Bernardone seemed to know the most influential among them.

A child does not judge any kind of adult behavior as wrong unless he is directly hurt by it, or has already absorbed the framework of an ethical system from his elders. There is no indication that Peter was especially concerned with the moral education of his son, or with using the journeys as pretexts for instruction; in fact, the contrary seems true. The course of the rest of Francis's youth suggested the family's indifference to this sort of training, for it must be kept in mind that the father had the right of absolute control over virtually every aspect of a son's life until he reached maturity and obtained manumission. If Peter had in fact objected to Francis's subsequent indolence and frivolity, he had only to say so to put a halt to it. But that was the business of religion, and Peter's religion was business. His son was now in training to become a successful man of the world, and conspicuous consumption and the accumulation of pleasurable experiences were a necessary part of that training.

§

After several such journeys, the teenage Francis was prepared to assume the role of apprentice in his father's shop at home, and thus was heir presumptive to the family business and fortune. Early in 1196, at the age of 13, he was invited to join the merchants' guild, of which his father was a proud member. Watching and heeding Peter, Francis acquired the special skills required in the trade, the fine points of weights and measures, of pricing and the art of bartering. He also learned the potent effect of dress: liveries, badges, hoods, stockings, cloaks, capes and hats—all of them in richly hued fabrics and fine textures. The tint and cut of each was particular to every individual and family, and to each station in society.

For the first time in history, fashion itself had become fashionable, and at work in their shop with their knives, measuring rods, awls and scissors, Bernardone and son were on the forefront of this trend. But according to the earliest accounts of Francis's life, he did not share Peter's work ethic.

Francis was, according to one early source for his life and times, "vastly different from his father—more good-natured and generous, given over to revelry and song with his friends, roaming day and night throughout the city of Assisi."

Lavish in spending, Francis squandered everything on parties, feasts and revels, while the Bernardones seem to have been the archetype of coddling, spoiling parents: "Since [they] were wealthy and loved him very much, they tolerated all these things to avoid upsetting him," as an early source put it. Indeed, when neighbors commented on the boy's extravagance, Pica replied defensively, like a good Italian mother: "He will still be a godly child, through grace."

For the present, however, young Francis Bernardone was (according to friends) "so vain in seeking to stand out that sometimes he had the most expensive material sewn together with the cheapest cloth onto the same garment"—an attention-getting, patchwork costume typical of the time.

A lively, slim young man, Francis had grown by his mid-teens to his full adult height of five feet three inches. Thomas of Celano, a contemporary who compiled several important documents about Francis within a few years of his death, provided several vivid details about him. Francis had a slender face with clear, black eyes; dark hair and a sparse, dark beard; a narrow nose; fine and pale skin; thin lips and good teeth; long and expressive fingers; and an appealing, musical voice. Lighthearted but undisciplined, he was courteous to everyone even when at his most rambunctious, and he was likewise unfailingly generous to everyone, unlike the sons of many parvenus, who were as greedy and selfish as their fathers. He was, in other words, the sort of teenager with whom it was easy to become impatient but who was difficult to dislike.

But he was also something of a spendthrift, and as time passed, often became a kind of benign embarrassment to his parents. As the scion of the wealthy and respected Bernardones, serious accomplishments were expected of him. Because Peter was now extremely wealthy, he had purchased pasturelands, orchards and territories outside Assisi, and revenues were pouring in tidily from farms and forests, gardens and streams. He was required to make regular visits to his holdings, and at such times stewardship of the shop naturally passed to Francis, who demonstrated diminishing interest in it. We have no information about Francis's half brother, Angelo, who would have been about 18 in 1196, or about any other siblings who are sometimes said to have been born to Pica and her first or second husband. The silence of early sources may betoken the obvious: that Angelo was absent from Assisi, and that in fact there were no other siblings.

And so, while Peter and Pica grew more concerned, disappointed and finally ineffectual in controlling their prodigal son, a merry band always seemed to form around Francis. In the squares and alleys of Assisi, the lad was quickly gaining a reputation as an expert party giver, a jovial companion and an accomplished minstrel—in effect, a popular and endlessly inventive wastrel.

THREE

1196–1205

S HORTLY BEFORE HIS DEATH, Francis of Assisi dictated reflections on his life and his vision for the future of his companions. He began by referring to his youth as a time when he was "in sin." This was no expression of false humility, but the objective assessment of almost a decade of his life passed amid "the seductions of the world," as his good friend Cardinal Ugolino, later Pope Gregory IX, said in the document of canonization.

All the earliest literary sources and even his religious companions later acknowledged the fact of Francis's confused and dissipated youth. Two years after Francis's death, for example, the friar Thomas of Celano put the matter directly: the young man was raised "indulgently and carelessly . . . [and was] taught shameful and detestable things full of excess and lewdness. . . . He boiled in the sins of youthful heat" and was steeped in "every kind of debauchery."

Cardinal Eudes of Châteauroux, who died in 1273, referred often in his sermons to the fact that Francis, "steeped in luxury, led a life given over to the flesh—he was really a great sinner." Henry of Avranches, composing a life of Francis at the same time, added that Francis's youth had been spoiled by the early lessons in greed he received from his father, who was "a deceitful huckster." And among the most fascinating early descriptions of Francis was this bit of Latin poetry, sung by his religious brothers in church soon after his death:

Hic vir in vanitatibus, nutritus indecenter—
Plus suis nutritoribus, se gessit insolenter

—a succinct bit of double-rhyming verse that can be rendered, "He was raised shamefully amid all sorts of folly, and as he grew up he surpassed those who raised him in even worse folly." It is doubtful that friars would have included idle gossip in their prayers, and while some religious rhetoric typical of the time may be involved here (perhaps to establish a contrast with Francis's later conversion), it is interesting that no early sources present an exaggerated account of his youthful piety. That is the usual custom in the lives of the saints—not the frank admission of the subject's dissipation.

Perhaps the most persuasive indication of Francis's youthful decadence is the fact that the Latin lines quoted above were completely revised by Franciscan leaders in 1260. The adjustment was significant:

> *Hic vir in vanitatibus, nutritus indecenter—*
> *Divinis charismatibus, preventus est clementer*

—"He was raised shamefully amid all sorts of folly, but by God's grace he mercifully kept himself free of contamination." Such a sentiment was thought to be more appropriate, for it reflected a more pious, if unrealistic, view of the youthful Francis. According to the approved life written by Saint Bonaventure, he never yielded to the seductions of the flesh. Were that the unlikely case, it would be hard to understand what Francis himself meant by his years "in sin," words he himself never used lightly.

More to the point, the putative innocence of Francis would make it almost impossible to account for his popularity as a young man. He was at the head of a somewhat wild pack of Assisi youths who caroused around town, often causing young and old alike to leap out of their way; this is not the sort of group that would be inclined to choose a pious lad as its leader. And while we should guard against overstating the extent of his sexual experience, it would be difficult to think of him as diverging from his comrades in only this one area of adolescent experimentation. This was a sexually anarchic era, and the town was full of randy, undisciplined and hedonistic youngsters.

Admired by his peers for his wit, practical jokes and bawdy songs and stories, Francis also conspired to be as unlike his thrifty, work-obsessed father as possible. He continued to spend everything his father paid him on frequent feasts and his wardrobe, for which Peter, despairing, soon demanded compensation.

Matters turned even worse when Francis began simply to remove fabrics and clothes from the family shop, using them for his own and his friends' amusement. "Because of the senseless waste of his wealth," according to Julian of Speyer, "he seemed affable and obliging [to his friends], but he dragged behind him many who clung to him for this reason, and they followed him as their guide and leader headlong into ruin."

All during adolescence, Francis was bursting with ordinary adolescent energy, and because he also had style and money, he attracted the most unsavory element in town. Social activities varied according to the season. There were late suppers in the town squares and picnics outside the city walls; there were raucous gatherings at any hour, serenades of nubile maidens, dances and sport, games and laughter and, of course, real disorder when the wine flowed too freely or someone's jealousy was roused. The high spirits of night prowlers like Francis Bernardone often brought out the commune guardians to drag them home or douse their giddy heads in a fountain.

At this time there also flourished the notorious *tripudianti*, a singing and dancing group popular in Umbria and Tuscany, led by young men of wealth and position. Their passionate, bawdy songs described bitter quarrels, miserable marriages and frustrated lovers. The Assisi *tripudianti* were especially celebrated for their dance on the feast of the city's second bishop-martyr, Saint Victorinus, celebrated on June 13. A spectacle depicting both faith and violence, it inevitably concluded with a banquet and a licentious brawl. The entire event was led by a *signore* who held aloft a kind of conductor's baton—and who was none other than Francis Bernardone.

Several times a year, the festivities got especially rough and even dangerous. One such occasion took place annually on December 6, the feast of Saint Nicholas, the patron of students and of Francis's parish church. In a parody of religious ceremonies, teenagers chose a local boy, dressed him up as a bishop, dragged the poor child into the church, led him in a sacrilegious ceremony and then through the streets, and finally put him at the center of a riotous and licentious orgy. In keeping with medieval incongruities, bawdy clerics and half-nude women often joined the throng in a cacophony of cymbals and castanets. Later in the evening, some women were crowned with garlands and sold to the highest bidders for a night or a weekend. With its origins in the ancient pagan Saturnalia (the so-called December liberties), this affair became such a scandal that Pope Innocent III condemned and forbade it in 1207.

§

The lyrics, melodies and stories popular during this period were not only bawdy tales and improvised drinking songs, for the youth of southern France and northern Italy were also hearing and learning the troubadour songs and the elaborate poetry of courtly love. Composed in new verse forms that flourished from the late 11th to the late 13th centuries, these ballads and songs were much favored at court—particularly at that of the troubadours' great patron, Eleanor of Aquitaine, who encouraged both the courtly love tradition and lyrics about the great legends of Brittany.

Eleanor was in her late 70s when Francis was a teenager; she had been, successively, queen consort of Louis VII of France and of Henry II of England, and she was the mother of (among other children) two English kings, Richard the Lion-Hearted and John. The most powerful woman of 12th-century Europe, she was a brilliant politician, a tenacious administrator and a patroness of music, the arts and literature; she also turned the court of Poitiers into the most famous center of troubadour poetry and courtly life and manners. When Francis and his crowd were roaming the streets of Assisi, the songs and stories created under Eleanor's patronage were the popular odes of the day, and his knowledge of French enabled him easily to memorize them:

> So pleases me the gentle season,
> And pleases me the gentle summer weather,
> And please me the birds, singing so much,
> And please me the flowers in bud—
> So pleases me all that pleases the courtly,
> And most of all please me deeds of chivalry:
> I undertake them joyfully,
> Bending all my heart and mind to them right willingly.

Another, freely translated, was sung by renegade students:

> Time for gladness, time for play,
> Holiday we keep today:
> Let the fiddle sound the strain,
> Sing the good old songs again.
> Hearts must beat in time with voices
> Till the dancing blood rejoices;
> Come, you scholars—most of all
> Who best love a festival.
> Pen and ink and copybook,
> How funereal they look;
> Ovid's songs, how dull with age,
> Still more any other's page.
> Never mind what's not allowed,
> Love is youth's temptation:
> Here we go, a glorious crowd,
> Hell-bent for vacation.

The works of Marie de France, the earliest known woman poet of that country, also flourished during Francis's adolescence and circulated all over Europe. They represented the highest achievement of the conventions of the *lais*, or poems of courtly love: from afar, lovers worshiped their ladies (usually already married to another), and both looked forward to a future colored by the delights of longing and the torments of inaccessibility.

One of Marie's most popular poems described two barons who lived in neighboring houses in a Breton town. One had a beautiful and courteous wife, who was adored by the other baron. The frustrated lovers talked for hours at their windows and for a time were happy—"but lovers can't be satisfied when love's true pleasure is denied."

Time passed, love deepened and the woman at last went to her lover at night; when she returned, she told her husband that she had gone outside to hear the nightingale. He, rightly suspicious, had the bird captured and brought to her. "Your nights will be more peaceful now that the bird can't awaken you anymore!" With that, he killed the nightingale and threw it at his wife's feet. Stricken, she sent it to her lover with a heartbreaking note of farewell, and he placed the dead bird inside a gold case that he carried everywhere.

§

In addition to love songs, seasonal ballads and poems of courtly love, the other popular narrative form of the era was the great medieval epics, which celebrated knighthood and chivalry. Wandering Provençal minstrels, whom Francis had already encountered in his travels with Peter, regularly passed through Assisi with pilgrims heading to Rome, declaiming the exploits of Roland and Arthur.

La Chanson de Roland, almost a century old when Francis was a teenager, was a widely known and sung epic poem. It tells of the recklessly brave warrior Roland, who is preoccupied with renown and glory during the reign of Charlemagne. Trapped against crushing odds by Saracen forces, he is contrasted with his sensible friend Oliver, whose sister he has betrothed and who urges him to seek help against the overwhelming odds of battle. But Roland refuses, and both men are among thousands killed. On hearing this news, his beloved falls dead.

The appeal of *The Song of Roland*, then as now, derives very much from a masterfully romantic yet sober tale, interwoven with the themes of tragic love, fatal pride and glorious battles—in other words, all the elements of chivalry to which both knights and ordinary young men believed themselves summoned. Turold, the likely author of the epic, became a name widely known in France and abroad, and the character of Roland was so familiar in Italy that local poets created supplementary tales of his exploits in their own country.

In fact, a widely known Umbrian romance of this period described visits to nearby Perugia by Roland and Oliver. Years later, when Francis urged his companions to value noble actions more than mere pious words, he reminded them that "the emperor Charles, Roland and Oliver, and all the paladins and valiant knights . . . were mighty in battle . . . [but] now there are many who want to receive honor and praise by only relating what they did," rather than by following their example of courage.

The various forms of the Arthurian legend, with their stories of Arthur's court, the Round Table, the rebellion of Mordred, the quest of Galahad for the Holy Grail and the forbidden passion of Guinevere and Lancelot, circulated even before the 11th century and achieved wide popularity via Geoffrey of Monmouth's histories a half century before Francis's birth. During Francis's youth, the versions set down by Chrétien de Troyes between 1165 and 1180 were also in circulation. Later in his life, after a group of religious companions had gathered round him, Francis referred to them as "my Knights of the Round Table."

Francis made a number of allusions to these tales later on in his preaching and letters, and he seems to have learned as much from the minstrels and troubadours as he did from the priests at San Giorgio, for the spirit of chivalry was to form a motif of his deepest spirituality.

Like the martyrs of old, the heroes of chivalry proved themselves and won their status by endurance—by suffering and risking death. As the single controlling social metaphor of the 12th and 13th centuries, chivalry in battles both temporal and spiritual was taken for granted as the aspiration of every honorable man. And the highest aspirations began with the simple knightly gesture of courtesy, manifest not only in a courtly manner but also, especially for the knight who had the resources, in generosity to everyone.

While Francis was still a teenager, occasionally working for Peter but mostly leading a carefree existence, something significant happened to him, though like many critical moments in life, it seemed not to have meant very much to him at the time. With good reason, all the earliest sources document the event.

One day in his father's shop, Francis looked up to see a beggar who had wandered in, seeking alms. Preoccupied with business and his own need for cash, he dismissed the man. Later, however, he confided to friends that he was bothered by a sense of remorse: "If that poor man had asked something from you for a great count or baron, you would certainly have granted his request. How much more should you have done this for the love of God!" In some way, he realized that he had been unfailingly generous to himself and his friends—but what of generosity and courtesy to those truly in need? The moment passed, and Francis returned to work; although his conduct was unaltered, at least he recognized how a real knight would have behaved in the circumstances.

§

Chivalry was not the prerogative only of aristocrats, for even those of the rising merchant class could aspire to its code of behavior if they were deemed worthy and were able to provide their armor.

Being knighted involved a solemn ritual. A candidate spent a night in prayer before an altar on which was placed his armor; in the morning, he attended Mass and, kneeling, swore to use armor and sword to honor God and aid the oppressed. His sponsor then gave him a symbolic blow on the shoulder and embraced him, saying, "In the name of God, of Saint Michael and Saint George, I dub you knight. Be brave, courageous and loyal."

The cult of knighthood was an aesthetic ideal assuming the appearance of an ethical ideal, and as such, membership in it was coveted by every young man of means. While nobility in service and constancy in love were among its most highly regarded themes, valor in battle was perhaps the most obvious and reasonable path toward knightly perfection, and in the spring of 1198, Francis saw his chance to achieve it.

At that time the members of the commune of Assisi—the rising middle class to which the Bernardones belonged—attacked the imperial keeps and threatened the Rocca Maggiore, the fortress high above town that was the stronghold of the emperor's legate. Carried by a wave of enthusiasm for their cause, the mob of new bourgeoisie was essentially declaring civil war against the feudal lords. The issue here was not one of social revolution or the rights of man, nor was the uprising concerned with class equality or solidarity with the poor and oppressed. Quite the contrary: what motivated these men was an obsession with material gain and a hunger for commercial success. Those who were getting more now wanted the most. Every healthy young man in the commune joined the siege, and Francis, as a member of a prestigious merchant family and of the guild, could not and would not have excused himself from participating.

It eventually fell to the new pope to intervene in the conflict, and he proved to be up to the task. Perhaps the cardinals had grown weary of appointing aged and ailing men to the position, for in January of that year they had elected the handsome, witty, 37-year-old Lotario di Segni, who took the name Innocent III. He at once ordered Duke Conrad, the imperial legate, to turn over control of the duchy of Spoleto, thus adding it to the Papal States. Abandoning his loyalty to the empire, Conrad hastened south to meet Innocent's representatives at Narni, where he surrendered the entire duchy, including Assisi.*

That was the moment for which the burghers had waited. Paying no heed to the threat of excommunication, they laid waste the Rocca Maggiore and formed a stronger communal government, and with astonishing speed, the youngest of the burghers (Francis among them) surrounded the city with new ramparts, which they built from the stones of the fortress. A dreadful massacre of revenge then ensued, during which the aristocracy and knights were evicted from their urban towers and rural castles and killed outright. Those nobles who could fled to nearby Perugia, 12 miles west, where they joined forces with Perugian aristocrats who already had an age-old hatred for Assisi.

After this unfortunate episode, the citizens of Assisi may well have expected some tranquillity, not to say autonomy, but skirmishes continued across the Umbrian plains from 1198 to 1200. Some merchants, like Peter and Pica, tried to get on with their lives and business interests. Francis, forced to spend more time in the shop, became ever more bored and disaffected. As he approached 20, he had not the remotest idea of what to do with his life.

§

By November 1202, the exiled nobility had mustered their allies in Perugia and stormed toward Assisi. Francis and his friends, naturally eager to join the glorious battle, mounted their horses and joined a ragtag group of mer-

---

*Emperor Frederick Barbarossa had been succeeded by his son Henry VI, who reigned from 1190 to his death in 1197, after which began a series of rivalries that placed German supremacy in jeopardy. Henry's widow entrusted the tutelage of their two-year-old son, the future Frederick II, to Pope Innocent III, while in Germany two rival kings claimed power. Although king of Germany from 1212, Frederick II was not declared Holy Roman Emperor until 1220.

chants, shoemakers, butchers, notaries, archers and cavaliers, departing the city as the church bells tolled slowly, solemnly. The official chariot of the commune, drawn by white oxen and draped in the town's red-and-blue flag, came at the end of this procession, escorting the fighters to war. Very likely, the proud young men on horseback joined their voices in one of the most popular paeans to battle:

> Nothing cheers my soul like the cry of "Charge!"
> And the cry "Help!" echoing loudly—
> Nothing is so welcome as to see the lowly and the proud
> Lying in a ditch together . . .

A company of Assisians with crossbows and arrows managed to take a Perugian stronghold on the Collestrada hilltop, three miles outside Assisi, doubtless believing that a swift victory would soon be theirs. Nothing could have prepared them for what followed, however, for when the Perugians saw what had happened, they advanced at once and attacked ferociously. The men of Assisi were overwhelmed, and the slaughter was enormous. Men and boys were tracked down and hacked to death, and the vineyards and fields were littered with the bodies of the dead and dying. Assisi had been resoundingly defeated.

Francis, an early casualty, was among the survivors who were dragged off to Perugia. Meanwhile, the parents, wives and grandparents of Assisi's soldiers remained uncertain of the fate of loved ones whose bodies they could not locate. After six months of silence, the captors sent word that the wealthy merchants of Assisi would have to pay large ransoms for their friends or sons. While messages were exchanged and negotiations continued, Francis languished for a year in a damp and polluted prison improvised from underground Etruscan ruins.

Conditions were appalling by any standard. Prisoners were confined in almost perpetual darkness in a subterranean vault and subsisted on a meager diet of stale leftovers and tainted water; there was nothing like a latrine or facilities for washing; and the place was brutally cold in winter and cruelly airless in summer. It was an ideal incubator for malaria, tuberculosis and all manner of bacterial and viral diseases; as it happened, many prisoners did not survive the ordeal.

It is difficult to imagine anyone but an adept mystic finding the equanimity and patience to survive such circumstances, and Francis had neither of those qualities at this point in life—much less is there any evidence that he had the slightest religious sensibility. Conditioned to a life of luxury and caprice and unaccustomed to suffering or deprivation, this privileged young man must have been in a state of constant anxiety. His comfortable family home, his fine clothes and his privacy were now all but memories, and he would have been heroic indeed not to have longed for death.

Some of the less sober early accounts of this episode in Francis's life present him as a buoyant and irrepressible prisoner, cheering his companions, making peace amid quarreling comrades and gamely awaiting release. But this retrojection of his mature character only serves to diminish the real misery of this year and our understanding of almost everything that followed.

By the end of 1203, a temporary truce was announced after the terms of ransom had been settled. Freed after his father paid the agreed-upon amount, Francis returned to Assisi, where his parents were relieved to see him alive but alarmed at his severely compromised health. Always small and slim, and doubtless weakened by his profligate life even before joining battle, Francis was now so frail that he could barely walk or speak. His face was drawn and sallow, his digestion was impaired, and he often shook for hours with fever. The young man had contracted malaria, of which there were several virulent occurrences in Italy during the Middle Ages, especially from 1100 to 1300. He was bedridden under his parents' care for an entire year, until the end of 1204.

§

During his recuperation, Francis retained his aspiration toward knightly glory, but he was physically unable to answer Innocent III's misguided and mismanaged call for the Fourth Crusade. Once again, Crusaders trekked over thousands of miles with few provisions; as one Church historian and theologian has written, their efforts "would not have been possible without real religious enthusiasm, passion, and often almost mass psychosis." This campaign ultimately led to the plunder of Constantinople and to the establishment of both a Latin empire in the East and the imposition of a Latin ecclesiastical system on the Byzantine Church, thus reinforcing a permanent schism between Eastern and Western Christians.

If Francis looked to his commune to provide a sense of purpose and the hope for a secure life after he recovered, he was bitterly disappointed. Despite curfews, murders were commonplace at night, and gangs of thugs attacked in broad daylight. Criminals were subject to ever more barbarous punishments: liars had their tongues torn away; forgers lost their hands to the axe, and looters their feet; a minor thief had his eyes gouged out; those even suspected of betraying the commune were strangled almost to death, then cut down while alive and slowly flayed. But the more extreme the remedy, the greater number of crimes were committed. *"Sanguis exivit,"* wrote the chroniclers and judges, describing both crime and punishment— "blood flowed."

If, on the other hand, Francis had turned from the commune to the local clergy and religious for comfort and counsel during his recuperation, he would have found considerable disorder there, as well. Innocent III had just begun a major reform of the clergy, and to his credit, he outlined some of the abuses of the time in a document crisp with moral outrage:

> Many priests have lived luxuriously. They have passed the time in drunken revels, neglecting religious rites. When they have been at Mass, they have chatted about commercial affairs. They have left churches and tabernacles in an indecent state, sold posts and sacraments, promoted ignorant and unworthy people to the clerical state, though they had others better suited for it. Many bishops have appropriated the income of a parish for themselves, leaving the parish indigent. They have gone to the enormous abuse of forcing parishioners to make special payments so as to have still more income. They have extorted money from the faithful on every pretext. They have made a scandalous commerce of relics. They have allowed the illegitimate children of a canon to succeed the father in the benefice.

Francis's convalescence was slow and painful. "When he had recovered a little," according to Celano, "he began to walk about through the house with the support of a cane . . . [and] one day, he went outside and began to gaze upon the surrounding countryside. But the beauty of the fields, the delight of the vineyards and whatever else was beautiful to see, could offer him no delight at all [and he] considered those who loved these things quite foolish."

For an entire year, physical weakness, intellectual boredom, spiritual confusion and a kind of postwar cynicism left him sick in body and soul—a condition that moderated every desire, including sex. Francis had no interest in pursuing love, whether courtly or carnal. Of this time, Francis later said simply, "I was very frail." As for Peter and Pica, they wished only for his recovery so that he might resume his career in the shop. As he gradually regained strength in the summer of 1204, he began to rejoin his friends for festivals and parties, but without much enthusiasm. Now in his 22nd year, Francis found nothing to be of much consequence and, as his earliest chronicler records, "began to regard himself as worthless."

§

By the autumn, he had regained some strength but found no solace for his apathy. He had grown bored with his friends and their hedonism, but he saw no alternatives. "It is difficult to leave familiar things behind," observed Celano; "vice, with enough custom and practice, becomes second nature." As for the family business, constantly set before him by his benevolent and patient father, Francis viewed the prospect of a greater involvement in it as even more tiresome. Even so, he had not lost his taste for colorful costumes and the latest fashions.

Still longing for chivalric glory in some form—especially after the failure of the Perugian expedition and his degrading stay in prison—Francis decided, early in 1205, to accompany a nobleman going to join the papal forces of the great Norman captain Walter of Brienne, in Apulia. Thus engaged, Francis was confident of earning his knighthood. In addition, at Apulia's port of Brindisi, Crusaders would depart for Constantinople and Jerusalem, which might afford another opportunity for heroism. Success in battle would redound to Francis's credit, and was sure to please his father even as it gave the son a way out of the shop.

As an early source records, Francis "prepared clothing as expensive as possible," befitting a prospective hero. Just before his departure, he dreamed that a man led him into a palace filled with knightly armor, saddles, shields and spears. This vision Francis interpreted as a divine endorsement of his plans, and in the morning he set out, more optimistic than he had felt since the siege of Rocca Maggiore six years earlier. When family and friends asked the reason for his obvious joy, he replied, "I know that I will become a great prince!"

So convinced was he that there would be no return to his old life after the achievement of his knightly quest, Francis made a grand gesture—a generous one, but also theatrically self-indulgent. An older knight was then returning to Assisi poor, dejected and wearing only the tattered remnants of his once glorious uniform. With a great flourish, Francis gave the knight the fine garments he had accumulated. Perhaps he recalled the story of Martin of Tours; but he may also have believed that he would return victorious, with no further need of his father's help.

Francis may also have remembered the poor beggar he had years earlier dismissed from the shop, and seen this as his chance to reverse a previous unkindness by present charity. But human motivation is rarely pure—as Thomas More famously said, "Only God is love right through"— and there was, it seems, more than a touch of noblesse oblige in the donation. Francis's behavior was that of a medieval prince in whom the passionate desire for virtue coexisted with the longing for praise. He was a living embodiment of the subtle justification of self-glory by a yearning for heroism: "My soul to God, my life to the king, my heart to my lady, honor for me!" was the knight's motto, and at this time, also that of Francis.

Twenty-two miles south of Assisi, he and his companion had to stop for a night at Spoleto; Francis had developed a spiking fever, a recurrence of the malaria that would remain in his system and cause illness for the rest of his life. Half delirious, he shivered, then perspired profusely and endured hours of nausea, and was clearly in no condition to continue on his mission.

Then, not quite conscious, Francis heard a voice asking him where he intended to go. Francis described his plans for battle and knighthood, and then he heard the question "Who can do more good for you—the master, or the servant?"

"The master," Francis replied.

"Then why are you abandoning the master for the servant, the patron for the client?"

"Sir, what do you want me to do?"

"Go back to your own home and you will be told what to do. You must understand in another way the vision you had."

It is interesting to note that the sources do not describe this experience as a dream revelation; Francis, ill with fever, simply heard someone asking his plans for the future. The voice may well have been that of his unidentified companion, but in light of what subsequently occurred, his own followers much later interpreted this moment as the means God chose to announce His will.

There are, after all, no mere synchronicities for those who believe that throughout time God discloses Himself by working through human events and human agents. After all, the guidance of the people of Israel from creation through the prophets, and the event of Jesus, too, were so "ordinary" that even eyewitnesses could underestimate and dismiss them.

This was the unexpected message that uprooted Francis; indeed, it seemed to contradict his interpretation of the dream of the palace filled with armor and weapons for which, he once believed, he had been destined. Now he was caught short—by illness and perhaps by his companion, who understandably realized that the frail young man would be more a burden than a partner.

(Revelations through dreams are a commonplace in the Bible, and this means of divine communication was taken very seriously in medieval life, especially in writings about the saints. People in the Middle Ages were familiar with the motif of dreams in the Hebrew and Christian scriptures. The Old Testament dreams of Abimelech, Jacob, Solomon, Laban, the pharaoh and Nebuchadnezzar, for example, were as much in currency as the New Testament dreams of Joseph, Pilate's wife and Paul.)

❦

And so, in the spring of 1205, Francis turned back to Assisi—arriving home, we can be sure, not only weakened again by his recurrent malaria and its effects but also humiliated at the failure of another undertaking and just as unsure of his future as before. Depressed and forlorn, he had once more to rely on his father's largesse and his mother's care.

Most of his old friends were now engaged in their own or their families' trades, or were married or betrothed or had set out to join the Crusades or for adventure elsewhere. Francis waited to hear what he would be "told to do," but there was only silence—no voices came to him at night, no inner hint or intuition occurred to him by day. Even more than the previous year, he was an aimless wanderer, a man in his 20s mired in the confusions of youth.

Younger men in the commune were well aware of Francis's reputation for fun and his old habit of supplying everyone with money for good food and wine. Hence, by the time of the summer festivities, he was made the official master of the revels, a title he accepted in the absence of any more meaningful purpose in life. The *rex convivii* (king of the banquets) was a role that had survived from Roman antiquity; in Assisi, a fellow who played the host and underwrote the banquets became honorary monarch, complete with a baton for scepter. All that summer and up to the time of his 23rd birthday, in early autumn, he reigned without rival but with increasing torpor and disaffection.

Prowling about with his company of revelers one summer evening, Francis began to trail behind. One of his companions noted his jaded, distracted appearance and mocked him: "What were you thinking about, that you couldn't keep up with us? Are you thinking of taking a wife?"

Unable to reply that he was thinking of nothing specific and unwilling to admit that he was bored and depressed to those who were neither, Francis quickly turned to his questioner and replied sharply: "Yes, you're right! I am thinking of taking a wife—and one more noble, wealthier and more beautiful than you have ever seen!"

That must have provoked a response of loud hoots and whistles. Here was Francis the dreamer, Francis the boaster, who was now going to achieve his desired social status by marriage to a noble, beautiful, wealthy wife. Who would have this melancholic fellow, who seemed to do everything in his power to alienate people and was not glad to share in a family business that guaranteed real security, even a fortune?

His friends continued on their way, singing and joking, looking for more fun, unaware that Francis had turned aside into an alley toward the piazza and found his way home. As Peter and Pica knew, there was no woman in his life at all, and certainly none he intended to marry. In fact, there seemed to be neither a person nor a purpose that mattered to him at all.

1205

A S THE INDOLENT SUMMER of 1205 turned into autumn, Francis continued to work with his father in a kind of quiet, resigned desperation, unable to envision either a bright future or a chance at either knighthood or nobility.

Late one afternoon, he was returning from an errand to one of the properties his father owned outside the city walls, south of town. Having grown weary after hours of walking in the bright sunlight, he wandered into the cool refuge of San Damiano, which stood a mile from the city walls, at the foot of the hill on which Assisi was built. San Damiano was a small church, and over its doorway Francis could make out the faded words often inscribed in country chapels: *Domus Mea* (My House). Once inside, Francis sat alone, his eyes gradually adjusting to the dark.

The place seemed on the verge of collapse from old age and neglect. The walls were cracked, the low vault was crumbling, the beams were rotting. Wild grass sprouted along a narrow window, and the crescent-shaped apse, once bright blue with painted stars, was faded and peeling. No one had worshiped at San Damiano for years.

Over the abandoned altar, a crucifix had somehow survived the decay. Painted on linen stretched taut over a walnut frame, it was a striking image in the tradition of Syrian-influenced 12th-century iconography, the eyes of Christ gazing serenely and directly toward the viewer.

In the stillness of the small church, Francis felt, as an early source described, "different from when he had entered."

And then, "the image of Christ crucified spoke to him in a tender and kind voice: 'Francis, don't you see that my house is being destroyed? Go, then, and rebuild it for me.'"

History offers many accounts of people catching glimpses of the world beyond, of being addressed by some unknown presence. Moses before the burning bush; Isaiah awed by his vision of the majesty of God's court; Jesus aware of a profound sense of mission at the time of his baptism; the Buddha beholding the universe in a bouquet of flowers and Julian of Norwich seeing it in a hazelnut; Saints Paul and John astonished by unexpected visions; Saint Augustine hearing a child's voice whisper, "Take up and read"—these moments changed the world and revealed the intersection of the timeless with time, of this world with another.

The two earliest accounts of Francis's experience at San Damiano are far less dramatic than some might wish. Yet the simple description—the image spoke to him "in a tender voice"—is in keeping with the most traditional image of Christian faith, that of the rejected, outcast Jesus addressing a man broken by disappointment and estranged from himself. What more apt icon could God use to reach out to a man of Francis's time and place?

"He felt this mysterious change in himself," Thomas of Celano concluded, "but he could not describe it. So it is better for us to remain silent about it, too." Thomas's report of this event is likewise remarkably measured, offering no praise of Francis, and nothing designed to raise him in the estimation of readers or to present the moment as a miracle. It is merely an episode in which a man knows that he has been touched and changed, and sets out to respond by action.

Francis could only interpret the message literally: he was sitting in a collapsing church, and he had been told to rebuild it. Immediately, he left San Damiano and set about finding ways to attend to its disrepair. Now at last, he had found a focus and a remedy for his present bewilderment.

§

Francis of Assisi lacked any of the formal language necessary to describe mystical experiences. Neither theologian nor philosopher, he had no religious education apart from an abbreviated time in a makeshift classroom and the ordinary layman's exposure to sermons.

But what did God mean to him? And how did he imagine or represent God to himself?

First of all, God was the Being Who had reached out to Francis precisely in the image of the one who had been crucified. The medieval Christian knew and proclaimed the faith that Jesus was God's ultimate disclosure and revelation of Himself to the world—that Jesus was God's own Word, His extension of Himself into time and space. But now the figure of God in Christ came alive for him. The Jesus on whom Francis gazed was stretching out loving arms on the hard wood of the cross; the Jesus he beheld appealed to Francis. How could this request be ignored?

In a mysterious moment, the fog of confusion broke, and Francis had been given a task. Whereas he had previously been obsessed with social status and the acquisition of personal glory, he now accepted a humble and demanding assignment. This was the beginning of a new stage of his life: he would no longer be concerned with seeking glory, privilege or nobility—he would no longer (to use the modern terms) be driven to try to find himself or to improve his self-esteem. To state the matter succinctly: he had heard; now he longed to respond, and so to keep up the dialogue.

As his relationship with God grew to become more intimate and profound, Francis came to believe that he had to articulate his experience of God's presence. But this is something that defies human expression, and so Francis would often burst into poetry and song; he also acted and gestured in ways that communicated his awareness of the enormity of God, Who defies comprehension.

However, this immense and unimaginably good God, Who addressed Francis in the image of the poor, crucified one, also brought him to life, gave him purpose, rescued him from chaos. In other words, God was his Creator and Redeemer not in some theoretical, academic or analytical sense, but because Francis had *experienced* God as author, renewer and savior. He knew—in a way that was deeper and that surpassed all other modes of knowing—that God had saved him from turmoil and given him meaning. Francis had not only been lifted from the depths of depression, he had been lifted out of the prison of self.

Henceforth his life would no longer be centered on himself, his needs, his past, his pleasure, his pain, his glory, his fulfillment. From this time forward, he had one goal in mind: to remain accessible to the voice that had just addressed him—to enable the conversation to continue. Francis had been touched by the concrete image of the poor and humble Jesus, rejected and outcast, dying alone, convicted of perfidy and convinced that he had let God down. Francis wanted to be warmed and embraced forever by that touch.

It had only been a moment, but it represented the first major step in turning everything over to God. To commemorate the day, Francis later composed a short Prayer Before a Crucifix: "Most High, glorious God: enlighten the darkness of my heart and give me true faith, certain hope and perfect charity, sense and knowledge, Lord—that I may carry out Your holy and true command."

What had happened in that dark, decrepit abandoned little church was nothing less than the beginning of a lifelong process: the conversion of Francis Bernardone.

§

For most people, the word "conversion" means the finding of religion or a change from one to another; one converts for this or that reason—personal or social, profound or shallow, to please others or to find inner peace. Whatever the motivation, it is a process that is self-contained and reaches a logical end point. So understood, however, conversion evokes merely simplistic notions about what is one of the most mysterious adventures in human experience. This idea deserves some consideration if we are to understand the development of the complex character of Francis of Assisi, whose conversion was really the arduous work of a lifetime, not the settled, simple effect of a single moment.

Too often, "conversion" connotes some sort of defining moment that seems to come out of the blue, with no advance warning or promise. In fact, sometimes the most significant shifts in consciousness and life direction begin with a long-standing conviction that one's direction has been lost, that existence itself has no purpose. The biographies of many great people in history describe just such a critical point after episodes of painful emotional unrest, depression and crisis.

To convert is to embark on a process; in religious terms, this involves a decision to commit the whole of life to God. But this cannot be achieved by a single act of the will, nor does it occur in a day, or after a single event, however dramatic and life-altering that event may be. Conversion, in other words, often involves isolated moments of incandescence, but it is finally an ongoing project.

The moment when a person first becomes aware of a great Power is essentially passive: something *happens* to someone—it is not a matter of what one chooses to do or refuses to do. Nor does it involve thinking beneficent thoughts or being kind to others or planning for the future, although some of these elements may follow in various forms during the process. It does, however, require entrusting all that is one's life and security to God, Who is faithful and acts only out of love for us.

Conversion is, then, a response to God, Who invites us to a state of complete freedom, away from everything that is hostile to His goodness and mercy. The call one hears is not primarily or simply an encouragement to amend one's life or to follow a particular religious path. The call Jesus extended to his disciples, for example, was not religious—it was resoundingly secular. It was a summons to acknowledge God's unconditional love of us as individuals; and it was an invitation to proclaim that love to the world by acts of caring, forgiveness and compassion for others, by refusing to demand one's prerogatives at the expense of others and by rejecting vengeance and reprisal. The New Testament summarizes the entire mission and message of Jesus in one calm phrase that is deeply moving in its secular simplicity: "He went about doing good."

We begin to acknowledge, accept and know God—always imperfectly and darkly—when we seek to be free of our idolatry of self, love others unselfishly and accept our existence as meaningful, despite its unmanageability. When we renounce our fear of life and give up trying to have it under our control—that is, when we acknowledge our contingency and utter dependence on God—then God comes to us and turns us toward Himself. Seen in this light, conversion means not only a turning away from one's past but entrusting oneself to the unexpected, uncharted way into the incalculable future in which God comes to us.

Conversion then becomes a radical and uniquely personal adoption of a new life. It is a fundamental experience of the inescapably true orientation of every human being toward the mystery we call God. We cannot produce this experience at will by some arcane mystical methods. We can ask, we can seek, but essentially we must wait.

The obstacles an individual faces in the continuing conversion process come not only from the selfishness of a world intent mostly on the pursuit of goods, power and pleasure. There are dangers, too, in religious legalism, and in taking false comfort from traditional religious practices, which can lead to a sense of smug superiority. When faith ceases to be a challenge to the standards of polite society, it is no longer, or has not yet become, faith.

§

Although Francis now had a concrete goal, he did not immediately abandon his accustomed way of life. He was still a rich merchant's son, and so when he considered what he had to do to repair San Damiano, he naturally turned first to the family coffers. After racing home, he gathered up some bolts of cloth from the shop, mounted his steed and rode to the nearby town of Foligno, where he sold the fabric, the horse and even his own fine outfit and brought the proceeds to a priest he found sitting near San Damiano.

"I beg you," he said as he handed him the coins, "buy some oil and keep the lamp burning before the image of the crucified. When this money runs out, I will again give you as much as you need."

But the astonished clergyman knew that Peter Bernardone would be furious at San Damiano's ill-gotten gains; he also knew that Francis had been (as Celano tells us) "living outrageously among his relatives and acquaintances and exalting his stupidity." In addition, he suspected that Francis, who was wearing only a peasant's smock he had found in Foligno, was probably either drunk or mad. Accordingly, the priest refused the donation and Francis—angry, disappointed and offended—tossed the money aside.

Fearing the tempest he would face at home, Francis hid in the underground chamber of one of his father's properties for almost two weeks, sustaining himself on wild berries and handouts from passersby. Meanwhile, Peter and Pica grew understandably more anxious by the day. Eventually, his father located him and dragged him back to town.

Pica wept with relief and ran to prepare a meal; Peter, on the other hand, was speechless with rage. Francis was a pathetic sight, dirty, pale and thin, with a sickly, distracted and frightened appearance. Earlier, he could be tolerated as a spoiled, overgrown rich boy, but now, in this condition, he was a profound embarrassment to his father. Some Assisians considered Francis ill, some called him a lunatic or an ingrate, and some even proclaimed him a sinner, now firmly within the devil's grip.

Francis needed to be taught a lesson, that much was clear. Peter knew he had to accomplish two things. He had to reform his son once and for all; and he had to resolve the shame of his son and the humiliating pity of his friends—he had, in other words, to put a good public face on the matter for the consuls and the people of Assisi. And so he dragged Francis to the San Giorgio *trivium*—the place for adjudicating public disputes.

After thrashing Francis in the sight of all, Peter was reminded by one of the city fathers that the statutes of the commune gave a father the right to chain up a recalcitrant child. This idea repelled Peter, who then changed his tactic. In public that afternoon and over the course of the following week at home, he pleaded with Francis to behave reasonably. There was nothing he would not do for his beloved son, he promised, if only the boy would come to his senses.

Francis, however, was adamant. His entire universe had been shaken, his sense of possibility completely renewed since that afternoon in San Damiano. God, he insisted, was waiting for him to repair the little church.

With no options remaining, Peter locked his son in a dark, airless storage room, where Francis languished, seeing light only when his father unbolted the door for his mother to hand him a bowl of soup and some bread. The house arrest continued for weeks, until Peter departed "on pressing family business," according to Celano, and Pica released her son. But where would he go, what would he do?

He slipped out quietly that night and took refuge in a cave outside the city, away from the public taunts, the whispered comments, the mockery and the pity. Fearful of confronting his father, he knew he had to leave home for good. There was nothing left to him but his task, no one to rely on but the God Who had spoken to his heart a few weeks earlier. In the solitude of the cave, Francis listened.

FIVE

1206–1208

I‌T WOULD BE COMFORTING to imagine Francis of Assisi, calm and confident in his rustic retreat, breathing the heady air of spiritual ecstasy, emotionally buoyed by a newfound awareness of the presence of God, embarking in the direction of sainthood and certain of the route that would take him there.

But such was not the case. After the experience at San Damiano, there was a painful interval during which he took no comfort from any pious practices, and the nature of his vocation remained unclear. The late autumn of 1205 and the new year 1206 were frosty and damp, and Francis, alone in his cave, found prayer almost impossible; early sources add that he often wept with fear. Finally, in February, he convinced the priest who was caretaker of San Damiano to let him sweep the church and begin repairs.

By now Peter had returned from trading to learn that his boy had left home, and while Pica tried to defend her son, she was as usual ineffective against her husband's outrage. Later, pious romantics argued that Pica had always had an intuitive comprehension of her son's mystic journey. But there is no evidence for this pleasant invention: no one, in fact, understood Francis's youthful odyssey, least of all himself.

Peter rushed to San Damiano, where he found Francis, shivering with cold as he scrubbed and swept. At the sight of his son, Peter "was touched with sorrow and deeply disturbed by this sudden turn of events," as Francis's friends movingly recalled a few years later. Few moments in the Bernardone family history are as poignant as this picture of a desperate father, trying one last time to rescue his son from folly and bring him to what he believed was a sensible life. But Francis was unmoved by any of his arguments.

For all he cared, Peter then said desperately, the boy could pursue any crazy scheme that came into his head, or he could simply live off his friends just as he had freeloaded at home. Whatever the case, his father intended to claim what was justly due to him: the money Francis had obtained by selling the fabric and the horse, which he demanded be repaid at once. That was impossible, Francis replied: he no longer had the money, for he had given it to the Church. His father would have to retrieve it from the bishop.

To excuse Francis's behavior as simply unfair would be to minimize the insensitivity of his conduct. First, he had stolen from his own family. Second, he had blithely tossed the money aside. Third, indifferent to his father's patience and property, Francis spoke with astonishing guile. Because he knew that the priest at San Damiano had eventually collected the money, Francis insisted it was now officially Church goods. With no regard for family obligations or secular law, he presumed that a churchman would invoke canon law to defend a contributor against a rich merchant.

But here he miscalculated badly, for Peter went to the city magistrates to ask them to force restitution of the money from San Damiano. The consuls, however, were prohibited by statute from interfering in family quarrels. Peter then brought criminal proceedings against Francis for rebellion, larceny and public humiliation—offenses punishable by banishment or imprisonment. But that matter, too, was not within the purview of the law, for Francis's bequest to San Damiano and his work there put him legally in the service of the Church: "He no longer falls within our power," as the communal leaders explained. The case would have to be brought before the bishop of Assisi, the formidable Guido, and messengers were dispatched to bring Francis into town.

At nine o'clock on a cold, windy morning in early March—the time fixed for disputes in which the bishop adjudicated—a great crowd gathered in the Piazza di Santa Maria Maggiore to watch the proceedings of Bernardone against his son. Staying back among the throng, Pica kept her distance, as Peter stepped forward, solemn, respectable and proud in the garments that marked his success.

At the sound of a bell, Bishop Guido appeared at the top of the grand staircase of the church. Wearing a miter of silk fabric and a blue velvet mantle fastened with gold clasps, he was an imposing figure, surrounded by canons and acolytes, the public assessor and the notaries. The crowd must have fallen silent, for Guido was not a man to tolerate disrespect, much less contradiction.

A man of violent temper and imperious conduct, he had since 1204 commanded the diocese of Assisi, of which he owned about half the property. In only two years, he made his mark by ruling in an abundance of litigations and arbitrations and by issuing many important pronouncements and sentences. Occasionally, he sought out an antagonist and punched him to the ground, thus exploiting the prohibition against laymen striking back against a clergyman. Sometimes Pope Innocent III himself had to warn the bishop to moderate his behavior.

But Guido also followed to the letter a directive he had received from the pope to the effect that "all the goods that the church possessed, or would acquire in the future with the help of God, must remain in the hands of the Bishop of Assisi and his successors."

Guido took his seat and nodded at Peter Bernardone before turning to acknowledge the arrival of Francis, whose appearance must have shocked even his father. He had washed, trimmed his beard and surreptitiously obtained from his mother the kind of elegant outfit that he once customarily wore.

Peter stated his case, repeating his accusations of theft and dishonor, seeking redress and compensation.

Guido turned to Francis, whom many people still knew and liked, and spoke calmly to him. "Your father is infuriated and extremely scandalized. If you wish to serve God, return to him the money you have, because God does not want you to spend unjustly acquired money on the church. [Your father's] anger will diminish once he gets the money back. My son, have confidence in the Lord and act courageously. Do not be afraid, for He will be your help and will abundantly provide you with whatever is necessary for the work of His church."

And that, everyone must have believed, would be the end of the matter: Francis Bernardone would soon be back in the bosom of his family, and his parents—as so often in the past—would forgive and embrace him.

But the day's surprises had just begun.

With remarkable composure, Francis rose from his place and approached the bishop. "My lord," he said, raising his voice, "I will gladly give back to my father not only the money acquired from his things, but even all my clothes." With that, Francis slipped through a side door of the cathedral, only to appear moments later stark naked, standing before the bishop and holding out all his clothes, with a cash purse placed on top of them. The astonished bishop took the garments and the money, handing them over to an acolyte.

Francis now turned to the crowd and said, "Listen to me, all of you, and understand. Until now, I have called Peter Bernardone my father. But because I have proposed to serve God, I return to him the money on account of which he was so upset, and also all the clothing which is his, and I want only to say from now on, 'Our Father, Who art in heaven,' and not, 'My father, Peter Bernardone.' "

Peter, "overcome with unbearable pain and anger, took the money and all the clothing," and there was no further need of a formal judgment. With that, Bishop Guido stepped toward Francis and covered his nakedness with his ample cloak. From that day, Peter and Pica Bernardone disappear completely from every account of their son's life: there is no evidence of any reconciliation, and the circumstances of their later lives and of their deaths are unknown.

§

The scene of the judgment before the bishop is among the most famous in religious history and has often been represented in art, from the 13th century up to the present, but much of it remains painful to read and difficult to comprehend.

At the moment of disrobing, Francis was in fact engaging in the *ars concionandi*, the craft and skill of oratory—the popular medieval method of argument and persuasion in the public assembly, or *concione*, where citizens discussed and decided matters of importance to the commune. This technique aimed to persuade not so much by rational discourse or verbal rhetoric alone but by a dramatic manner, by the physical actions that accompanied the words and finally by some gesture that would attract an audience's attention.

That morning, Francis may have been thinking of Christ's nakedness on the cross when he startled the crowd by this grand theatrical action.

Medieval piety saw valuable symbolism in nakedness; monks often quoted the injunction of Saint Jerome that the follower of Jesus, "being naked [that is, not dependent on possessions], follows the naked Christ—that is, the bare cross." Similarly, the evangelical movements that renewed popular devotion from the 11th to the 13th centuries stressed the necessity of spurning anything superfluous in one's life.

Francis must have realized the profound meaning of his gesture—which, given his choice of clothing for the occasion, could hardly have been the inspiration of the moment. Whereas he knew what he was abandoning, what he was forever giving up, he could not foresee what his lot would be once the moment of renunciation had passed. For that, he had to rely on Providence; fortunately, Guido rose to the occasion and provided Francis's immediate need for clothing against the winter chill by giving him a tunic.

It was not Francis's nudity that startled the crowd; people in the Middle Ages had little shame about the body and sexuality. In Francis's time, there was little possibility to develop a sense of shame about the flesh: rooms were crowded, privacy was rare, and because there was no indoor plumbing, toilet facilities were improvised wherever one happened to be.

That morning in the piazza, what did shock the Assisians was Francis's willingness to make a complete break with his family, its structure, its security and its support. Nakedness was thus a powerful symbol of what Francis desired: freedom, like that of the naked newborn, without the burden of worldly goods or privileges, without the pleasures and responsibility of possessions and fine clothes. However lost he had been until then, he had always kept the ties of attachment to his family's influence and money, but now he was throwing in his lot with all those who had nothing—and in 1206, to have nothing meant literally to have nothing, not simply less. From that day, he would take his place with the disenfranchised, with the poor and with the Christ whom he had seen on the crucifix at San Damiano.

His actions that morning can only be appreciated in context and as part of an ongoing process. His conversion had begun with a crisis of meaning following imprisonment, illness and long recuperation. Then, he had experienced a profound disconnection from life and a concurrent disillusionment with earthly glory and riches. After that, he had been disabused of his desire for knightly status, and following his return to his old ways of indolence and empty distraction, he found life more empty and purposeless than ever. In other words, the spiritual divestment preceded its physical counterpart.

§

For all their value, the earliest documents about Francis must be read with a degree of skepticism, particularly where this episode of his life is concerned. His illness, his return from Spoleto, his disgust with the emptiness of social life, the moment at San Damiano: the original sources and the subsequent tradition of pious preachers tend to reduce these stages to the logical unfolding of a coherently constructed narrative. But if that was the case, and if one occurrence with its clear purpose followed another event with its evident meaning, then one must ask why Francis himself took so long a time to discern the obvious course of his life.

The answer lies in what happened soon afterward. Francis knew that he could never turn again to his earthly father for support, given his cruel remark that henceforth only God was his father, not Peter Bernardone. That, of course, was a specious argument, for Peter was his father and forever would be. One can neither deny nor replace a human relationship, however inadequate or painful, by asserting that a relationship with God will fill its function or substitute for it.

Human motivations are nothing if not complex, and Francis—who must have realized the humiliation he had caused his parents—also accepted the fact that he could not continue to keep a link to his family and rely on their support only when it was convenient. In some way, he perhaps recognized that it would have been the greater insult to his parents *not* to break with them, given how much he had already asked them to endure. If his method was surely insensitive, offensive and self-dramatizing, it was also extremely risky—perhaps the bravest thing he had done in his life thus far. He at last forced himself to perform a public act that was as uncompromising to himself as it was to his parents.

We should be very clear on one particular matter: Francis did not condemn the material possessions so frantically accumulated by his father. To claim this about him is an error that has been made frequently by his admirers. He did not, after all, burn his father's shop or sabotage his business. Material things were not, in and of themselves, the problem; rather, Francis's attitude to them was. At last he himself had come to understand that the impediment to his happiness lay not in his father's profession or riches but within himself.

Implicitly, however, he was indeed rejecting something unhealthy in society, and in this regard he was a true visionary.

Precisely at this time, money was becoming more than simply a social convention, a medium of economic exchange. People were beginning to pursue money as a primary goal; and the amount of money one acquired determined one's status in the community. Society in the 21st century, in fact, operates on the same tacit assumption that began in the 13th—namely, that money can indeed buy happiness, or at least rent it.

Francis's era was the first time in history, since the Roman Empire, that costly items were purchased for no other purpose than to publicize the surplus wealth of the owner—and these items were, for the most part, clothing. Expensive garments were identified with status, and status with social importance. People began to know the price of a great deal, but the real value of very little. Thus began what Thorstein Veblen, 700 years later, famously termed "conspicuous consumption."

After Bishop Guido gave Francis an old hermit's tunic, he counseled him to make a pilgrimage to Rome, which he did that spring of 1206. Saint Peter's Basilica, built over the saint's traditional burial site, was not yet the grand structure that was begun in 1506, whose final design owed to Michelangelo, Maderno and Bernini, and which survives to this day. Francis prayed at the former church, which dated from the fourth century and had a large atrium at its entrance. While there he gave to a group of sick beggars the remnants of a small purse Guido had provided. With that spontaneous, generous bequest, Francis was literally both impoverished and homeless—a condition made even more serious by his fragile health and recurring bouts of malarial fever, which left him utterly exhausted.

Making his way slowly north from Rome on foot, he came upon a colony of lepers. Many such communities existed, most of them in isolated rural areas. Lepers were considered legally dead; they had no rights under any law, and while the Church opened many hospices to care for them, it did so with the contradiction of invariably citing them as examples of the deformity of sin.

The numbers of such poor, lame people were legion, for they included not only those suffering from leprosy itself but also from the widespread effects of consuming contaminated grains, always a consequence of famine. These included eczemas and shingles, skin cancers and putrefying limbs, facial ulcers and blindness. Travel to and from the East and the importing of pathogens by ship, more frequent since the onset of the Crusades, also introduced various new forms of sickness into Europe.

People with hideous deformities were required to live among themselves, were forbidden to enter towns and cities, and were prevented from making any contact with the rest of society. If they limped along the road or came close to town to beg, they had to cover themselves with their pathetic rags, which did little to stifle the appalling stench emanating from suppurating wounds; they were also required by law to sound a clapper or a bell to warn of their proximity. Everyone kept a distance from lepers, for their condition was considered both highly contagious and a sign of dreadful sinfulness.

Since the time of his youthful travels with his father, Francis had known about lepers, for it was impossible to avoid them on country roads from Italy through France and Flanders. Like everyone else, Francis would never come too near to them; if passersby had a few coins or some bread to spare, they flung the offering from what was considered a safe distance.

But this time his encounter was very different. Perhaps he had a lingering memory of the dying at the little clinic of San Giorgio; in any case, he did not flee in horror as before, but instead approached one of the most lame and pathetic of the group. With no money to give and no food to share—for he, too, was now reduced to begging—Francis knelt down and gave what he could: an embrace, a bit of comfort, a few sympathetic words. Francis would almost certainly have remembered the New Testament accounts in which Jesus healed a leper. "Moved with pity, Jesus stretched out his hand and touched him," which must have shocked bystanders as much as the cure itself did.

With this single act of charity, Francis was apparently transformed, for when he returned to Umbria he not only resumed his restoration of San Damiano but also began to nurse lepers, a task rarely undertaken by anyone. This involved not only begging food on their behalf and feeding them, but carrying them to a nearby brook or stream to wash their sores. "For God's sake, he served all of them with great love. He washed all the filth from them, and even cleaned out the pus of their sores." His care, in other words, meant more than merely not showing revulsion. It meant a willingness to be with them precisely because they were outcast. It meant taking with grave literalness the standard of the Gospel that to minister to the needy was to minister to the lonely, naked and dying Christ.

The importance of these acts of compassion for the progress of Francis's conversion cannot be overestimated. Later, he came to recognize that the courage given to him that enabled him to minister to these pariahs marked a moment of extraordinary grace. He referred to this period in the final days of his life, when he began to dictate his final *Testament* with the following words: "The Lord gave me, Brother Francis, thus to begin doing penance in this way: for when I was in sin, it seemed too bitter for me to see lepers. [But then] the Lord Himself led me among them, and I showed mercy to them."

There existed a rich biblical and medieval tradition that "showing mercy" to the desperate was a sign of changing one's life. That this marked the beginning of a turn toward God—that is, of conversion—is also a belief that has endured down through the centuries. After World War II, for example, an Albanian grocer's daughter named Agnes Bojaxhiu decided to care for the dying poor in Calcutta by simply being with them, so that they would not die alone, without the warmth of a human embrace. Later known as Mother Teresa, she said (when awarded the Nobel Peace Prize): "I choose the poverty of our poor people. But I am grateful to receive [the prize money] in the name of the hungry, the naked, the homeless, the crippled, the blind, the lepers and all those people who feel unwanted, unloved, uncared for throughout society—people who have become a burden to society and are shunned by everyone."

§

What, then, enabled Francis to perform actions that at first must have been repellent to his refined sensibility and his constitutional frailty? The answer is both simple and inexhaustibly mysterious: only the quiet, sudden infusion of some power beyond himself made it possible, and this the believer calls grace—the unbidden, unsought, unexpected emergence in the soul of a capacity hitherto unacknowledged.

We have come to accept the inscrutability of inspiration, the sudden moment of illumination, the unforeseen leap of imagination that occurs in the expression of human genius. Archimedes, Kepler, Newton and Einstein in science have their artistic counterparts in Homer, Shakespeare, Mozart and Monet. The only thing we can say for certain about their moments of epiphany is that their precise source cannot be rationally explained; the person enlightened is perhaps astonished most of all. There are many such stories throughout history and in every culture; each of them changed lives past counting.

In the benighted leper, Francis saw at last the fullest meaning of the suffering Christ, a meaning that had eluded him at the crucifix at San Damiano. Then, his inspiration was immediate, concrete, outer-directed: "Repair my house." For a time, he would continue to do that literally, by restoring crumbling churches. But thenceforth, he perceived a deeper meaning in that instruction. By extending himself in compassion to the neediest, he would in fact undertake a more extensive repair and reform of the larger "house"—the community, the institution so critically in need of renovation.

In nursing the world's outcasts, Francis had begun to rise to the genuine nobility he had long sought, which was to be discovered not in armor, or in titles or battles, glory or contests. Honor would be found not in associating with the strongest, the most attractive, the best dressed or the most secure people in society, but with the weakest, the most disfigured, those who were marginalized, dependent and despised.

In prison, the rich young man of Assisi had, it seemed, suffered without purpose, for his consequent illness temporarily had left him apathetic and depressed, with nothing to alleviate a sense of futility. The subsequent quest for knightly glory in battle had proven fruitless. But now, among the feeble and the powerless, Francis realized that the quest for glory would not lead to happiness, nor would the mere pursuit of pleasure or even a good reputation provide any real security.

In embracing and attending lepers, he went beyond knowledge to experience. In their unimaginable suffering, he saw the ultimate agony of

Christ crucified—Christ abandoned and rejected, alone in his death, apparently rendered powerless against the triumphant malice of the world. But that, faith insisted, was not the end of the story.

§

When he returned to Umbria late in the spring of 1206, Francis resumed the repairs to San Damiano. It was work for which he had some training, since he had once helped to build the new city wall for Assisi from the ruins of the Rocca Maggiore. He relied on his experience in business, in bartering and trading, and in using his natural charm and courtesy to the best effect. He found stones in fields and streams, and when he needed timber, heavy boulders or other supplies, he did not hesitate simply to ask for them. Sometimes people were eager to offer donations for a church; just as often, he was dismissed as some sort of eccentric vagrant.

In addition to San Damiano, he also turned his attention to two other small, derelict churches—San Pietro della Spina, in the fields beyond Assisi, and the chapel of Santa Maria della Porziuncula, two miles south of the city. Given his dedication to these tasks, it is not surprising that for several years Francis regarded this work as his permanent vocation. Rebuilding churches was in fact a pious medieval tradition, and Francis imagined that for the rest of his life he would be little more than a day laborer—a prospect from which he derived only the profoundest joy. Passing Francis at work on San Damiano, his half brother, Angelo, remarked loudly and sarcastically to a friend, "You might tell Francis to sell you a small coin's worth of his sweat"—to which Francis replied politely, "Oh, I will sell that sweat to my Lord at a high price!" He had not lost his sense of humor.

Without home or possessions, he worked alone at San Damiano and then retired to a shed nearby, or to the cave in which he had formerly taken refuge from his father. And here, according to all the early sources, his prayer intensified. "I left the world," he said of this time—that is, he stepped away from both the business and the busyness of society.

He did not, however, abandon the natural world, the handiwork of God's creation; on the contrary, he embraced it ever more and more deeply. With his talk of "leaving the world," Francis allied himself to the tradition of the ancient desert hermits, renouncing the values of the society in which he had been born and raised.

§

During this time Francis continued to dress in the burlap tunic that Guido had provided, along with leather sandals, a belt and a staff for walking. It was the simple garb of a lay hermit, clothing that marked its wearer with a particular status in the Middle Ages. First of all, it signified a juridical change, in that the wearer was now under Church protection. Since the fourth century, a number of both men and women had chosen a hermit's existence, seeking solitude to pursue their spiritual lives without distraction. Beginning in the early 11th century, the hermit's vocation became newly popular, offering an alternative to the ways of monks and the proliferation of monasteries, where life had become rich and indolent. Hermits lived alone, following the customs of the Byzantine tradition, which included solitude, silence, fasting on bread and water, prayer vigils and, to avoid idleness, craft work.

In Francis's time, the ranks of new European hermits included layfolk, clergy and monks who turned their backs on the comfortable lives they had enjoyed and withdrew to the countryside. They were, therefore, essentially penitents who wished to live out the *metanoia*, or conversion, they had experienced. Heedless of their appearance, some sought shelter in caves or huts, lived entirely on raw produce and did manual work. But their desire for solitude did not mean they turned their backs on the world completely, for they were much involved in trying to alleviate society's problems, serving as wandering preachers, aiding visitors, helping weary travelers and generally assisting the needy.

Francis made a significant addition to the hermit's garb. With a jagged piece of limestone or chalk, he marked the back of his tunic with what henceforth became his sign—a large **T**, the letter tau, which marked his service to the poor.

"He favored the sign of the Tau over all others," according to Celano. "With it alone he signed letters he sent, and he painted it on the walls of [monastic] cells everywhere." It became a kind of coat of arms for Francis.

The letter **T**, found in both the Hebrew and Greek alphabets (as taw and tau, respectively), symbolized the fulfillment of the message of the patriarchs and prophets. Ezekiel the prophet had been commanded to place this mark on the foreheads of all those who hated iniquity. The imagery was repeated in the visions of Revelation, wherein the "seal on the foreheads" of God's servants signifies His protection of them. Quite naturally, Christians viewed **T** as the mark of the crucifixion and resurrection of Jesus, which itself was believed to be the fulfillment of everything promised to Israel. By the time of the Middle Ages, the tau in the form of a cross appeared widely in manuscripts and was a popular motif in art. Many Christians also traced the sign of the cross on the foreheads of families, friends and those setting out on journeys. The Hospitalers of Saint Antony the Hermit, a group of itinerant monks dedicated to the care of lepers and plague victims, wore the **T** on amulets, on their staff and on their habits as a kind of symbolic prayer for divine protection against epidemic.

Francis not only adopted this widely popular sign for his own emblem and signature, but often knelt with arms outstretched, consecrating himself in imitation of the crucified and offering himself entirely to God. He was also known to prostrate himself on the ground with his arms similarly outstretched.

His life was spent in the quietest simplicity: building, begging and praying. In a way, he had now become both the beggar he had dismissed from his father's shop and the knight in tatters to whom he had once given his own fine garments. From moment to moment, Francis was dependent on the mercy of God. And here we touch on the deepest meaning of poverty of spirit. Those who strive for that sublime dependence are the true recipients of God's friendship—"Blessed are the poor in spirit," we read in Scripture, "for theirs is the kingdom of heaven."

§

An important element of medieval spiritual life was its ascetical aspect— that is, its emphasis on discipline and self-control, the subjugation of the body and its desires and the practice of certain exercises designed to inculcate virtue. Fasting, for example, was a central fact of Christian life, and even ordinary laypeople fasted for the entire 40 days of Lent as well as on the eve of many feasts throughout the year.

As perhaps was to be expected of so enthusiastic a convert, Francis developed the custom, in his 20s, of extremes of mortification: "He inflicted his flesh with such fasting," according to a frank account offered by his first companions, "that, whether healthy or sick, this excessively austere man hardly ever or never wanted to indulge his body. Because of this, he confessed on his deathbed that he had greatly sinned against [what he called] 'Brother Body.' "

"He rarely or hardly ever ate cooked foods," according to Celano, "but if he did, he would sprinkle them with ashes or dampen the flavor of spices with cold water." And if invited to a dinner "given by great princes who venerated him with much fondness, he would taste some meat, [but] the rest, which he appeared to eat, he put in his lap, raising his hand to his mouth so that no one could know what he was doing . . . [and] he would not allow himself to drink even enough water when he was burning with thirst." As for sexual temptation, his antidote was also typically medieval: "He would immerse himself in a ditch filled in winter with ice, remaining in it until every seduction of the flesh went away."

In addition to intermittent bouts of recurrent malaria, Francis began to suffer from chronic gastritis and, because of insufficient and unhealthy food, a gastric ulcer that never healed and caused frequent attacks of acute pain and anorexia, which were perilous for an already slender and frail young man.

To his credit, he later acknowledged the harm he had done himself with the regimen of self-affliction that he had begun in 1206. In discrediting these measures, he was also discouraging his companions and followers from imitating them. Today we are inclined to view such medieval practices as neurotic, and even masochistic. But they must be judged according to the context of their times, and if we do not choose to imitate them, we can still come to appreciate that they were part of an ideal that brooked no compromise. Francis's intention was clearly to give birth to a new life, enveloped in what today we call a new lifestyle: it would feature no more revels, no culinary caprices, no tippling at wine for the sheer pleasure it brought. For him there had to be a complete break so that he could be winnowed like ground wheat, the old man ready to be made over into the new.

But why such contempt for the body? people object. How can this mode of conduct be called service of God? It is probably best to acknowledge immediately that there is simply no justification, according to our modern understanding of a healthy spirituality, for penances such as those often assumed by Francis and others during the Middle Ages.

Fasting and control of the body were then seen to be part (but only part) of a program by which people could overcome the inclination to luxury so that the soul could the more readily rise to consider the things of God. Even those who did not practice heroic fasting or penance took for granted that the flesh had, at least occasionally, to be denied so that the spirit could flourish.

Is our contemporary obsession with physical perfection any less pathological than the conduct of the ascetic? Nine hundred years after Francis, people want to feel good about themselves—a longing doomed to disappointment, or at least only temporary satisfaction. But in an age of faith, physical denial was aimed at toning the spirit, not the body—so that, freed from sluggishness and dependence on the comfort of rich food and drink, the spirit would be fit and ready not for a new wardrobe or ideal romance but for inner clarity, a prelude to prayer. On this point every religion in the history of the world agrees: a certain mastery over the inclinations of the flesh is always in order if the spiritual life is to flourish.

As for Francis, we might wish his self-inflicted penances had not been so imprudent. That may be because we prefer saints to be either perfect in every way or so ordinary that they conform to our own stature and do not challenge our spiritual indolence. But saints are in fact heroically in love, and like lovers, they sometimes become eccentric, and even overstep themselves; holiness does not preclude humanity, after all. Above everything, however, saints keep God firmly in sight. They remain faithful, and that is why they are saints—not because they are invariably models of polite or even imitable conduct.

§

While restoring San Damiano, San Pietro and Saint Mary of the Angels chapel (the Porziuncula)—tasks that took from the summer of 1206 to early 1208—Francis regularly traveled to attend lepers in Gubbio, a town about 20 miles north of Assisi's walls. Once, during his solitary journey, he was singing French melodies when highwaymen accosted him, taking his fluency in French song for a sure sign that he was a wandering minstrel with a purse. They demanded to know his identity, and Francis must have been about to give his legal baptismal name, for he replied (in the spirit of John the Baptist), "I am the herald of the great king! What is that to you?" His boldness, and probably his lack of anything they could purloin, much annoyed the men, who tossed him into a ravine as they departed.

Francis collected himself and made his way to the lepers, and from Gubbio, when heavy rains brought flash floods, sought refuge in the Benedictine monastery of Santa Maria di Valfabbrica. The unexpected guest looked to the monks like nothing so much as a hapless beggar, and so he was hustled off to the kitchens, where he was put to work and finally given a bowl of cold remnants from their supper. Two days later, having decided he was a nuisance, they sent him off into the night.

SIX

1208–1209

BY EARLY 1208, Francis had completed the repairs to the small church of San Pietro della Spina, and he began work on a place the locals called the *porʒucle*, literally a "little portion" of land belonging to the Benedictine monks of Mount Subasio. The monks had abandoned the property and a chapel called Saint Mary of the Little Portion, or Saint Mary of the Angels, which stood in a clearing in the middle of a forest. Francis, and later his friends, took to referring to it as the Porziuncula and considered it something like God's little share. It was commonly called simply "Santa Maria," and so it will be designated here—Saint Mary's.

Francis labored quickly, and after only six weeks the altar was usable once again, and services could be held. On the morning of February 24, Francis stopped work on the broken stones and deteriorating walls to attend Mass in the cold, dark chapel. The Church's calendar on that date honored Saint Matthias, chosen to replace Judas among the original apostles. The priest read aloud the New Testament account of Jesus sending out his company of 12, and the passage forcefully struck Francis, who was kneeling quietly in his hermit's tunic: "As you go, proclaim the good news, 'The kingdom of heaven has come near.' . . . Take no gold or silver or copper in your belts, no bag for your journey, nor two tunics nor sandals nor a staff."

At the end of Mass, Francis approached the priest and asked him for an explanation of these words. Are they not self-evident? asked the cleric. The apostles were to travel completely unencumbered by excess and were to make themselves entirely dependent, even from moment to moment, on the mercy of God.

Pondering this reading, Francis considered his own garb and then looked at the priest. "This is what I want," he said quietly. "This is what I seek, this is what I desire with all my heart." And so, acting to obey the injunction literally, Francis removed his makeshift shoes and set aside his staff, exchanged his leather belt for a piece of rope and discarded one of his two tunics. "He was no deaf hearer of the Gospel," observed one account; "he was careful to carry it out to the letter."

Francis could not but surrender to the immediate impact of Jesus' words: indeed, he approached them simply but fully, putting into practice the biblical counsels without waiting to consider their every implication. In other words, in following the lessons of the New Testament he pursued the reverse of the usual means of pedagogy. He did not try to understand what the Gospel meant and then attempt to find ways of carrying out its message. Rather, he dared the experiment of first living that message, and from living it, discovered a new and practical way of understanding it.

Discarding even the humble garments he had been wearing, Francis left himself only a tattered cloth tunic with a capuche, or hood, a short undergarment and a piece of knotted cord for a belt; henceforth he went without shoes, until he grew quite ill one winter and friends begged him to avoid frostbite. The tunic itself was made of coarse material, and when the hood was raised over his head and his arms were extended, Francis appeared to be embraced by the cross. This was by no means a uniform: he simply meant to dress like a very poor man, and no longer even a hermit. He (and eventually his companions) wore whatever muted colors they could find—gray, brown, black, dark green—and Francis never bothered to choose a common color for a religious habit. (That occurred only well after his death; one group of Franciscan friars eventually chose a hood that reminded some people of coffee mixed with foaming milk: cappuccino derives its name from these Capuchin friars and their capuche.)

Francis's simplicity was an implicit correction to the luxury and privilege that defined much ecclesiastical life. There were already movements within the Church to address these abuses, and groups had sprung up to offset them by contrary action. Francis had no intention of joining such a group, however, nor was he going to play into the hands of those angry heretics who rejected the Church because of corrupt churchmen. He simply made a radical effort to practice the Gospel uncompromisingly at a time when the institution seemed hopelessly wayward.

Francis recognized that without the Church there would have been no Mass that February day. Sinful though it was, he was entirely devoted to it, for it was the guardian and repository of a tradition that had to be kept alive. Francis had none of the smug superiority with which some people consider themselves outside and above a sinful Church, for he was all too aware of his own frailty. In any case, he could never have conceived of abandoning the Church, which had never, during his youth, abandoned him. One might say that he took it seriously but not too seriously: it was the footsteps of Christ that he sought to follow, not the lead of any churchman, cleric or saint.

§

From that February day, Francis added to his duties the calling of the first disciples of Jesus. When he finished his day's work, or a portion of his repairs, he wandered about the plain and the valley, urging people to turn their hearts toward God, to reform their lives by prayer, simplicity and concern for the poor, and begging them not to follow the ways of the rich and content.

"His words," according to his friends, "were neither hollow nor ridiculous . . . [and] he inspired his listeners with words that were simple and a heart that was heroic." Of his exact speech and expressions we know very little, for there are only brief, synthetic summaries and no direct transcriptions of his spontaneous sermons and the brief conversations he had with strangers he met en route. We do know, however, that his customary greeting to everyone was, "May the Lord give you peace!" As for his attitude toward public sinners, reprobates and felons, Francis was almost revolutionary in his counsel, much like Jesus of Nazareth. He and his companions, he said, "must be careful not to be angry or disturbed at the sin of another, for anger and disturbance impede charity in [ourselves] and others."

That in itself must have sounded odd to people, for this was not an era when peace reigned anywhere—not among kingdoms, not within the

Church, not in communes, counties or cities. But peace was the message of the prophets of Israel and the goal of Christ's ministry, and the New Testament letters (of Paul, Peter, John and Jude, for example) typically conclude with prayers and blessings for peace. Forgiveness, the calming of strife, lasting harmony among people, the thirst for justice—all these effected peace among individuals and communities.

When Francis insisted on the need for peace, it was more than just a sentimental wish; it was a prayer for the human condition. It derived from his acquaintanceship with Scripture, from hearing the words spoken at worship, and from his direct inner experience of the peace of God, which had changed and was continuing to change his life as his own conversion continued. "Live in peace, and the God of love and peace will be with you." With those words, Saint Paul concluded his second letter to the Corinthians; with those same words, Francis embarked each day on his mission to proclaim God's peace to a violent world. Much more than the mere absence of conflict, peace was to be the result of better relationships with God and neighbor, and was therefore necessarily linked to justice and love.

When the early documents add that Francis "preached penance," the meaning of that phrase was clear to his contemporaries: it signified an invitation to reform one's life, to convert and be reconciled to God by living joyfully in His presence. That, after all, is the meaning of the biblical notion of justification—to be justified is to have one's relationship with God made right, to accept the divine offer of friendship, which bestows meaning in this world and the promise that death will not finally conquer, that life endures eternally in God.

§

From February to mid-April 1208, Francis continued his ceaseless round of work, prayer, tending the sick and barefoot preaching in the vicinity of the chapel of Saint Mary's. His sympathy for the suffering was deep and immediate, his manner was always courteous, his presence undemanding and his message quietly joyful.

It was perhaps inevitable that the people of Assisi would soon want to see for themselves this enthusiastic and charismatic young man, once so well known as a hedonist. In his new life, as they witnessed, his energy was even more astounding than before, especially because he was not at all robust. It was perhaps also to be expected that so engaging a person would begin to attract both the transiently curious and some serious followers, although Francis flatly refused to see them as anything other than companions in faith. He had no desire to be anyone's leader; he wanted only to serve.

One young man who found Francis at Saint Mary's announced with great fervor that he wished to live an identical life of simplicity, work and sacrifice—and then, after a few days, promptly vanished. In late March, a young merchant named Bernard Quintavalle, who like Francis was from one of Assisi's wealthiest families, heard about the former rake's new life. He and a friend named Peter Catanio were curious to learn the truth about the rumors of conversion, and so Bernard invited Francis to his home, a grand palazzo in the city.

Their conversation lasted all through the night, and at one point Bernard asked, "If someone had held a certain [feudal] lord's possessions for a long time and no longer wished to keep them, what would be the best thing to do?" The solution was obvious, Francis replied: he had to give everything back to their owner.

"I acknowledge, then," Bernard continued, "that everything I own was given to me by God, and now I am ready to return it all to Him." In that case, Francis said, they would go to church in the morning and consult a missal in order to discern the will of God in the gospels.

The random opening of the Scriptures for spiritual advice was a common but not entirely sanctioned practice in the Middle Ages: called the *sortes apostolorum,* it was a custom based on the devout (if somewhat superstitious) belief that if one by chance turned to the same or similar passages three consecutive times, it was a clear sign of God's plan. The following morning, Bernard sent for Peter Catanio, who joined them at the Church of San Nicolò in Assisi's market square and, as it happened, very near the former Bernardone residence.

Of the ages and appearances of Bernard and Peter (and subsequent companions of Francis) we know almost nothing: as was typical of the time, the earliest sources had no interest in providing biographical details of anyone other than Francis. His friends and allies feature in the various accounts of his life only when an oral tradition exists for an event in which they participated. Some appear more frequently than others, and a few were closer to Francis than most. But it is important to emphasize that, like him, each of the first Franciscans (as they came to be known) was ultimately a contemplative with a private and solitary life to which he returned almost as often as he undertook work as a preacher and caregiver for the poor and sick.

That April morning, Francis, Bernard and Peter gathered in the church, and after a few moments of silent prayer, Francis opened the missal. The three men read together the first passage they chanced upon—verses in which Jesus invites a rich young man to join the fellowship of his disciples: "Go, sell what you own, and give to the poor, and you will have treasure in heaven; then come, follow me."

The next passage to which they turned at random was Jesus' counsel to the first disciples as they set out to proclaim the reign of God in the world: "Take nothing for your journey—no staff, nor bag, nor bread, nor money—not even an extra tunic."

And the third was another saying of Jesus: "If any want to become my followers, let them deny themselves"—that is, let them put others first and be always ready to sacrifice themselves.

The unanimity in the sentiment expressed in the three passages left no doubt in the minds of the three men, and Francis said that these simple lessons of Jesus were to be the outline of their lives, the sole norm for their conduct. Fulfilling the letter of the biblical counsel, Bernard sold his impressive palazzo and his business. Peter, who seems to have been a candidate for the priesthood, likewise changed his plans; very soon after, he and Bernard joined Francis at Saint Mary's, where they both assumed the simplest garb and set to work.

A week later, on the feast of Saint George, April 23, an earnest 18-year-old named Giles heard about the group living in simplicity near Saint Mary's. He hurried to find Francis, to whom he confided that he was more concerned about the state of his soul than about any future career, and because he had no family, he was free to become the fourth in the small band of men.

According to some admiring chronicles, this assembly represented the beginning of the Franciscan Order. In fact, nothing could have been more remote from Francis's intentions. He wanted only a group of poor, unen-cumbered men like himself to proclaim God's mercy by good example and sometimes by preaching. The formal establishment of a Franciscan Order within the Church was a long time in coming, and it happened despite the expressed wishes of the so-called founder, Francis of Assisi.

The lives of those who seek God rarely follow the tidy outlines of pious scripts fashioned centuries later, and Francis and his followers were no exception. Instead of receiving a warm welcome when they went about their preaching, or gratitude when they distributed the proceeds of Bernard's fortune among the poor, the group found itself resented just about everywhere that year. In an era that was so obsessed with wealth, to give money away to those who had not worked for it seemed sheer folly.

Also contrary to the accepted social standards of the day was the fact that there was no discrimination, no class division among the members of the group. Bernard had been a rich merchant (perhaps even a knight); Peter had had experience as a canon, or ecclesiastical, lawyer; Giles was a peas-ant. To their number would be added clerics, nobles, scholars and illiter-ates. Their only common denominator was radical poverty and a highly refined sense of fraternity.

"Some declared that they were fools or drunkards," according to one early source, "and others in the city mocked them as senseless and stupid." Most people tried to ignore them, and sometimes rocks were thrown.

They faced hostility from the clergy, as well. When Francis, Bernard, Peter and Giles went to distribute the proceeds from the sale of Bernard's property among the sick and poor, a priest named Sylvester recognized Francis as the man to whom he had given stones for repairing Saint Mary's. "You did not pay me very well for the stones you took from me," Sylvester said angrily.

With that, Francis knelt at the priest's feet and set down a large share of the coins from Bernard's cloak. "Do you now have full payment, Father?" Francis asked ingenuously.

"I have it fully," Sylvester replied, gathering the money and returning to his residence.

Over the next several months, many priests of Assisi avoided Francis and his band, and some may have felt shamed by the integrity of the men's

lives. Sylvester, meanwhile, had a goodly share of Bernard's money but little serenity, while Francis and company had nothing and seemed to lead
lives rich with meaning. A year later, Sylvester gave the money to the poor
and shyly approached Francis. He started to kneel to make his apology, but
before he could do so, Francis bent to lift him up, respectfully kissed his
hands and, hearing his request, welcomed him without question into their
company. Sylvester was the first priest to join them.

Before a year had passed, Francis had about a dozen faithful companions. There was no doubt that, slowly and according to no clear plan, a kind
of society was forming around a man who was a contemplative hermit, an
itinerant preacher and a restorer of churches.

In light of the rapid growth of the group, it seems clear that Francis
must have been an especially charismatic individual, one who had an abundance of intelligence, warmth and insight. He offered his followers, quite
simply, a better life, a more joyful life, one that provided the kind of satisfaction that comes from a commitment to something other than money.
They found him and his message irresistible.

They also found him constantly surprising. While he insisted on their
dedicating themselves to poverty in their own lives, he also admonished
them "not to look down upon or judge those whom they see dressed in soft
and fine clothes and enjoying the choicest food and drink—rather, let
everyone judge and look down upon himself!" Judgment was the prerogative of God. There was in Francis nothing of the sanctimonious censor; he
rarely alluded to damnation, and unlike many wandering reformers of his
time, he pronounced no condemnations against any person or any specific
belief. Such a positive, loving embrace of the Gospel had not been heard of
in anyone's memory.

Referring to the greeting they always offered ("May the Lord give you
peace"), Francis reminded his companions, "As you announce peace with
your mouth, make sure that greater peace is in your hearts. Everyone
should be attracted to peace, kindness and harmony through your gentleness. We have been called to this: to heal the wounded, to bind up the broken and recall the erring."

In fact, it was precisely the engagement of Francis and his religious
brothers with the world, their presence among people they pledged to

serve, that saved them from a particularly subtle and dangerous form of fanaticism.

The idea of Christian perfection, which began in the ancient monasteries and spread to the world as an ideal, is one of the most appealing, demanding and ultimately hopeless notions of the spiritual life. By definition, only God is perfect—that is, complete and independent unto Himself. Humans, on the other hand, are radically imperfect, and that, paradoxically, is welcome news, for the recognition of our incompleteness throws us on the mercy of God and enables us, as Saint Paul stressed, to put up with one another's faults.

But the idea and ideal of perfection were still taken for granted as a spiritual aspiration in the Middle Ages. For Francis, it took the form of radical poverty, like that of hermits. The recorded lives of the saints tell us about the hermits who were successful in that quest, but we have no idea how many failed. We know nothing of those who were broken in body and soul by their inability to lead isolated, destitute existences, or how many lost their minds or starved to death in the process.

While Francis had a contemplative, even a mystic, character, he was not born for the hermit's life, which was at least partly a reaction against monastic excess. In addition, by virtue of their very distance from people, hermits were unable to remedy the evils they condemned. And so, as monasteries proliferated, most hermits simply returned to the common monastic life they had once abandoned. The Carthusians and the Camaldolese did survive as hermits but gathered once weekly for common prayer.

Although Francis pledged himself and his fraternity to freely elected deprivation, they may have been spared the worst psychological effects of it by their simultaneous commitment to serve others. It was their sense of human solidarity, in other words, that enabled them to preserve their own humanity. Later spiritual writers would designate Francis's life as "mixed"—that is, he combined the contemplative's dedication to prayer with the activist's commitment to practical work on behalf of the needy.

As word of Francis and his companions began to swirl throughout Assisi and the Spoleto valley, a number of Assisi's priests insisted that Bishop Guido summon the man who had once stood naked before him.

"It seems to me that your life is very rough and hard," the bishop said, wearing the formal, bejeweled robes and gemstone ring with which he met visitors, "especially because you do not possess anything."

"If we had possessions, my lord bishop," Francis replied respectfully but pointedly, "we would need arms for our protection—because disputes and lawsuits, as you know, usually arise out of possessions. And so, love of God and neighbor are greatly impeded. Therefore, we do not want to possess anything." Guido, the wealthiest landowner and most litigious man in Assisi, had no retort.

§

"After the Lord gave me some brothers," Francis recalled later, "no one showed me what I had to do, but the Most High Himself revealed to me that I should live according to the pattern of the Holy Gospel. . . . And those who came, gave whatever they had to the poor and were content with one tunic, patched inside and out, with a cord and short trousers. We desired nothing more. . . . And we were simple and subject to all."

It would take a very narrow and churlish spirit to object to this humbly stated program, which had no real structure and was grounded in goodwill. But we must face in all its complexity the problem of the total destitution Francis enjoined on his companions. There is, for example, no biblical evidence that Jesus and his companions lived in absolute poverty, as though it were something to be constantly refined, like a talent. On the contrary, they had a common purse for their modest daily needs, even though they chose the wrong man to look after it.

After Constantine made Christianity the official religion of the Roman Empire in the fourth century, martyrdom was no longer the ultimate demonstration of fidelity to Christ. Vowed chastity and committed poverty took its place, and the desert hermits imitated Christ by imitating the radical poverty of the prophets and of John the Baptist. But the separation of self from material goods per se may be more a nonchristian than a specifically Christian gesture. The basis of Christian faith is the Incarnation: the belief that the material world and everything in it is good, and that God has chosen to enter the world by uniting Himself to human flesh. Christian life, therefore, is concerned with the *right use* of the things of the world, not contempt for them. To be sure, excess (especially to the detriment of others) can never be acceptable, but "excess" is a problematic word and can be honestly assessed only by each individual.

In the Middle Ages, however, Christian spirituality was tainted with the Manichean and Cathar heresy, which proclaimed that because the material world was fundamentally opposed to the world of God, and hence evil, Christians had to pass through it having as little contact with it as possible. This was an unfortunate deviation, but it is also understandable if we examine the logic of radically spiritual people of the time. They believed that churchmen were rich and clearly not very good; therefore they were not like Christ, who was goodness incarnate. Hence they presumed that Christ must have been deliberately poor—and "poor" became equated with "good" and absolute poverty with Christlike perfection. Just as Francis was saved from the dangers of total isolation by his fraternity, so, too, did they eventually temper his practices—which led, of course, to the loss of precisely the single-minded, absolutely pure commitment that Francis brought to his practice of poverty.

§

By the summer of 1208, the repairs to Saint Mary's were completed, and Francis and his friends moved to an adjacent shack, devoting themselves by day to itinerant preaching and caring for lepers, and in the evening to prayer. Although they built makeshift huts for shelter here and there throughout the countryside, they had no permanent home (much less a church) and they earned their simple meals by hard manual labor in fields and vineyards, by hauling water or firewood in the cities and building walls and houses.

"I worked with my hands," Francis said of this time, "and I earnestly desire all brothers to give themselves to honest work. Let those who do not know how to work learn, not from desire to receive wages, but for example and to avoid idleness." Any follower of Francis who did not join in these labors could not remain, like the nameless and indolent young man who was with them for a time, refusing to share in their toil but eating heartily from the common, meager supply. "Go on your way, Brother Fly," Francis said, dismissing him with an epithet indicating the fellow's status as a mere parasite, "because you want to feed on the labors of your brothers, but wish to be idle in the work of God—like Brother Drone, who does not want to gather or work, yet eats the work and gain of the good bees."

During late spring and early summer, Francis traveled northeast to the Marches, the region fronting on the Adriatic, where he simply counseled anyone who would listen: "Love and fear God, and reform your lives." Giles, who accompanied him, called out candidly, "Do what my spiritual father here tells you, because he speaks most wisely!" Francis would have preferred less of such reinforcement, but Giles was something of a character—and so benevolent that Francis had no heart to correct him.

"Some people willingly and joyfully listened," according to one account; "others, however, jeered at them. Many people repeatedly badgered them, and it was extremely wearisome to answer so many questions because new situations gave rise to new questions. Some asked them, 'Where do you come from?' while others asked, 'To which [religious] Order do you belong?' They answered simply: 'We are penitents from Assisi.' "

That, for the moment, was all that Francis would allow. He and his companions formed a fraternity like many others then proliferating throughout Christian Europe. Because they were bound by no vows or ties to any bishop, much less to superiors in Rome, they faced none of the problems of organization, of structure or of churchly legality. They were simply workingmen who begged for food as compensation and devoted private time to prayer.

However modest were the group's aims, it nonetheless began to encounter an increasing amount of hostility in its travels. "Many who saw and heard them considered them impostors or fools. Some remarked, 'I wouldn't care to invite them into my house—they would probably steal my belongings.' Because of this, many insults were inflicted on them in many places. Therefore, they very frequently sought lodging in the porticos of churches or houses." Even from these, they were often evicted—as occurred once when a man returned to find that his wife had permitted them to sleep against an outside wall of their house near a woodshed, and he banished them immediately. "In short, people considered them most despicable and persecuted them as though they were criminals."

This did not dissuade Francis, however. As he persisted in his work, people very gradually began to notice that, unlike so many clergymen and monastic preachers, he and his friends lived in a manner consistent with their teaching. In urging others to a new commitment to the Gospel, they had obviously first embraced that commitment themselves; their kindness, their refusal to accept any money as compensation, their constant vigilance in relieving the sufferings of others—these made an impression on people who were unaccustomed to seeing such integrity from the typical representatives of religion.

Returning from their journey in Ancona, they found that four more men had joined the company at Saint Mary's. By now, they needed a place to pray and to sleep when they were not out begging, and the Benedictine owner of Saint Mary's gave the tiny chapel to Francis, who insisted on paying the monks a yearly fee of a basket of fish caught in nearby Lake Trasimeno. Not to be outdone, the bishop responded to that gift by sending a jar of oil. And so it went for many years.

By early 1209, Francis had 10 companions: in addition to Bernard, Peter, Giles and Sylvester, there were added the names of Morico, who had been with a religious order that cared for the sick at a leprosarium; Philip, who had a natural gift for preaching Scripture in a lively, intimate way; Juniper, known for his humor and patience; Leo, who had been ordained a priest just before joining Francis and who became his confessor, secretary and good friend; Masseo, whose pleasant disposition and common sense Francis often held up as exemplary; and Rufino, a shy man much admired by Francis.

Over the next few years, the fraternity grew to include Elias, a man of tyrannical temperament who later became a serious problem; Illuminatus, Pacificus and Leonard, who often accompanied Francis on his travels; John of Cappella, a dyspeptic elderly man who betrayed Francis's ideals, left the group and was considered a Judas to the brothers; and Barbaro, Sabbatino and Bernard Vigilante, a trio of whom we know nothing. Even as it increased in size, the fraternity avoided the complications of an organized religious order by maintaining a simple life and by following Francis's example, as a contemporary described: "He instructed [his companions] not so much in words and speech, but in deed and truth."

In the autumn of 1208, Francis took the entire group to the Rieti valley and to Poggio Bustone, where they set up small huts and a place for prayer, which they used as a base from which to care for the many lepers nearby. Many people in the area were impressed, their hearts touched by the simple acts of kindness and caring to which this band of men devoted themselves.

SEVEN

1209

AS HIS CONVERSION continued mysteriously, and with very little sense of what direction his future would take, Francis became ever more haunted by the image of the crucified Christ. Paintings, icons and carvings of the crucifixion were ubiquitous in medieval Europe, of course, but it may have been the very familiarity of the representation that had weakened its impact for so many.

The image of the crucified savior had preoccupied him since that day in 1205 at San Damiano: it was the face of Christ he saw on the twisted features of despised lepers; the tortured bodies he knelt to wash and comfort were one body, that of his wounded Lord. It was in this spirit that, reworking an ancient prayer, Francis often recited and taught his companions the simple oration that he repeated in his *Testament:* "We adore You, Lord Jesus Christ, in all Your churches throughout the world and we bless [that is, honor] You, because by Your holy cross You have redeemed the world." What was the nature of the Jesus to whom Francis committed himself? The man from Nazareth was neither a political revolutionary nor a benevolent preacher of some vague ideal of brotherly love; nor was he a man who coveted any kind of power. In himself, what was he—and more to the point, for our purposes, what was he for Francis of Assisi?

§

"My God, my God, why have You forsaken me?" Jesus cried out on the cross, and the question must be examined with a full appreciation for its implications of abandonment. Christ's words express no confidence that God would vindicate him (although vindication seems to be implied by later words in the psalm of which this is the first verse), nor is this a shout of despair. It is, simply, an appeal, a supplication.

Jesus himself was no Stoic: he did not seek to suffer, nor did he accept death patiently. He endured it in all its agony, screaming out to God. Jesus felt the profoundest sense that he himself had let God down. Abandoned by his friends, he was, by any standards of this world, an utter failure. Cut down in his prime, his work suppressed, his honor destroyed, his loved ones alienated, he was, at the end, subjected to a method of execution reserved for the worst criminals. He who abandoned everything to God seemed abandoned by God. His existence seemed drenched in futility.

The Jewish nation from which he came was of bygone grandeur, its magnificence diminished by the victories of occupying Romans. There were no concrete achievements in his own life to speak of, either—he left no work as a monument, no coherent philosophy, no handbook of morals, no school of teachers to assume his position. Anyone who claims to admire Jesus as a philosopher has probably never read the New Testament, for all the elements that traditionally define a philosopher's life and legacy are absent. His followers were a diverse crew of ordinary people—fishermen, a tax collector, itinerant workers, a prostitute—and they lacked any remarkable gifts or talents; at the end, they had no very clear idea of what he had been about.

The question cannot be avoided, and it has been asked with respect to others in equally tragic circumstances at every point of history: what sort of God would allow His people to be treated so cruelly?

A God, in fact, Who takes human suffering with absolute seriousness. A God Who enters fully into agony and death and does not allow it the final victory. A God Who completely transforms the meaning of suffering and death.

Good Friday was not, after all, the end. The proclamation continues with the experience of the complete transformation of Jesus to the world beyond death, in a new and permanent mode of existence by which (thus Saint Paul to the Corinthians) "he is alive now with the power of God." The Resurrection reveals precisely what was not to be expected: that this rejected, murdered Jesus, was right in what he proclaimed about God. In raising him up beyond death forever, God thus vindicated the one who had given himself totally to Himself and to humanity.

One of the aims of Christianity is to continue to proclaim that God has approved of Jesus—his message, his deeds, his teaching. The God of the beginning—of Creation, of the call to Israel, of the prophets—is also the God of the end: the living God Who creates also completes. Death does not have the last word; suffering is not the final experience. There is, we might say, a profound logic in all this: the Creator God reveals Himself; the revealing God embraces and summons; the summoning God finally acts in love to save what He has created. Nothing is lost. As was true of the first Good Friday, so (faith asserts) it will be forever: God will make all the difference, for finally He summons from death to life.

Without at least some comprehension of this mystery, we cannot hope to understand the life of Francis of Assisi. He can be respected as a man who appreciated the beauty of all creation; he can be admired as a man who was compassionate, who lived simply, who loved animals and elements. But the same can be said of countless others. In Francis's case, we have to perceive what lay at the deepest core of his being: a constant, constantly maturing reliance on the God he experienced as unimaginable love and mercy—a God Who asked him to collaborate in the healing of the world. And that healing could not ignore the mystery of the cross.

It was this mission of mercy that Francis and his friends offered. While their itinerant life explicitly rejected the monastic ideal of stability for the peripatetic life of Jesus, Francis likewise remained a paradox to the established religious communities with their vast properties. And whereas the tendency in formal religious life was either to flee from the world into the monasteries or to be involved wholly in pastoral work among the people, Francis, without specifically planning to do so, combined both the contemplative and active lives into one.

By vivid lessons and informal exhortations, by acts of kindness and charity, he offered an approach to the Gospel that was not new but that he presented in original and joyful terms. Christian life was not a fairy tale—Francis's rigorous life countered that idea. It was, rather, a summons and a challenge. With that in mind, Francis spoke to the crowds "not in the usual

manner of preaching," according to an eyewitness, "but like a political orator." In other words, he used both word and gesture (the *ars concionandi*),
so well learned in his youth during the political struggles in his hometown,
gestures first manifest when he shed his clothing before Guido and the
crowd that cold day in 1206.

§

When the Roman Empire collapsed in the fourth and fifth centuries, social
power passed to a group of wealthy Christian families, who were in fact the
foundation of a new aristocracy. They established monasteries, composed
mostly of noblemen, in southern France, and although these were certainly
the most civilizing institutions of the Middle Ages, the system was seriously flawed. Although religious life was always to have been modeled on
the original apostolic community in Jerusalem, in practice a ladder of superiority based on noble birth was put in place, and the communities became
dependent on money and gifts.

By the time of Francis, the leaders of monasteries were typically
selected by the head of the wealthy family that owned and endowed each
one. The ideologies and interests of the rich and powerful were supported,
and superiors often ruled in a secular (even military) style. Their monks, or
"subjects," like peasants in fealty to a king or emperor, were compelled to
comply in blind obedience; this led to what pious men sometimes called
heroic submission. It also led to complaints and rebellion.

Francis would have none of this, and he prepared himself to resist it as
an organizational standard. He took steps to assure there was nothing too
solemn about his program. Sometimes he leavened his exhortations with
well-known French songs people would understand; "other times, picking
up a stick from the ground and putting it over his left arm, he would draw
another stick across it with his right hand, like a bow on a viola. Performing all the right movements, he would sing in French about the Lord Jesus."

By the spring of 1209, however, it had become increasingly clear to
Francis and his companions that some form of official approval was necessary for what they were undertaking—specifically, some sort of papal
approval. Bishop Guido, recognizing the authenticity of Francis's devotion
and the value of his modest society, urged him and his companions to pre-

sent themselves in Rome—the better to forestall the charge of heresy that was so quickly leveled against the many religious individuals and sub-groups that were then so popular in society. Like Francis, but far more vocally, many of them were of goodwill but were highly critical of ecclesiastical decadence.

One such figure was Arnold of Brescia, who died in 1155. A devout abbot who believed the only way to reform the clergy was for the Church to abandon completely any claim to temporal influence, he failed to see that this scheme would only make the emperor all the more powerful. Arnold was a well-meaning ascetic who was unfortunately compelled by political circumstances (in the imperial contest with the papacy) to become a violent revolutionary. He eventually suffered the heretic's fate of excommunication and execution.

A number of organized groups wandered throughout Europe, proclaiming all manner of quite unchristian ideas, more often fomenting dissent than inciting people to service, and preaching a religion that undermined the core of orthodox faith. But at the same time, some of them identified strongly with the poor and were quick to aid the destitute.

That was true of the Cathari, for example, a sect that originated in the Middle East and, in Francis's time, flourished throughout southern France (where they were known as Albigensians) and northern Italy (where they were called Patarini). The Cathari believed that the world of matter and everything physical were the creation of an evil god eternally at war with the spiritual, transcendent world of the good God; hence they held that Jesus could not have been a human being but was an angelic illusion, a phantom who only seemed fleshly. Precisely because they, too, lived in absolute poverty, they believed that they alone were following the path of the poor, divine (but not human) Jesus.

The Cathari gathered in communities, where they led rigorous lives. They condemned marriage and all contact between the sexes, believing procreation to be wicked and sinful because it contributed to more souls captured in evil flesh. In their highly structured hierarchy, the Cathari divided their adherents into the *credentes,* ordinary believers who acted as servants, and the *perfecti,* those who were the most advanced and enlightened. They were, of course, highly critical of the Church: merely by virtue of the fact that it blessed marriage and sex, it was to be rejected. In response, the Cathari set up their own pope and bishops, with a diocese in the Spoleto valley that was closely organized according to the Roman model. Partly because their preaching about ecclesiastical decadence was so self-evident a truth, they spread rapidly.

In 1208 Pope Innocent III attempted to counter the Cathari the only way he knew: by launching what became known as the Albigensian Crusade, a battle against heretics in which brutality was routine and that led ultimately to a system of inquisitions.

Panic stricken and determined to preserve the apostolic faith, the institutional Church fell into the unfortunate trap of offsetting error with error. Heretics were tortured and burned in alarming numbers; after the Church turned them over to civil authorities, even the general population witnessed with equanimity and approval the appalling punishments applied to those considered beyond redemption. By the 15th century, the Cathari, or Albigensians, had all but disappeared, though their influence lingers even to this day among those Christians who condemn the body, who see wickedness everywhere, who make sexual matters the only gauge of morality, and who forget that the world of matter is the work of a loving God.

Another reformer popular at the time was a benevolent Frenchman named Peter Valdes (or Waldo) of Lyons, a wealthy merchant who at first glance seems a spiritual father to Francis of Assisi. Less than a decade before Francis's birth, he divested himself of all wealth and possessions, opened a soup kitchen during the famine of 1176, and went to live as a wandering beggar and preacher. He had the benefit of an important teaching tool, a vernacular translation of the Bible and the writings of the early Church Fathers that he had commissioned. Such a version was contrary to canon law, which permitted only the approved Latin rendering of Scripture.

Peter defied the regulation against laymen preaching doctrine; he also actively sought followers to do the same, and he continued to use his Bible translation. Eventually, due to the ignorance of a few myopic bishops, he was proclaimed a heretic and excommunicated. To the end of his life, he courageously maintained that one was obliged to obey God rather than men; in our own time, he might well have been regarded as an enlightened ecumenical leader and invited to address interfaith groups.

The Humiliati fared better within the institutional Church. A reform-minded 12th-century group of mostly Italian laity, they did not share the Cathari's belief in a dualistic world of evil against good. Remaining with their families, they met for work and prayer, were eminently honest and debated intelligently with heretics. The Humiliati also practiced poverty, sharing their goods with the destitute; they devoutly read Scripture in the approved Latin translation and exhorted the faithful informally, outside churches.

Adhering to the papal regulation that they limit their sermons to moral encouragement and avoid all discussion of theological matters, they sought and received papal approval for status as a religious Order; for a time they flourished in northern Italy.

Francis could not have been unaware of the Humiliati, and in fact he seems to have been inspired by many of their practices. Unfortunately, they did not remain faithful to their origins: they grew in both numbers and wealth until, by the 16th century, they disbanded.

Some groups came into conflict with Rome not only because they preached against a clergy that had become largely dissolute but because they went so far as to proclaim that sinful priests were invalid priests—that is, that their celebration of Church services must be avoided by the faithful. This degree of moral righteousness was ultimately counterproductive, for if churches were abandoned because the clergy were condemned as sinful, then both the clergy and the laity would suffer: there would be no witness to the need for reform.

Francis, in contrast, insisted that clerical sinners be treated with respect, not only because of their sacred office but because on principle he condemned no one; he also dismissed criticisms about their learning or their virtue. Their task, he insisted, was to administer sacraments, and it was not anyone's prerogative to judge their consciences. When he did encounter priests who were derelict in their simplest duties, Francis's tactic was to respond with pointed action: he took a broom and a pail of water to a grimy church and then spoke to the priest privately.

It needs to be emphasized, in this brief outline of some contemporary heresies, that whatever their shortcomings, the radical poverty movements of Francis's time brought a new vitality and energy to the spiritual life of the Church by insisting on living the Gospel, and not just emptily preach-ing it. "Unfortunately," as one Franciscan scholar has recently observed, "the extremists failed to see that the Word is more than the preaching and that Scripture does not derive its power from the sanctity of the one who preaches it, no matter how holy [or unholy] his life may be."

It takes a certain kind of courage to be a heretic, to stand by one's con-viction, and each of these groups and individuals in fact did the Church a great service by proclaiming in word and action that Christianity is a viable way of life, a plan for living, and not just a romantic fantasy of unattainable ideals. Their radicalism met with fierce opposition from the Church long before they attempted to dilute doctrine; they were excommunicated and harassed merely for their insistence on living the Gospel as the disciples of Jesus had lived it, which was an implicit condemnation of ecclesiastical decadence.

In this context it was important that Francis demonstrate that his wan-dering group of poor men was free of the taint of Cathar heresy; to that end, he constantly proclaimed his love and gratitude for the material world, and he condemned neither sex, nor marriage nor the clergy. And unlike Peter Waldo, he did not seek followers but merely accepted them. Francis also hastened to make it clear that he was faithful to the apostolic creeds, that he had no intention of putting vernacular Bibles in the hands of his companions and that he was not assuming the right to teach doctrine (for which he had neither talent nor academic preparation).

Hence, in the spring of 1209, Francis heeded the counsel of Guido and went to Rome for approval for his program and his fraternity. Because of the bishop's influence at the papal court, they were promised an audience with the formidable Pope Innocent III.

Forty-nine-year-old Innocent was a superb lawyer and brilliant admin-istrator, a shrewd diplomat, a persuasive speaker and a born ruler. One of the most powerful leaders in the history of the Church, he thought of him-self as less than God, to be sure, but as much more than an ordinary man—as the ruler not only of the Church but of the entire Christian world. A century later, Pope Boniface VIII carried this preposterously unbiblical and unchristian idea of power to its extreme: the pope, he declared, was the only true and rightful ruler of the entire universe, with dominion over every living creature in every sphere of reality. Dante, Boniface's contemporary, consigned him to hell in the *Commedia*.

At the time, some felt that Innocent behaved more like an emperor than a priest: in some respects, at least, he succeeded in imposing his will in every country of the world. In Italy, he drove out the German emperor and expelled his legates from the Papal States. In Sicily, he had charge of the regent's son, the emperor-to-be. In Germany, he placed Otto of Brunswick on the throne and then excommunicated him in favor of Frederick II. He also obtained, as papal fiefs, the kingdoms of Aragon, Portugal, Sicily and Poland and wielded strong power in Scandinavia, Spain, the Balkans, Bulgaria, Cyprus, Armenia and Prussia. Only France resisted his dominion.

Like many people who loved exercising power and are gifted with a keen mind, Innocent III lacked warmth and spontaneous compassion— hardly negligible deficiencies in one who is called to be the spiritual father and servant of all. In fact, he also had a profound humanity, a deep piety and a keen recognition of the need for Church reform. In his private life, this diminutive man with intense eyes and great dignity was quite frugal, modest and, paradoxically, without pretense, and by example as well as decree he encouraged a spirit of honor among the clergy and simplicity of life among the bishops. It was he who prudently allowed the Humiliati to preach penance, and in so doing he far exceeded his predecessors in promoting lay associations that could benefit the spiritual life of the Church.

In addition, Innocent was, for his time, remarkably restrained in the matter of heretics. He knew that bishops could be overzealous in their pursuit of the unorthodox, and Innocent reminded them that mercy and caution were in order: God cannot err, he rightly asserted, but the judgment of the Church and churchmen is fallible (which was sound Catholic teaching from the time of the apostles until 1870, when the doctrine of papal infallibility was proclaimed). Every time a heretic or an unorthodox group was reported to him, Innocent responded with a warning to the local bishops that severity must be avoided. Alas, the pope was not always obeyed in such matters, and his temperate attitude was overridden by zealots in Rome and beyond.

§

As it happened, Bishop Guido received a summons to attend certain meetings, or synods, in Rome at the same time Francis planned his trip, and so he arranged to meet his protégé there. Francis set out with his companions, and on the way he suggested that they select one of them to be a leader, to decide the route, the times for rest and so forth. They chose Bernard Quintavalle, and (according to one of the earliest witnesses) "they did as he said." However much Francis was honored, he obviously had no intention of functioning like a religious superior.

They reached Rome in April 1209 and found it a disorderly society of only about 100,000 citizens (its population had been more than a million at the time of the apostles), most of whom were bankers and merchants, clerics and pilgrims and beggars. Rule of the city was in the hands of noblemen in constant conflict with popes, and the atmosphere was one of both fierce greed and dangerous abandon.

The group arrived at the pope's residence, the Lateran Palace. They brought no extended document or anything like a formal religious Rule such as govern the Benedictines, Augustinians or Cistercians. Francis brought along a more or less hastily drafted paper (soon after lost) with a few gospel passages designed to inculcate a simple life of faith, and some broad guidelines about manual labor and common prayer. As Francis himself later said, he had compiled a few verses from the New Testament (among them were most likely the sections chosen at random a year earlier by him, Bernard and Peter Catanio), "and I had this written down simply and in a few words."

Since it soon became clear that Francis's fraternity could indeed become a new religious Order, its distinctiveness was immediately evident—there was nothing monastic about it. It had a revolutionary freedom precisely because it was apostolic in form.

But Francis did not legislate exactly what his order would do, as the established religious had, providing detailed regulations for daily conduct. Typical monastic rules were gravid with directives adjudicating every aspect of both common and private life. The Benedictine Rule, for example, evolved into a book of no less than 73 chapters dictating what a monk wore during the day and at night; what he ate at which hour; how he should pray; when he should or should not speak; on which topics he should meditate.

In fact, this oldest Western and most revered monastic Rule allowed none of the freedom and discretion Jesus had granted the apostles. As one modern scholar has accurately written:

> Detailed practical guidance on the right course from day to day, such as is found in Saint Benedict's Rule, can safeguard a high standard of conduct and give a feeling of security, but it provides limited opportunities for moral growth. Saint Benedict performed a great service to the Church, but it seems to many people, looking back on it now, that the Benedictine interpretation of the Christian life, as it was lived by most monks, lacked some of the elements we would consider essential to Christian living.

Without specifically naming it so, Francis clearly envisioned a code for spiritual living that left his companions remarkably free—they could live in hermitages when they felt the need for intense prayer, or they could choose to be day laborers, nurses or wandering preachers.

This degree of freedom alone comprised a quiet revolution. Up to this time, those who wanted to devote themselves to a religious life had to join a formal religious Order and obey its particular system of laws and regulations. To his credit, however, Pope Innocent III tried to resolve the challenge presented by new groups like the Humiliati and (he was about to learn) Francis of Assisi. Sensitive to the new Gospel movements, he distinguished between heretics and the orthodox and approved lay organizations without requiring them to be religious Orders.

Before Francis and his friends were admitted to Innocent's presence, they met with a curial prelate and friend of Guido's named John Colonna, a kindly, discerning man and a member of that relatively new group of administrators known as cardinals—the pope's senate or cabinet of advisers. (By this time cardinals had been papal electors for only 150 years; before then, the people and clergy of Rome had always chosen their bishop—the pope—by voice acclamation.) John, impressed with Francis's simplicity and humility, at first recommended that he join a monastery or a hermitage—not surprising advice from a cardinal who was also a Benedictine monk. "But Francis refused his urging," according to Thomas of Celano. His humility notwithstanding, Francis was also tenacious and had a strong sense of his calling—which was not, he believed, to live in isolation and apart from ordinary from people.

That evening, while Francis prayed, John Colonna met with other members of the papal household, who were firmly convinced that any sort of approval of Francis would only set him on an independent path, on which he would soon veer off into the thickets of heresy.

But John went directly to the pope with his recommendation: "If we refuse the request of this poor man as novel or too difficult, when all he asks is to be allowed to lead the Gospel life, we must be on our guard lest we commit an offense against Christ's Gospel itself. For if anyone says that there is something novel or irrational or impossible to observe in this man's desire to live according to the Gospel, he would be guilty of blasphemy against Christ, the very author of that Gospel!"

§

The following day Francis and his company were ushered to the Belvedere gallery, called the Hall of Mirrors, where Innocent sat surrounded by all the symbols of his authority. Francis respectfully made his brief *propositum*, which he had committed to memory, and he asked formal permission to preach everywhere, not just within the confines of the diocese of Assisi. Innocent listened intently and then asked a few questions.

"Your life is too hard and severe," said the pope, "if you wish to found a congregation possessing nothing in this world. Where will you obtain the necessities of life?"

"I trust in my Lord Jesus Christ," was the response of Francis. "He will not deprive us of our bodily necessities when we need them."

"So much is true," the pope continued, "but human nature is weak. Go and pray to the Lord with all your might, so that He may show you what is better and more beneficial. Then come back and tell me, and I will grant it."

The companions in their threadbare tunics left the great pontifical hall, crossed through the grand chambers studded with mosaics and shining with marble, descended a wide staircase crowded with guards, important visitors and lackeys and found themselves in the great, sun-drenched piazza.

Impressed by the men's faith and simplicity, one of the cardinals had followed them outside, where he stopped Giles to ask for prayers. "What need have you of my prayers?" Giles asked. "You have more faith and hope than I!" The cardinal was puzzled. Giles pointed first to his own patched garments and then to the prelate's sumptuous robes: "You, sir," said the fearless Giles, "with your wealth, honors and worldly power hope to save your immortal soul. I, with my simpler life, am afraid I'll be damned. Yes, you obviously have more faith and hope than I have!" The cardinal's reaction has not been recorded.

Someone had arranged lodgings at a local monastery, and after another night of prayer, Francis returned and made the same petition, asking Innocent to approve his group of penitential preachers. No doubt persuaded as much by the charismatic appeal of Francis as by his seriousness of purpose, the pope acquiesced, granting the company permission to preach anywhere—an unusual dispensation, for it exempted Francis from the jurisdiction of Guido. Unconcerned with formalities and the fine points of administration, Francis departed without a written commitment; he had only a verbal authorization granting him and his band the right to publicly incite to virtue and discourage vice, thus summoning the faithful to penance and a reformation of life. They were not, however, allowed to deliver formal sermons on matters doctrinal.

Once again, Innocent proved himself a master of political diplomacy as well as a serious reformer. Assured by Guido and by his own observation that the 26-year-old former merchant from Assisi never attacked churchmen or Church practice and in fact won some heretics back from their errors, Innocent saw a potential ally—and one with whom he could work without resorting to force. It would be far better to strengthen Francis's loyalty to the Church by approving his fraternity.

§

An interesting paradox emerges here—the simultaneous attitude of dissent and conformity that seems to have characterized Francis. He had already rejected the acceptable standards of status and riches; he had given up his arms, clothing and money; and he did not wish to formalize his dedication to God in a conventional religious Order. Yet here he was in Rome, seeking approval for himself, his companions and his future plans: he was literally kneeling before the leading representative of the official faith, which was itself an institution that exploited both money and power.

If Innocent had rejected his petition and said, "No, this is not a good idea—go back home and forget about this idea of yours, for it leads to heresy," it is almost impossible to imagine Francis proceeding with his plan. He may well have joined a monastery and perhaps have found his way to God along more traditional lines. Sooner or later, however, someone else would have taken up his standard.

But there is a second, purely practical, element to consider in understanding Francis's submission to Rome. He knew that to forestall the suspicions and opposition of bishops, cardinals and the pontiff himself, and to proceed without harassment, he had to have his program validated; the alternative could have eventually been a charge of heresy, or at least insubordination.

We should not, however, judge Francis's obeisance as hypocrisy: on the contrary, he was a savvy Italian politician who knew how to use the system literally for the love of God and not for his own benefit. There was in his plan nothing to be gained for himself, nothing certain, really, except risk and failure.

1209–1210

As Francis prepared to depart Rome, he was forced to deal with one final detail he had not anticipated. The papal personnel, despite objections from the sensible John Colonna, decided to ensure that Francis and his companions would promise obedience to Rome, and the way to guarantee that was to induct them into the clerical state. The dozen men were therefore asked to submit to the tonsure—the ceremonial cutting of the hair on the crown of the head, to signify admission to the lowest (nonpriestly) rank of clerical status and as an injunction to institutional loyalty. Originally a monastic procedure, the tonsure had been administered as a first step toward the priesthood since the seventh century.

This demand must have caused Francis and his friends some dismay, for he had no desire to become a cleric and would in fact never become a priest, and although many later Franciscans were ordained, he neither required, expected nor preferred candidates for his company of men to take that step.

Francis never believed that he had to be a cleric, or pronounce formal vows, in order to commit himself entirely to God. "No one showed me what to do but the Most High Himself." His words ring down through the ages with an assuredness very like that of Saint Paul himself, who proclaimed that the revelation about the inclusion of Gentiles into the Christian community came from God Himself.

In the core of his being, Francis knew that his vocation had not come from the encouragement of churchmen, and he would not permit it to be configured by ecclesiastics or ecclesiastical politics. As for the tonsure, it sometimes, paradoxically, made Francis's public preaching a little easier,

since with it people were able to recognize him and his company as orthodox, official and approved.

However, this visible symbol at once clericalized, and therefore began
the first steps of gradually controlling, the fledgling society. Francis had
offered an alternative to the centralized, legalistic, politicized, militarized
Roman system; in time, and quite against his will, his society would indeed
be severely compromised. But we can only speculate what would have happened if Innocent III, instead of coopting Francis by integrating him into
the system, had really listened attentively to him and had taken the Gospel
seriously—if he had adopted by imitation Francis's guiding philosophy
instead of dismissing him with a blessing and a slightly condescending
approval within the standard limits.

Whatever concessions he was forced to make, Francis's visit to Rome
fixed him resolutely in his commitment to poverty. Francis sensed what the
hierarchy did not: the more that laymen grew to resent the Church's wealth
and demanded a poor, apostolic clergy who would meet them on their own
terms and represent the simplicity of the Gospel, the richer the institution
became. The Church of Rome was simply not prepared to abandon its
assets: instead, it had become ever more convinced that the respect of the
masses could be sustained only by pomp and circumstance. Yet as the institution strengthened its economic and social power, it lost the respect of vast
numbers of people.

Medieval culture was virtually defined by its obsession with categoriz-
ing, classifying and naming everything, and religious groups of any size
were no exception. What would Francis call his company? Once they designated themselves "poor men from Assisi." But when he was now asked to
identify himself and the others, he said simply, "I want this fraternity to be
called the Lesser Brothers"—*fratres minores*. Later, the official designation
became Ordo Fratrum Minorum—translated into English as the Order of
Friars Minor, which does not quite communicate what its founder wished,
for it replaces the word "brothers" and the idea of fraternity with the more
clerical word "friars" and the formal designation of an Order. Also, the
significance of the key word—that his fraternity was composed of those
who made themselves *minores*, less important than everyone else—was virtually lost. The English expression "Friars Minor" sounds almost coy and

polite, and does not at all suggest the threat to pride and primacy that Francis intended.

"We were simple and subject to all," Francis said—and that was the point of his "lesser brothers." There was to be no power structure, no quest for leadership inside or outside the fraternity. Francis's exploitation of the word *minores* alluded not to the rising group of middle-class merchants of the commune, who revolted because they wanted a larger slice of the pizza. His *minores* were to be literally that, the humblest servants of all.

℘

For several weeks, Francis and his companions wandered about Rome, inviting people to reform, proclaiming the presence of God and His infinite friendliness in their lives, and summoning them to honesty and kindness in their dealings with one another. Today, it is perhaps difficult to imagine how revolutionary this program sounded. Their task, as Francis said later, was "the benefit and edification of the people, announcing to them vices and virtues with brevity, because our Lord when on earth kept his word brief."

Their spontaneous sermons were not theoretical, nor did they allude to complex philosophical or theological matters. Addressing their audiences in a mixture of medieval Latin and the new Italian dialect, they were more like street-corner speakers than clergymen in pulpits. Francis did not develop some new method of religious rhetoric: he preached by simply being who and what he was, and by explaining to his hearers why he lived as he did. And he was able to communicate with ordinary people because he was one of them, as the hierarchy and much of the clergy were not—hence the rise of heresies, which crudely attempted (in the absence of the witness of orthodoxy) to satisfy the deepest and truest longings people always have.

The content of his presentation was invariable: peace among individuals (which meant, in practical terms, the refusal to take vengeance, to defraud or hurt others in any way) and the conformity of every life to the spirit of the Gospel, which meant an ethic of loving service. Perhaps no other excerpt from his preachings captures better his evangelical spirit than his invocation on one verse of the Lord's Prayer ("as we forgive those who trespass against us"): "What we do not completely forgive, make us, Lord, forgive completely—that we may truly love our enemies because of You, and that we may fervently intercede for them before You, returning no one evil for evil, and striving to help everyone in You." As Chesterton said centuries later of Christianity itself, what a wonderful idea—and a great pity so few people have ever tried it!

People noticed at once the major difference between Francis and other itinerant preachers. The themes of judgment, penance and the risk of damnation characterized most public preaching in medieval Europe, and the fear of hell was much exploited by Rome in an attempt to keep the faithful in line. Demons are shown torturing the damned in just about every archivolt, tympanum and capital of medieval cathedrals.

But in this respect, Francis understood the human heart better. He knew that love of God and the joy of commitment to Him could not be motivated by fear, which bred only resentment and remorse. On the contrary, he knew that people would be attracted to the truth of the Gospel by hearing that it brought a measure of serenity and happiness. His message, in other words, was neither gloomy nor colored by doom and threats, for Francis could only preach the God he knew—one of infinite patience and fidelity, Who wishes to draw near and embrace all people in the particularities of their lives.

Unlike the Cathari, the Waldensians and others, Francis also did not impose his own radical poverty or style of Christian living on others unless they expressly wanted to join his fraternity. He believed that each person was responsible for discerning the circumstances of his own personal fidelity to the Gospel.

He left us an outline of this preaching, and it is virtually a summary of the key sayings of Jesus in the four written gospels: "Do penance—change your lives—by performing good works, since we will all soon die. Give to others, and it shall be given to you. Forgive and you shall be forgiven. And if you do not forgive others their sins, the Lord will not forgive you your sins."

§

What was the reaction of people to this radically different kind of proclamation—a preaching that summoned courteously instead of threatening angrily, an advocacy accompanied by an example of service and of sharing with those less fortunate even his own meager supply of food? It would be comforting to discover that many lives were changed by Francis's words and example, but we have no evidence for that, and no objective measurement can reliably assess either the life of the spirit or the changes effected by the long process of conversion. It seems that Francis, like Jesus himself, had considerable difficulty getting people to listen and hence very little practical success, at least in terms of dramatic and immediate changes in the lives of most people. The message was simply too astonishing.

Both society and the Church regarded Francis with suspicion for a very long time, mostly because his way of life and his message were deeply subversive and in evident conflict with contemporary values. And so both clergy and laity often felt uneasy in his presence and regarded him and his friends as mad or fantasists; that, as history clearly shows, is often the reaction to authentic prophets. During his lifetime, Jesus himself was not highly regarded, and even his closest companions had serious doubts about him—to the extent that they abandoned him at the time of his arrest and execution.

While we lack immediate and demonstrable results of his preaching, it is impossible to overestimate the revolution that Francis effected. In the Middle Ages, as we have seen, the primary means of proclaiming the Gospel was through the monasteries, and people could learn Christian culture only by joining them. Francis, on the other hand, embraced a new, nonmonastic mode of evangelization. Rather than inviting people out of the world and into the places where he and his fraternity lived (as did cloistered monks), they went out to the people, meeting them wherever they were and speaking to them in their own language and style. Only 70 years after Francis's death, his friars were preaching in Asia and establishing Christian faith in China. By their very nature, Benedictines and Cistercians, as well as Carthusian and Camaldolese hermits, could not have made such an impact. To be sure, Francis was not the only one to engage in this revolutionary model, for the Dominicans also lived and worked outside monasteries, as did the many itinerant preachers. But in time, the Dominicans (by choice and papal persuasion) chose mostly the life of the university, which had its own form of enclosure. Franciscans were every-where.

§

As they headed back to Assisi, Francis stopped on the road between Bevagna and Cannara, about six miles south of Assisi. Annoyed at the indifference of so many people and dejected at the apparent failure of all their efforts, Francis announced that he would probably have a more respectful hearing from the birds—which is exactly what happened. The event, one of the oldest documented in his life and perhaps the most often represented in art, has been sentimentalized out of all proportion to its deeper truth. But once the veil of romance has been lifted, it reveals an important motif in Francis's life:

> There was a great multitude of birds of different types gathered, including doves, crows and others commonly called *monaclae* [jack-daws or magpies]. When Francis saw them, he ran swiftly toward them, leaving his companions on the road. He was a man of great fer-vor, feeling much sweetness and tenderness even toward lesser, irra-tional creatures. When he was already very close, seeing that they awaited him, he greeted them in his usual way ["The Lord give you peace"]. He was quite surprised, however, because the birds did not take flight, as they usually do. Filled with great joy, he humbly requested that they listen to the word of God:
>
> "My brother birds [he said], you should greatly praise your Cre-ator and love Him always. He gave you feathers to wear, wings to fly, and whatever you need. God made you noble among His creatures and gave you a home in the purity of the air, so that, though you nei-ther sow nor reap, He nevertheless protects and governs you without your least care."
>
> The birds stretched their necks, spread their wings, opened their beaks and looked at him. He passed through their midst, coming and going, touching their heads and bodies with his tunic. Then he blessed them, and having made the sign of the cross, gave them permission to fly off to another place. . . . And from that day on, he carefully exhorted all birds, all animals, all reptiles, and also insensible crea-tures, to praise and love the Creator.

On another occasion, at a village called Alviano, Francis was about to preach to a crowd:

> But a large number of swallows nesting there were shrieking and chirping. Since the people could not hear Francis, he said to the noisy birds: "My sister swallows, now it is time for me to speak, since you have already said enough. Listen to the word of the Lord and stay quiet and calm. . . ." Immediately those little birds fell silent, to the amazement and surprise of all present, and they did not move from that place until the sermon was over.

Birds were not the only beneficiaries of Francis's extraordinary attention:

> The wild beasts harmed by others used to flee to him and they found in his presence solace amid their trials. . . . He often freed lambs and sheep from the threat of slaughter because of the graciousness he felt towards the simplicity of their nature; he even picked worms out of the roadway so that they would not be harmed by passersby. . . . All creatures tried to return the saint's love and to respond to his kindness with their gratitude. They smiled when he petted them, they granted his requests and they obeyed when he commanded them. . . . He called all animals by the name of brother and sister, although he preferred the gentle kinds [of animals] above all others.

The accounts of Francis's life are all filled with such moments: he frees a rabbit captured in a trap; he returns to the water some struggling fish trapped in nets; he asks that honey be supplied for bees in wintertime; he tames a killer wolf, turning the beast into a town pet for the people of Gubbio. In all these tales, the animal world seems to respond immediately and naturally to him, as if the saint had reestablished a kind of prelapsarian Eden, in which (it was believed) man and beast existed in an ideal, harmonious state. This motif was reinforced by medieval piety, which represented the spiritual life as a return to Paradise—an idea developed as early as the desert hermits, eight centuries earlier.

The idea of concord between saints and animals was not new. An 11th-century legend told of the hermit Saint Aventin of Troyes, who was so generous in feeding the birds that they became daily visitors to his hut. Likewise, just a few years before Francis, an account of the life of William of Malavalle remarked that

> he dwelt securely, unharmed and untouched, in the midst of wild beasts, serpents and dragons. The birds of heaven ate with him. The fierce beasts approached him meekly, laying aside their natural feroc-ity, and without doing him any harm, revered him as if they were rational beings. The animals of the wilderness fell to the ground to kiss his holy footprints, and all the reptiles came and went obediently at his command.

Similar tales occur in the life of the French saint Girard of Saint-Aubin d'Angers, who died in 1123—and also apparently formed friendships with birds. Likewise, Francis's contemporary Caesarius of Heisterbach describes a group of storks asking an abbot's permission to depart from monastery grounds: the superior blesses them, and they depart happily. Such legends abound, as do tales of saints releasing hunted or trapped animals, defending those about to be killed and sheltering those who shiver in wintertime. But they were artistically rendered for the first time when they were linked to Francis in about 1260, by an unknown painter known as the Saint Francis Master, whose work is still visible in a fresco of the lower church of the Basilica of Saint Francis in Assisi; and by Giotto, in about 1299, in the basil-ica's upper church. Both are visual narratives of a human being who is especially attuned to creatures, who seems to have a mystic communication with them.

It is a commonplace today that some men and women have a unique bond with animals, which in fact sense human sympathy or gentleness or goodwill and so respond to them in ways that most people would consider marvelous or even miraculous. A good veterinarian, for example, will have an especially strong connection to animals, but even people with no special training often seem to know what gestures and tone of voice are reassuring or threatening.

Remarkable correspondences often occur between men and women and the being of all other things—connections unimaginable to those who lead only an inexpectant, ordinary life of the senses. Francis's connection to wildlife was not merely an expression of his love of nature: it was the product of a profound bond with everything that lived.

In that light, rather than asking, "Did this happen as it is described?" it would be more valuable to consider, "What significance did birds have for Francis's world, for his chroniclers and for him?"

In the 14th-century work *Les Livres du roy Modus et de la royne Ratio*, the traditional medieval division of society into those who pray, those who go to battle and those who work is represented by particular categories of birds. Doves, crows and magpies—precisely the birds whom Francis is said to have addressed—are symbols of all those who do manual labor. While this treatise appeared after the earlier accounts of the saint's life, since the birds mentioned are exactly the same, it seems as if the chronicles of Francis were exploiting a well-established medieval metaphor or fable, which was only later codified by the unknown author of *Les Livres*.

In addition, throughout the Middle Ages, birds were often used to represent souls, because they can fly up to God. They were also potent symbols of freedom. In the feudal system, the majority of people were tied to the land, and almost no one was mobile. But birds were unfettered, cheerful, singing, hopeful—everything workers aspired to be. As scholars have also long pointed out, the brilliant colors and intricate markings of birds were often regarded as parallels to the complex and colorful details of medieval heraldry.

The metaphorical point of the incident of Francis and the birds, then, may well be that in his preaching and in his fraternity, he often had more success with the lowest level of society—the poor and disenfranchised manual workers, poetically symbolized by birds—than with the rich and powerful (the clergy and nobility). This interpretation assigns Francis a far richer and more compassionate sensibility than being simply a friend of birds, and thus offers a view consistent with his concern for and identification with the poor.

Any overly literal reading of the episode of the preaching to the birds risks trivializing the importance Francis had for those without power, influence, prestige or political strength—precisely the people symbolized by the birds, and the group that most welcomed his message. And is it not far more compelling to know that besides loving all creatures, he communicated with the marginalized and downtrodden and delivered a message that they took to heart? Finally, it is interesting to note that there are no artistic representations of Francis preaching to people—simply because, as everyone understood, the birds stood in for all of poor, dependent humanity.

֍

By the autumn of 1209, Francis and his companions were back in the environs of Assisi. The weather turned unusually cold, and the hut near Saint Mary's had become dangerously damp and frigid in their absence. Accordingly, some of them made tents in the forest, while Francis (who was often ill that season) took a few others and moved to a pair of abandoned shacks a mile and a half from town, next to a narrow, winding stream called, aptly, the Rivo Torto; the place was very near the leper hospice of San Lazzaro. "Well," he said to his friends when they arrived, "it's easier to get to heaven from a shed than from a palace!"

Not long after their return, the Holy Roman Emperor and his caravan passed nearby. As was customary, people were able to get handouts from one of his minions if they jostled for position and cheered the emperor. But the clamor and celebration was of no importance to Francis, who did not interrupt his prayer to join the crowd; besides, he told his companions, there were certainly needier people than they.

The shacks consisted of two small rooms, one for eating and one for sleeping, although the brother friars—as they were now called—did little of either. By day they worked with farmers in nearby fields or cared for lepers; in the evening they went to Assisi and preached in the squares and then returned to pass several hours in the space between the shacks, praying.

On Saturday nights, Francis walked to Assisi, spent the night in a hut in the cathedral garden, and preached early Sunday morning in the Church of San Rufino. There, he distinguished himself by his kindness to the clergy. Francis refused to treat wayward priests with anything but enormous gentleness and utterly without condescension. "Woe to those who look down on the clergy," he said, "for even though they be sinners, no one should judge them because the Lord alone reserves judgment on them to Himself."

The fraternity owned absolutely nothing but the tunics on their backs, and their food consisted of wild fruit from the fields or a few turnips that grew near the shack. Thus their common life continued for almost a year in this place for which the word "modest" is an understatement: Francis had to write the brothers' names with chalk on the beams of the hut, so that when they wished to pray or sleep, each could find his place without disturbing the others. But he liked it there, not least of all because, by following the course of the stream, Francis could easily arrive at some caves on Mount Subasio, where he could make time for prayerful solitude—places so narrow he called them prison cells (*celle* or *carceri*).

§

The winter was harsh, and all the brothers suffered from it in some way, especially because of the lack of food; for several days, they had only a few pieces of mealy fruit and melted snow for sustenance. Then, thanks to a generous benefactor, some eggs, cheese and fish arrived to save them from starvation. Still, Francis insisted that everyone fast on Wednesdays and Fridays, and that the food be parceled out in small servings at other times. For him, fasting was as essential an activity as prayer, and he was not yet open to compromise on the matter.

But then something took place that revealed both his essential humanity and the depth of the ongoing process of his own conversion.

One night when all were asleep, a brother awoke and began to cry out, and Francis ran to his side.

"I'm dying of hunger," moaned the friar. Indeed, the man was very pale, his mouth was dry from dehydration, and he may have been close to collapse. With that, Francis retrieved some of the stored food and invited everyone to a midnight meal; from then on he tempered the severe fasts he had been imposing on himself and his fraternity.

"My brothers," he said soon after, "each of you must consider his own constitution. Although one of you may be sustained with less food than another, I still do not want one who needs more food to try imitating him in this. Rather, considering his constitution, he should provide his body with what it needs. Just as we must beware of overindulgence in eating, which harms both body and soul, so we must beware of excessive abstinence even more, because the Lord desires mercy and not sacrifice."

This was a significant accommodation on his part, for that night Francis realized that he would have to adjust the rigors of penance and self-denial if his fraternity was to survive. From this time, he was on the alert never to set down or require adherence to an abstract set of laws; the norms of charity and good example would henceforth always take precedence.

This new approach to their common life was evident soon after, when the priest Sylvester fell ill with a stomach ailment. "If he could eat some ripe grapes," Francis whispered to another friar, "I believe it would help him." No such fruit could be found in the vineyards during the winter, so early next morning, Francis climbed up to town and begged a bunch of grapes and some wine from a merchant.

Returning to his friends, he distributed the treats to everyone and once again warned them against excessive austerities. "Our brother the body needs a certain ration of food and sleep," he said. "If you refuse him this, he will also refuse to serve you and, discouraged, will reply, 'How can you expect me to give myself up to vigils, prayer and good works when, because of you, I am too weak even to stand?' " As his friends recalled later, "He insisted that it was just as much a sin to deprive the body of what it really needed as, prompted by gluttony, to offer it too much."

Unlike many who were dedicated to pious ideals, Francis was as vigilant for the emotional as for the physical health of his fraternity. One of the newest friars, a young man named Riccerio, wanted so desperately to please Francis that he feared that anything other than explicit praise meant he had incurred disfavor. In fact, Francis rarely scolded or praised others, as he considered that such behavior would have marked him as a superior who had a right to be pleased or displeased by a subject. But the sensitive Riccerio was in such turmoil that he avoided even his teacher's glance. Finally, sensing his pain, Francis took him aside and assured him, "Listen, do not be troubled by any thought. You are very dear to me, and you may come to me confidently whenever you want, knowing that you are welcome and can speak freely." His counsel was invariably characterized by such healthy common sense, free of cant, hypocrisy, aloofness or any sense of his own importance in the group other than his duty to provide the best example.

§

Only one brother defected during those harsh days of 1209 and 1210, while at least 40 joined them and set up camp wherever they found work, coming together for prayer, counsel and what little food they could gather. Obviously, the message of Francis of Assisi was making great sense to this increasing band, many of whom were, like him, the sons of wealthy merchants or even noblemen.

Today, much in the lives of these men sounds harsh, crude and unappealing, and so it requires some effort to appreciate the great joy that they found in hard work, the care of others, prayer and mutual support. Even the clergy and laity who grumbled about the friars and misunderstood their purpose had to admit that this group was attentive to the needy, who responded gratefully. Francis and his companions were known by the fruits of their labor and the spiritual serenity their life clearly bestowed on them and those who met them.

Of course, at one time or another, there were problems within the fraternity. Brother John of Cappella left the brotherhood and after many misadventures committed suicide. Juniper may have been a mystic, but he also had an almost pathological obsession with the humiliated Christ. Masseo was something of an agoraphobe who spent much of his life in a grotto. Elias had a despotic character and later, as minister, or superior, of the group, oppressed many of Francis's friends and was eventually excommunicated.

One could almost say that the friars would have to have been somewhat mentally unhealthy to have sought out this form of life, and that so fierce a devotion to it indeed put some of them at risk of psychological unbalance. They may have been holy men, but they were also, as one historian has described them, "unorganized and unruly tramps."

Nevertheless, precisely what comprises a degree of lunacy in a world gone mad with the obsession for power and money? Should it be considered healthy, then or now, to give up one's life, to abandon everything, for the world of commerce, for the right clothes, for more and more expensive possessions? How many people asked, as Francis and his friends must have, "How much is too much?" or, "Do I own my possessions, or do they own me?" How much real serenity of spirit was found among those who were committed to money—not as a means to support themselves or their family, or to give to those in need, but as an end in itself, for the mere acquisition of property, public image and social status? And how much authentic freedom was found among those who were prepared to put other realities and other people ahead of money?

Throughout history it has never been easy to distinguish the socially acceptable, sane person from the eccentric, marginal saint. Among the latter, there are indeed certifiable neurotics to be found, often precisely because they have marginalized themselves by adhering to transcendent values that do not conform to the standards or expectations of a world driven only by what is tangible and by comfort or pleasure. Because they have fallen in love with ultimacy, saints are people of extreme behavior.

It is, of course, perfectly acceptable for those who are eccentric to be graced with holiness. The infirm, the marginal, the impolite, the mentally wounded—all are within God's embrace and can find their own brand of godliness. Just as we admit that physical suffering does not preclude sanctity, we ought to say the same of emotional or psychological suffering. The friends of God are not always polite or healthy; nor are they always to be imitated.

With specific regard to Francis, we may not, finally, be drawn to him because we want to imitate him. Imitation of his extreme, literal manner of following Christ would be, in our own time, both impossible and frankly undesirable. What matters, rather, is Francis's abandonment of himself to God and his offering of himself for the good of the world—a dedication that was itself a definition of conversion.

§

In the autumn of 1210, the group of friars left Rivo Torto, though not exactly by choice, as it happened.

One afternoon, a poor man came to the sheds, leading his donkey and perhaps hoping for a handout. In order not to be turned away, he pushed the animal inside, shouting, "Go on—we can manage in this place!"

It apparently never occurred to Francis to challenge him. "God did not summon us here to be innkeepers for donkeys, dear brothers," he said, perhaps with a smile, "nor to negotiate with strangers. Our task is to show men the way of salvation." And so, refusing to claim anything or any place as his own, he immediately announced that they were departing. Before nightfall, they had traveled the few miles back to Saint Mary's, where they were ready to undertake the necessary repairs to what would be more or less their primary residence, although Francis still considered it the property of the Benedictines and insisted on continuing to pay the annual rent of a basket of fish. For the rest of Francis's life, it was his favorite domicile. The stranger and his mule, meantime, occupied the huts at Rivo Torto.

1211–1212

THE PLACE MARKED as the cradle of Franciscanism stood in stark contrast to the vast abbeys and great cathedrals that were the centers of medieval religion. The "little portion," or *portiuncula*, of land, permanently loaned by the hermits of Mount Subasio to Francis and his company, stood in a forest, and it consisted of a chapel, a cabin for meetings and a hut with small cubicles for sleep. Meals were taken on the ground, sacks of straw served as beds, and the roof was made of mud and leaves. Francis thought the humility of the place absolutely fitting, and he did not resent that he had been denied a church or cloister by the bishop and canons of Assisi.

From early 1211, when the community settled in at this modest base camp, Francis continued to gather a motley band of friars: manual laborers, knights, former robbers, priests, teachers. He courteously accepted anyone who wanted to join, who professed the faith of the apostles and was willing to abandon everything he owned. Only men could join, of course: both Church and world would never have thought of including women. That not only would have risked and invited charges of concubinage, but would also have presumed equality between the sexes, a notion that was inconceivable in the 13th century.

§

Bernard Quintavalle, the first to join Francis and the man elected guide on the journey to Rome two years earlier, was now the first to be sent alone on a mission. Well bred and intelligent, once rich and influential, Bernard retained only his manners and civility—to which he added a deep sense of service. Early that year, Francis asked him to go north to Bologna to preach, and Bernard was on his way immediately.

On his arrival, he was at first mocked and attacked by a crowd before he could say a word: his lowly appearance led them to believe that he was a renegade or a brigand. But a magistrate listened, recognized Bernard's holiness and was impressed by his words. He not only wanted to join the friars but also wanted to introduce Bernard to the city fathers and to ensure that the visitor would be treated with respect and even veneration. With that, Bernard rushed back to Saint Mary's and told Francis that someone else would have to go to Bologna to continue the task; it was, he said, a place where he had more to lose than to gain—honor, respect, even fame (especially when offered in response to one's piety) were distinctions he shunned like a disease.

His life remained profoundly contemplative even as he worked among the poor. Bernard was with Francis at his death and survived him for about 20 years, after which, at the end of a long and bitter illness, he sat up in bed with great difficulty. Turning to the young friars around him, Bernard said, "Dear brothers, I cannot speak many words to you. I was once where you are now, and you will soon be where I am now. I tell you this: for nothing in this world, nor for a thousand beautiful worlds like this one, would I wish to have lived otherwise than I have done, nor to have served any other master than our Lord Jesus Christ. I beg pardon for every offense I have committed, and I ask you, my dear brothers, to love one another." Moments later, Bernard Quintavalle died—with all the deserved reverence and devotion he had so vigorously declined.

§

Also at Saint Mary's was a young man aptly named John the Simple, a teenage farmer who had lived with his parents until the morning he heard that the controversial Francis Bernardone was sweeping a nearby church. Leaving his oxen in the field, John found him, finished Francis's chores and then plied him with questions. Within hours, he was the latest candidate for the fledgling community. He raced back to the family farm, unyoked the oxen and brought one to Francis, saying: "Let's give this to the poor! I'm sure I deserve to have at least this much as my share of my father's things!"

That afternoon, his parents and brothers heard what John had done and hurried to Francis in tears, "grieving more over losing the ox than the man," wrote Celano with trenchant irony.

"Calm down!" said Francis to the hysterical family. "Here, I'll give you back the ox and take only the brother."

But John was not called the Simple for that day's deeds. Hearing from the other brothers that he should seek to imitate Francis, he did so—with unnerving literalness. If Francis raised his arms in prayer, John at once did the same; if Francis scratched his head, John repeated the action; if Francis coughed and spat, John could be counted on to mimic him. Finally, Francis had enough and asked what John was doing. "I promised to do everything you do," he replied artlessly. "It is dangerous for me to leave anything out." Francis set him right on the matter.

The following year, John grew very sick—a condition he tried to hide from the brothers. With astonishing courage and not a word of complaint, the boy finally succumbed to a ravaging illness. Dull-witted he may have been, but when he died, at the age of 18, he was deeply mourned by every-one in the community; Francis always referred to him as Saint John.

⸙

Masseo, a tall, handsome and sophisticated man, was a first-rate preacher and had the kind of vanity that comes from being admired all one's life; being held in such esteem enabled him to cultivate an effortlessly engaging personality. This quality must at least partly explain the fact that when he returned from work in the fields, farmers always gave Masseo the choicest bits of food and drafts of wine to take away.

Perhaps to no one's surprise, Masseo soon became almost unbearably self-centered—even to the point of begrudging Francis the respect he never sought but was always afforded. One day Francis was returning from work to Saint Mary's when Masseo approached him and demanded, "Why you, eh? Why you? Why you, I ask!"

Francis inquired what he meant.

"The whole world seems to be running after you!" Masseo replied. "Everyone wants to see you, to hear you, and even to join you. Why? You're not a handsome man, you have no great knowledge or wisdom, and you're not of noble birth! Why does the whole world come to *you?*"

Without a trace of annoyance, Francis said calmly, "You want to know why me, and well you should. Why me? I'll tell you why. It's because God could not have chosen anyone less qualified, or more of a sinner, than myself. And so, for this wonderful work He intends to perform through us, He selected me—for God always chooses the weak and the absurd, and those who count for nothing."

The consensus of the earliest documents is that this answer left Masseo so stupefied that his own authentic conversion began that day. He spent a
· great deal more private time in solitary prayer, withdrew for long periods to a grotto and fasted so much, as penance for his vanity, that he lost his good looks. For a while, he became almost dangerously eremitical; at least Francis seems to have thought so, for he had to counter Masseo's increasing aloofness by forcibly bringing him back into the fold, where his talents (and newfound humility) were much appreciated. Francis, who never harbored grudges and was not offended by the rude question of 1211, ultimately grew very fond of Masseo, who became one of his closest friends.

§

Angelo Tarlati was a former knight who retained his somewhat imperious nature in the fraternity. One day, a trio of violent robbers who had been terrorizing the countryside came to Saint Mary's. Only Angelo was there that afternoon and, impatient with their demands for food, surprised them with a violent rebuke: "Murderers like you? You're not satisfied with robbing honest folks, and now you want to take the little that belongs to God's servants! You have no respect for God or man and don't deserve your place on earth. Get out of here and don't let me see you again!"

When Francis returned, Angelo proudly told him what had occurred. "You've behaved like a man with no religion at all," Francis responded, and gathering some of the bread and wine he had received as wages that day, gave the food to Angelo and told him to take it to the robbers. "Serve these unfortunate men with humility and good humor until they are satisfied. Then—and not until then—tell them to stop robbing and killing." The sources describing this event differ in details, but they are unanimous in recounting the finale: the brigands were not only converted, they eventually joined the fraternity "and died the death of saints." It is not likely that the early chroniclers would have noted the presence of criminals among the band of friars unless they could not avoid including a fact everyone at the time knew to be true.

§

Surely one of the most unconventional among the early Franciscans was a young man named Juniper. "I wish I had a whole forest like him," said Francis, who knew how to turn a pun as well as how to tolerate Juniper's eccentricities.

Francis once sent Juniper on a mission to Viterbo, west of the Rieti valley. Taking seriously the biblical injunction against returning evil for evil, Juniper offered no protest when he was wrongly taken for a political spy and was forthwith escorted to the scaffold. He was saved only when another friar happened along, wearing the same kind of tunic; the crowd had heard him preach before, and so they took his word about Juniper's innocence.

But on other occasions Juniper demonstrated a certain kind of raw wisdom. When a group of the brothers was once solemnly discussing how they dealt with all kinds of fantasies and desires, Juniper stopped the conversation with a simple statement: "As for me, I simply crowd out such temptations with other thoughts, and when the devil knocks at my door, I shout, 'Be gone! The inn is full and we're not opening up to anyone!' "

His odd behavior sometimes had an underlying spiritual motive. On a visit to Rome, he learned that some people, believing he was a wise counselor, were seeking him out for advice. His companions assured him it was pointless trying to avoid such attention and admiration, but they had not taken Juniper's resourcefulness into full account. As he approached the eager crowd, he spotted a group of children on a seesaw. At once, he went over to them and joined the fun as if it were the most important item on his agenda. The enthusiasm of his admirers was at once checked, and they withdrew, disappointed that a holy man should act such a fool.

Of his good intentions there was never any doubt, even when they led to embarrassing moments. Faithful to Francis's example, he would cut pieces from his tunic to give to beggars, though the portions were sometimes so excessive that Francis had to reprimand him for his immoderation. But then, one cold afternoon, Juniper saw a shivering beggar. "You've come at a bad time, my man," he told the fellow. "I've just been forbidden to give away my tunic." He paused, bent over and whispered to the beggar, "But if you want to take it away from me, I won't stop you." The poor man immediately took the hint, and Juniper had to return home in his under-garments—to much laughter from the fraternity.

This time, Francis was exasperated. "Ah, Brother Juniper! I really don't know what penance to suggest to you for this bit of folly!"

"I have an idea," Juniper replied without a trace of guile. "Just tell me to go back where I came from in the same outfit!"

With that, Francis became genuinely annoyed and gave Juniper so stern a rebuke that he nearly lost his voice. That night, there was a knock at Francis's door, and he opened it to discover Juniper with a lighted candle in one hand and a dish of soup in the other.

"You shouted so, a few hours ago, that I thought you must be hoarse. So I've brought you some hot soup, which will do your throat a world of good."

Francis sighed, told Juniper to stop being so silly and dismissed him.

"Very well," replied Juniper. "Since you don't want my soup, which I didn't make to throw away, then please hold the candle for me, and I'll eat it myself."

At that, Francis had to yield, and he burst out laughing. The two men shared the soup and talked late into the night.

§

Taking his cue from popular legends, Francis called Giles "my knight of the Round Table." The young man had no gift for preaching but was industrious at manual labor and was willing to do anything to help support the common cause.

He also had what is sometimes called the wisdom of the simple. When one of the friars remarked that Giles ought to learn how to give a good sermon, he replied, "Isn't it better to go on a pilgrimage than to show others which road to take?" He added that he himself had heard very few good sermons. "I think it's a shame that men do not have long, curving necks like cranes."

What on earth could he mean? the other friar wanted to know.

"Well, many words would stick in their throats because of the difficulty they would have getting out."

For all his gentleness, Giles occasionally spoke with an honesty that verged on harshness. A local woman had been mourning for a very long time over the death of her adult son, and one day Giles asked her, "Which would you rather have—your son's body or his soul?"

Well, his body, of course, the old lady answered—she missed his physical presence.

"Then go to the cemetery," Giles said, "and find the body you loved so much, and you will see what has become of it."

Another time, Francis had preached on the dangers of sexual excess. Afterward a man came up to him and Giles and said, "This doesn't really concern me, for I have my wife, and I know no other woman."

Giles had a quick response. "Doesn't a man ever get drunk on the wine from his own cask?"

He spent most of his later life in prayerful solitude, but when the great basilica was constructed to honor Francis after his death, Giles came to Assisi and unequivocally stated his disapproval. "Now all you need are wives," he said bitterly to the friars living there in comparative splendor after 1230. They asked what he meant by that comment. "I mean that since you have forsaken your promise to live poorly, all you now need to do is to abandon chastity—after all, you made a commitment to that, too!"

❧

Bashful, inarticulate Rufino had come from a powerful Assisian family. Francis knew that his background could be an advantage in the city, if only Rufino would overcome his shyness and step forth to address a group. Rufino refused, and Francis—taking his demurral for arrogance—told him that for penance he ought to strip off his tunic and walk into town naked to the waist. This Rufino did at once and was met with hoots of disdain from the townspeople. When this was reported to Francis, he regretted having caused Rufino's humiliation. Rushing up to the square where Rufino stood in public embarrassment, he took off his own tunic and stood next to him, also bare to the waist. And then Francis put his arm on Rufino's shoulder and, exploiting the *ars concionandi,* delivered a haunting sermon about the symbolism of Christ's nakedness on the cross, to which the crowd listened rapt.

Not long afterward, Rufino had a frightening dream in which he was told by the devil that he should leave Saint Mary's and the fraternity. The following morning he quietly departed, and for several months was nowhere to be found. When Francis finally discovered him, he called out, "Rufino, what have you been up to?" On hearing the story of the dream, Francis—who knew when earthy candor was appropriate—led him back to Saint Mary's and said quietly, "Listen, Rufino, next time the devil appears to you in a dream like that, just tell him, 'Open your mouth like that once more and I'll shit in it!' "

§

With so much responsibility and a collection of such strong personalities around him, Francis required occasional periods of absolute quiet and solitude. Accordingly he spent the entire Lent of 1211 in fasting and prayer on a small, uninhabited island in Lake Trasimeno, just outside Perugia. At the end of that sojourn, he dictated to Leo—his confessor, confidant and amanuensis—a letter to be circulated among all those who were joining the fraternity near and far. The length of three modern book pages, it was to be addressed "to those who do penance," that is, those who wished to reform their lives. They are, Francis says, the very spouses, brothers and mothers of Christ:

We are spouses when the faithful soul is joined by the Holy Spirit to our Lord Jesus Christ. We are brothers to him when we do the will of the Father Who is in heaven. We are mothers when we carry him in our hearts and bodies through a divine love and a pure and sincere conscience and give birth to him through a holy activity that must shine as an example before others.

As always with Francis's letters and sayings, almost half the text cites biblical verses. The first part is an invitation, the second a warning, but Francis concludes with enormous tenderness for those who wish to undertake a life of constant conversion: "In the love which is God, we beg all those to whom these words reach to receive those fragrant words of our Lord Jesus Christ [from Scripture], written here with love and kindness."

§

In addition to solitary places like the isles of Trasimeno, Francis (and later one or another of his companions) also withdrew to the tiny caverns on Mount Subasio. Little more than stone grottoes, these *celle* or *carceri*, as they were known, still exist in an only slightly reconstructed form, an hour's walk from Assisi, and their setting and simplicity remain deeply impressive. With help from new friars, Francis also built similar retreat huts near Cortona, Sarteano and other towns.

In Assisi, meanwhile, an 18-year-old girl who had heard Francis preach wanted not only to meet him but also to join his company of penitents. A friar had already warned her that this would be impossible, since Francis not only excluded women from his fraternity but avoided their company whenever possible, for he was all too aware of his vulnerabilities from his earlier life as the rake of Assisi. But the friar underestimated the sheer persistence of this graceful, radiant young noblewoman. Quietly determined, she returned to her spacious, elegant family home in the Piazza San Rufino and considered her strategy.

TEN

1212–1213

FRANCIS OF ASSISI was not always a good judge of character. Precisely because he tended to see only a person's best potential, was disinclined to condemn and eager to extend compassion, he sometimes too readily accepted those who came to him—especially if they were intelligent, capable and tempered by time and experience. These qualities accurately describe Elias Bombarone, the well-born son of an Assisian consul. Elias joined the fraternity early on and attached himself to Francis, whom he defended and served for years. Everything augured well for his future among the Franciscans, and Francis had nothing but praise for him.

But in the early sources, Elias remains a shadowy, transient figure— perhaps because the chroniclers were aware of his subsequent history. Soon after Francis's death, Elias was elected minister general of the worldwide fraternity, and at once his true character emerged. Despotic and self-indulgent, he tyrannized the fledgling Order, led it away from its spirit of poverty and into a quest for wealth and power, imprisoned several of the original and most faithful friars and generally betrayed both Francis and the community. Eventually, Elias was forced to leave the Franciscans and was even excommunicated, although he was finally reconciled to the Church and presumably begged pardon for his maniacally ego-driven career, his blithe contempt for others and his comfortably affluent lifestyle.

In these first years of the fraternity, Francis impressed so many people with his preaching and dedicated life that the number of friars increased exponentially, to the point that keeping them all true to his spirit and teachings grew to be a problem. More formal codes were also necessary because of the inclusion of priests in the ranks, the establishment of permanent residences, the demands of training recruits and the nature of the group's

preaching. It was becoming clearer that he would have to do exactly what
he had hitherto avoided, and establish some sort of structure and Rule so
that the fraternity could grow prudently and eventually survive him. Gradually, a *forma vitae,* or loosely organized "form of life," was developed—
verbally at first, based on custom and practice.

Francis had always insisted on the example of Christ as the model he
and his friars would pursue, and so the idea of a Rule would always mean,
for him, following the path of this life and nothing else. The essential elements in the Franciscan Rule, he insisted, would be strict poverty, authority exercised as service, obedience for the good of the community, a
fraternal, democratic spirit and honest work.

§

In this regard, Francis always preferred action to analysis—which may
explain why he responded so passionately to the news that had recently
come from Germany and France. Great crowds of indigent people, surviving on the fringes of society but inspired by wandering preachers and the
increasingly popular ideal of early Christian poverty, believed that the mission of the Crusades could be accomplished only by God's poor, and not
by violence and armor.

And so they set out for ports on the eastern coast of Italy and the south
of France, from where they planned to make their way to the Holy Land.
Vast numbers died in the trek across the mountains from typhus, starvation
or dysentery. Those who reached the port of Brindisi were discouraged
from departing by the bishop, who rightly anticipated catastrophe; he was
ignored. Those who left from Ancona were forced back by storms at sea.
The entire venture, alas, turned tragic almost immediately. Many were
shipwrecked or died during the voyage, and most never arrived at their des-
tination.

Within a few years, however, this event had been transformed in the
popular imagination into the trappings of a medieval romance. As it happened, the majority of people who set out on the ill-conceived mission
were serfs or servants, for which the most common word in medieval Latin
was *pueri*—a word that can also connote young boys or, more generally,

children. And so arose the appealingly heartbreaking myth of the Children's Crusade, in which innocent youngsters, willing to abandon themselves to a religious ideal and to risk martyrdom, supposedly left their homes, singing and praying. In poignant accounts more remarkable for poetic imagination than historical accuracy, they were said to have endured great deprivation and to have fallen into the hands of swindlers, kidnappers and molesters, who herded them onto boats and sold them into slavery in Africa and the Near East.

From late-13th-century religious chroniclers up to 20th-century writers like Martinus Nijhoff and Bertolt Brecht, this tale of the Children's Crusade has been an irresistible subject; as recently as 1963, the composer Gian Carlo Menotti wrote a compelling oratorio, *The Death of the Bishop of Brindisi*, in which the dying, guilt-ridden prelate is haunted by the ghosts of the doomed young Crusaders.

It is worth calling attention to this popular misrepresentation because the actual moment in history is directly linked to the proclamation of poverty by Francis of Assisi and others. More to the point, the Children's Crusade is connected to Francis's own decision to join the Crusades that same year.

It was, not coincidentally, the prosperous abbeys (so often criticized in Francis's preaching) that produced the first romances of the Children's Crusade. Monks seized on the ambiguity of the word *pueri*, conveniently transforming the rash heroism of the poor into the idealism of boys and girls. The official accounts, in other words, glorified not the eagerness of poor wanderers to follow Christ but the putative courage of innocent martyrs obeying the pope's call to liberate Christian shrines. Such chronicles would embarrass neither the wealthy monasteries from which they originated nor the hierarchy with its riches, for they avoided praising the poor, whose very condition was an implicit indictment of them. Celebrating the deeds of children was a much safer alternative.

Francis, of course, had always believed the poor had a special place in Christian witness. The goal of his poverty movement was neither the glorification of the destitute nor the easing of their misery, but rather a return to Christ and the moral reform of all society, civil and ecclesiastical, by means of voluntarily chosen poverty. In his view, the poor could become spiritually rich by the patient endurance of sufferings, which was the ultimate imitation of Christ.

When Francis learned of the popular movement among laymen and -women to rescue the Holy Land, he immediately decided to join them. Rejecting arms and the Crusaders' quest for riches and honor as well as the desire for indulgences and thus heavenly rewards, he entertained higher goals—the establishment of peace and the conversion of Muslims, both of which meant risking his life for Christ in an ultimate act of chivalry.

In fact, the earliest accounts of his life provide no direct link between Francis and the campaign in the Holy Land. That is understandable, for none of his chroniclers, writing after both his death and the failure of the poor people's Crusade, would have wished to associate him with so fruitless an undertaking; according to these sources, he independently came up with the idea to sail away with one or two of his friars. But today we know the groups with whom he wanted to travel, the timing of his attempted journey and the port from which he departed.

It is inconceivable that Francis would have been unaware of the larger movement, for this Crusade was one of the two or three most important events of the year 1212, and all the pilgrims who were heading for departure points in Ancona and Brindisi would have traveled along established routes that passed through Tuscany, Umbria and the Marches.

§

But there were other matters requiring his attention—legislating for his followers and attending to the spiritual direction of a socially prominent young woman from Assisi. For the present, he avoided any executive decisions, perhaps naïvely hoping that organizational matters would resolve themselves. But he could not disregard the dogged determination of Clare Offreduccio to meet him after she had heard him preach at the Church of San Rufino that year, during Lent.

Born in 1193, Clare was the oldest of three daughters of a noble family of Assisi; she also had two older brothers, of whom nothing is known. Her mother, Ortola Fiumi, was apparently wealthy when she married the prosperous businessman Faverone Offreduccio. When Clare was only five, the Offreduccios had to flee to Perugia during the period of political violence when the *minores* rose up against the nobility. On their return to Assisi in 1205, they restored the family home facing the Piazza San Rufino, an area always boisterous with the cries of heralds and hawkers.

Clare's father died soon after their return, and she was placed under the protection of her uncles. Most wellborn girls were safely married to prominent men by the time they were 12 or 13, but Clare refused all such arrangements proposed by her family. By early 1212, 18-year-old Clare's chastity was an acute embarrassment, for custom required her to wed before her younger sisters, Catherine and Beatrice.

A number of young men found Clare's rejection frustrating: Ranieri Bernardo, for example, recalled that she was "lovely to look at. The matter of a husband for her was discussed, and many of her relatives urged her to choose one, but she did not want to consent to it. I myself many times implored her to agree to it, but she did not want to hear of it." A neighbor named Peter Damiano added that her family "wanted her to make a marriage suitable to her noble station, to a great and powerful man. But she could in no way be persuaded to do it."

The reason soon became clear. She had developed a life of intense prayer, and she had promised to give herself entirely to God. "She saved the food she was given to eat, put it aside and then sent it to the poor," recalled John Ventura, a servant in Clare's home. Clare also sent Francis some money from the sum of her inheritance so that he and his friars could have food when they were restoring Saint Mary's.

When she heard him speak at the Church of San Rufino, only steps from her home, she believed that God had chosen "to enlighten my heart to do penance according to the example and teaching of our most blessed father Francis." Now she had realized her true vocation—to follow his lead, abandoning wealth and position, sacrificing marriage and family and devoting her entire life to an imitation of Gospel poverty and the service of the poor.

This was a remarkably bold aspiration, for at that time the only possibility available to a devout woman who wished to dedicate herself to a religious and celibate life was the cloister—an existence of total enclosure as a nun, removed from the world. As both Church and society otherwise expected a woman to marry and bear as many children as possible, the single life, to whatever purpose it was dedicated, was simply not a viable alternative.

But Clare—by all accounts a young woman of beauty, charm and enormous self-confidence—also had a remarkably independent spirit and resolved that that an exception might be made in her case. She wanted to do what Francis and his fraternity did, and to do it in the world, not apart from it—in other words, she wished to join his revolution in an active religious life.

During Lent, Francis and Clare met—always with a friar and her sisters or friends present, as required by contemporary propriety. According to Clare's sister Beatrice and a family friend named Bona Guelfuccio, the two discussed the Gospel, the world of wealth and power that kept the poor oppressed and an alternative life of total service to others. Clare's understanding of Francis's aims was radically deepened, and on Palm Sunday night, March 18, she slipped out of the family home and ran down to Saint Mary's. Exactly what she would do and where she would go were not yet clear in her mind.

Francis had approved of her desire to sacrifice her life, but he had presumed that she would realize her vocation according to the tradition and regulation of the Church, as a cloistered nun—especially because she was a noblewoman. In any event, it would never have occurred to the chivalrous Francis to subject Clare to the difficult and dangerous life of an itinerant preacher living on the margins of society. His counsel to her to lead a conventional nun's life was based on respect, and not on any underestimation of her potential. Firm in her conviction that Francis was her guiding light, she followed the traditional path—with what initial reluctance we can never know, for she never wavered in her commitment.

§

As for religious women, their traditions can be traced back to before Scholastica, the sister of Saint Benedict and founder of the Benedictine nuns in the sixth century. In Clare's time, there were (among other groups) the Beguines—religious laywomen who lived in common quarters, prayed intensely and performed works of charity. They lived chastely while in community, but they took no vows and were free to depart and marry without censure. By the early 13th century, because of their profoundly mystical devotion, the Beguines were suspected of heresy, and soon they were all but suppressed. (The group was reestablished in more tolerant times, and today there are robust communities of Beguines in Belgium.)

Enclosed nuns of Clare's time lived in highly stratified monastic societies; noblewomen who joined their ranks usually did so with personal maids or servants accompanying them, and wealthy, influential abbesses were often "mitered"—that is, in their convents they were honored with the respect typically accorded bishops (but of course without any priestly consecration). And for both sexes, cloisters were officially seen as providing a program to discourage concubinage and to ensure fidelity to vows.

§

Since the time of Saints Jerome and Augustine, the Church not only feared that women were the cause of sexual profligacy; it also presumed that even the devout among them would be contaminated by the world. There was no notion that the work and example of dedicated women might actually benefit secular society.

The basis for this was the belief of both Church and secular society that woman were inferior to men, weak, dependent, more prone to sin (thanks to a misreading of the biblical story of Adam and Eve) and dangerous to men's virtue. By Clare's time, it was presumed that women "must not be left to govern themselves, given their natural tendency to fickleness and the temptations that come to them from outside, which they cannot resist on account of their weakness." This principle was articulated by no less than Thomas Aquinas, Bonaventure and Duns Scotus—all of them powerful voices in 13th-century theology.

It is important to note here that Francis did not, in principle, share the generally low view of women that prevailed at that time. Whereas all the biblical interpretations of Genesis up to his time described Eve as the cause of Adam's downfall, Francis had a quite different view: he saw Adam's sin as one of pride and self-will, and in his reading of Genesis he never mentioned Eve at all. Francis followed the Gospel of Jesus, who treated men and women as equals and who certainly had women among his closest friends and companions.

§

On the night of Clare's arrival at Saint Mary's, Francis cut off her hair, thus giving her the tonsure and the concomitant protection of the Church. He then covered her head with a veil, clothed her in a sackcloth tunic tied with a cord and outlined the terms of her future life. The friars escorted her to temporary refuge with a group of Benedictine nuns, who had agreed to take her in at their convent of San Paolo at Bastia, two miles west of Assisi.

The next morning, when Clare's family discovered her absence and learned of her actions, her uncles tracked her down, broke into the convent and tried to kidnap her and bring her home. Her uncle Monaldo, who led the group, shouted that they had just found the perfect husband for her at last (some other handsome and rich merchant destined for disappointment), and that she should therefore stop all this nonsense and return home. In response, Clare removed her veil, displayed her shorn head and sternly announced that she had found her true spouse in Christ the Lord. Clinging to the convent altar, she claimed the right of sanctuary, and Monaldo and company were afraid to commit sacrilege by laying hands on the holy table.

Understandably, the nuns wanted no more of this sort of excitement. They summoned Francis, who arrived the next day and took Clare to another nunnery, that of Sant'Angelo di Panzo, on the slopes of Mount Subasio. Her uncles pursued her there and made another attempt to persuade her, but she was so determined that they finally abandoned her to what they considered her madness. Soon after, Francis (with the permission and collaboration of Bishop Guido) moved Clare into some rooms he had renovated as a convent for her at San Damiano. Her life, at her own request, was extremely rigorous in every way. Clare's sister Catherine, several close friends and even her mother later joined her at what became the earliest Franciscan convent. Within 25 years, there were 50 nuns in the community.

At first, the women followed an unwritten Rule of life Francis devised for them, which was virtually modeled on what the friars were developing for their own *forma vitae*. But eventually she took another revolutionary step. Despite pressure from Rome for her to adopt regulations set down by one of its clerical leaders, Clare drafted her own Rule for her nuns, which was radically faithful to the primacy of poverty and the spirit of Franciscanism. She had lifelong battles with bishops trying to impose bureaucratic changes, but she persevered, and a platoon of churchmen, at first suspicious, made their way to her door but departed mute with admiration. They invariably returned for her wise counsel.

A few years later, Francis suggested to Clare that she become the abbess, or superior, of San Damiano—not because he enjoined on her any authority he himself did not covet, but because this position would have freed Clare from interference by outside Church authorities and vested in her a more direct responsibility for the guidance of her nuns. (Dominican nuns, in contrast, had to have a priest and later a bishop as their superiors.) Clare accepted the position with some diffidence, for she never had any pretensions to rule. As one of the nuns said later, "She would more readily do something herself than order others to do it." According to another, "She really made herself the servant of all the sisters. She served all the sick, and if she saw another in need, she was the first to respond."

Enclosed at San Damiano for the next 41 years, Clare and her nuns survived by their own labor (needlework, making altar linens, gardening), but they always remained very poor. This Convent of Poor Ladies, as they were first called, was ultimately replicated throughout Italy and in virtually every part of the world, where they became known as the Poor Clares. (To this day, they are a sturdy branch of the Franciscan tree.)

Literally hours before her death, she finally succeeded in winning the prerogative of establishing and regulating precisely the kind of existence she saw as appropriate for her nuns, when the pope gave formal approval to the Rule she had drafted. This was enormously important, for it allowed Clare and her nuns everywhere to live a life of radical poverty, and they were effectively free of the economic tyranny of the nobility, the wealthier Orders and Rome itself.

Clare outlived her spiritual mentor by 27 years, dying in 1253 at the age of 59, worn out by illnesses doubtless worsened by four decades of severe, self-imposed bodily penances. Before her canonization two years later, papal investigators interviewed many people who knew her. There was complete unanimity concerning her profound and humble dedication to her community, her exemplary life and her ability to shape an authentic renewal of cloistered nuns at a time when they were often as lax and renegade as their male counterparts.

None of this would have happened without the inspiration of Francis. An aristocrat who could not pursue her original plan for a vocation like his, Clare found the truth of herself in a life as revolutionary as Francis's, which was also an indictment of the new, money-driven economy. And as the first woman to define a religious life for women, she began a tradition that later flourished in the lives of the great religious women and mystics: Catherine of Siena, Teresa of Ávila, Mechtilde of Magdeburg, Angela Merici and, closer to our own time, Elizabeth Seton, Cornelia Connelly, Frances Cabrini and Katharine Drexel, to name but a few. Institutions may try time and again to subordinate women and restrict their influence, but somehow God outmaneuvers institutions.

§

For a few years after 1212, Francis and his religious brothers enjoyed a friendly and supportive relationship with Clare and her religious sisters. Although they both understood the necessity of discretion at a time of flagrant concubinage among clerics and a laxity even among cloistered nuns, they did not feel compelled to forego all visits.

Later, however, continuing their friendship became more and more awkward, until the formalities of their status as members of canonical religious Orders forced them to sacrifice merely personal visits. At the same time, Francis had no desire for Clare and her nuns to depend on him for the management and the focus of their lives. But it is poignant to think of these two close friends, deprived of honest and honorable affection because of the prevalent belief that any contact between the sexes was a likely route to eternal perdition—a belief which must have influenced Francis to some degree.

Many people have come to view Clare as a tragic victim of male prerogatives. Deprived of her wish to live an existence like the friars', the argument runs, she had to settle for life in the cloister. In fact, it would never have occurred to a devout woman in 13th-century Italy to question the counsel of a man like Francis. Yet, she was a remarkably independent woman, refusing to follow the enforced customs of marriage and family and devoting herself instead to a career of sacrifice. In any case, it would be profoundly unfair to judge her by the options women have in the Church and the world 800 years later.

In recent years, other writers have interpreted Clare's cloistered life as the result of a suppressed erotic love for Francis: clearly this man and woman were attracted to each other, but they forswore marriage or concubinage out of a kind of emotional paralysis caused by religious fanaticism. But this assertion presumes a great deal more than the evidence allows and oversteps the boundaries of history or biography.

The fundamental tenor of the relationship between Francis and Clare was that of a spiritual father or religious counselor to his spiritual daughter. There is not the remotest hint, in any of the sources, of a warm, egalitarian comradeship or a romantic impulse, much less an attachment; theirs was not the fate of Abelard and Héloïse. Moreover, both of them were remarkably focused in their commitments; their subsequent lives indicate less a crippling repression than a deliberate subordination of their entire selves to God.

⸎

With Clare and her companions safely lodged at San Damiano, Francis asked a few friars to visit them occasionally and see that their needs were provided for. He then departed for Rome, to preach and to ask permission to extend his preaching mission to the infidels. While he was there, a cardinal introduced him to a wealthy and devout young widow named Jacoba Settisoli (later, the French and English forms of the first name would be Jacqueline). She was about 22 at the time—intelligent, beautiful and the mother of two young sons.

Jacoba came from a high-ranking family of the old Roman nobility, descended on her father's side from Norman knights who had conquered Sicily. Her late husband, Graziano, was from one of Rome's most illustrious families, the Frangipani, who claimed to be descendants of an eighth-century Roman who saved the citizens from famine by harvesting enough wheat to provide bread (hence the name Frangipani—the *frangens panem*, or "bread-breaking," family). By the time of her marriage, the Frangipani had acquired the remains of the castle of Emperor Septimius Severus, a magnificent place called the Septizonium (thus "Settisoli").

Because her wealth and family connections gave her easy access to the papal court and because she was eager to meet Francis, Jacoba arranged an introduction. Very quickly, she became, like Clare, one of Francis's spiritual daughters. Their meetings in Rome early that summer of 1212 were brief but intense and left her with a profounder sense of prayer and even greater dedication to the needs of the poor in Rome.

After she offered several of her properties for the use of the friars and their works of charity, Francis—astonished by her outspoken manner, her sense of humor and her leadership qualities (traits then thought more suitable for a man)—nicknamed her Brother Jacoba. Each time he came to Rome, she prepared an irresistible dish she first set before him that season: *mostacciuoli*, an almond-cream confection, evidently an ancient recipe among the Bread Breakers. Courtesy and perhaps the sheer delight in such a rare treat obliged him to accept it with much pleasure.

§

As a result of his meetings with the papal court, Francis obtained permission to extend his preaching mission as a kind of crusading cleric. Although he had no intention of assuming arms or armament, Francis believed that somehow the Muslims could be converted, which would spell the end to their ongoing conflict with Christianity. As recently as July 16, there had been a savage encounter at Las Navas de Tolosa, in southern Spain: where Christian knights massacred Saracen forces, broke their European stronghold and convinced Rome that the tide had turned in favor of the Christian legions.

But Francis had another aim in this mission—or rather, his goal had two particular aspects. He not only wanted to know this so-called enemy, to actually meet them and to convert them to the poor Christ, but in the enormous risk of doing so he would put himself in the position of achieving the greatest honor that could come to a follower of Jesus: namely, martyrdom. This was a notion universally held among medieval Christians, whether they actively sought such a destiny or not.

Ever since the first two centuries of Christianity, the era of Roman persecutions against the followers of the crucified Jesus, the highest ideal of witness was considered to be the literal sacrifice of one's life. In fact, it was the very fidelity of Christians unto death that was one of the primary impetuses for the survival and spread of the faith: "The blood of martyrs is the seed of the Church," as Tertullian observed at the height of the atrocities against Christians.

With the Edict of Milan and the legalization of Christianity in 313, the threat of martyrdom was removed. Subsequently, the ascetical traditions of the spiritual life regarded heroic virtue, selfless acts of charity and the habit of self-denial as the equivalent of martyrdom, and so even those who did not die for their faith could be proclaimed saints as a result of their dedicated lives. More to the point, preachers everywhere (following the lead of the Irish monks) declared that mortifications and penances were the substitute for martyrdom. This became a major motif in, for example, the preaching of Saint Bernard.

But the initiation of the Crusades once again offered the faithful the prospect of literal martyrdom, the ultimate act of adoration and the definitive Christian pilgrimage. Following the image of the cross, on which died the perfect martyr, meant engaging in battle to win back the true cross on which he died.

"Always eager to try his hand at brave deeds," as Celano wrote, "Francis burned with the desire for holy martyrdom and longed to reach the summit of perfection." While Francis had always been somewhat impractical and disorganized, this scheme was, by any standard, the most foolhardy; no one had ever thought of sending an emissary to proclaim the Gospel to the Muslims.

Francis, who had so often dreamed of knightly glory, now saw the fulfillment of his dream of chivalry, but with a crucial difference: he would seek not his own credit now, but only the honor of God. He would confront the enemy armed only with the spirit of truth. If he died, he reasoned, God would use his death to buy the redemption of the infidels. Like his contemporaries, he considered fallen Crusaders as true martyrs.

And so he returned to Umbria that autumn, asked Peter Catanio to assume spiritual direction of the friars in his absence, and at once joined the vast crowds of people from Germany and France who were gathering at Ancona to set off for Syria and join the Crusades. But the ship on which he sailed, heading southeast, was blown off course by violent storms, and he and his hapless fellow passengers found themselves in Slavonia, on the Dalmatian coast, only 95 miles from Italy.

After several days of more foul weather, no sailors would head farther south. Francis, who was traveling with one companion (probably Giles or Leo), had no money for the return passage—he had, after all, anticipated a one-way journey ending in death. But as they prepared to stow away aboard a ship making for Italy, a good man offered them food and wine, which Francis bartered to pay the fare. They reached port safely.

Once again, his longing for spiritualized chivalry, now joined to the desire for martyrdom, ended in failure. As so often, God had other plans.

ELEVEN

1213–1218

*O*N HIS RETURN to Italy, Francis resumed his preaching, but for the first time, his companions noticed a certain detachment in his manner, as if he were confused and displeased with himself. As the winter of 1213 wore on, with sharp winds blowing across the valley and icy rain pelting Saint Mary's, he seemed to be slipping into what today might be diagnosed as clinical depression.

Still, he spoke to individuals and groups with his usual charm and persuasion, and the fraternity continued to increase—most notably that season with the addition of a man named Pacificus, a poet and musician known as "the king of verses," a polite title for one who improvised bawdy lyrics to popular melodies. A typical offering might concern an unhappy wife who bemoans the infidelities of her jealous lover; or a daughter who asks her mother to find her a lover; or a lady with a lover who has to convince her husband that her feigned illness is real, so she can avoid the marriage bed.

When Pacificus met Francis in a town square, he was already a well-known figure. He introduced himself by way of one of the risqué songs in his repertory, to which Francis courteously replied that Pacificus had a fine voice that he could put to better use. With that, Francis took the man's lute and accompanied himself in a merry tune to which he improvised lyrics about the love of Christ. His manner was so uncensorious, so gentle, that Pacificus sought him out a week later and joined the fraternity.

For all that the Lesser Brothers were much admired, they began to encounter the disapproval of a significant minority of critics. Boncampagno of Signa, who was a master of rhetoric at the University of Bologna at this time, dismissed the Franciscans as "in part mere youths or boys. If, then, the pliability of their years makes them inconstant and easily led, that is only to be expected. But they have already gone to an extreme of madness, since they wander through cities and towns and solitary places without any discretion, enduring horrible and inhuman sufferings."

While this was certainly a harsh assessment, and not typical of the reaction to the fraternity, it did reflect, as even the best modern Franciscan scholars have collectively admitted, "the ambivalence felt by many observers toward the new movement." Doubtless some of that ambivalence had to do with the revolution Francis and his companions were proclaiming by action, in their disorganized but benevolent ways.

It is especially not surprising that a negative reaction should have come from the university master Boncampagno, for it was widely known that Francis of Assisi had little regard for advanced education and bookishness: "Those brothers of mine who are led by curiosity for knowledge will find themselves empty-handed on the day of reckoning. I wish they would grow stronger in virtue, so that when the times of tribulation arrive, they may have the Lord with them in their distress." But the same early chronicler added, "He did not say these things out of dislike for the study of the Scriptures, but to draw all of them back from excessive concern for learning, because he preferred that they be good through charity, rather than dilettantes through curiosity."

Francis's distrust of mere learning was in fact consistent with his radical life and message and did not reflect any particular anti-intellectualism. "We must honor all theologians," he said in his final *Testament,* and Celano recalled that "he considered doctors of sacred theology to be worthy of even greater honor" than preachers.

In fact, Francis's antipathy to mere academism was rooted in the fact that books and scholarliness were, at that time, the métier of rich monasteries. Since the only ones who had books, which were rare and expensive, were abbots, noblemen and princes, Francis could only regard owning them as an insult to the poor and to his ideal of the renunciation of possessions. In addition, he had experienced enough academic arrogance to know that there was no direct relationship between learning and holiness. When scholars and educated priests joined the Lesser Brothers, they received neither deference nor (in the early days) special assignments.

This, too, set the Franciscans apart and often made them suspect. In the fight against heresy and the movement for clerical reform, the Church needed every educated man—particularly those who had theological learning—whom it could marshal. This helps to explain Rome's eager approval of the Dominicans, whose main task was to refute heresy.

Francis, however, had a very different program, and he was managing to accomplish it without requiring his recruits to be educated. As long as the fraternity remained a band of praying and working men united by a common goal, they did not need to supplement their learning. When the Lesser Brothers became a formal Order with a worldwide mission, however, that changed immediately.

§

Perhaps fearing the contagion his gray spirits might spread among the brothers in early 1213, Francis withdrew for all six weeks of Lent to Isola Maggiore, an island in Lake Trasimeno. "He sought out a place of rest and secret solitude . . . where he could join to God not only his spirit but every member of his body," wrote Celano. "He made himself insensible to all outside noise, gathering his external senses into his inner being and, checking the impetus of his spirit, he emptied himself for God alone." During this time, Francis subsisted on a single loaf of bread and some rainwater.

Francis came to Easter in far better spirits, and as springtime continued, he seemed to find enormous joy in his work and in the signs of new life, both in nature and his community. He and Leo preached in the Spoleto valley and on May 8 were on their way through Romagna when they heard of festivities at Montefeltro, a castle atop a sheer cliff. (Today it is known as San Leo and stands a short distance from the republic of San Marino.)

A great celebration was in progress following the investiture of a new young knight by the lord of the castle, Orlando di Chiusi, a nobleman from one of the wealthiest feudal landowning families of central Italy. A vast crowd had gathered at Orlando's invitation, drawn by the promise of a feast. Francis and Leo made a detour to the castle—not to attend the banquet, but for the opportunity to preach to a large throng that would be in a happy and receptive mood.

On arriving at the celebration, Francis climbed onto a wall, clapped his hands for attention, offered good wishes to the new knight and then, in the spirit of the minstrel and troubadour he had once been, happily entertained the guests by singing lyrics familiar to everyone in the crowd. His song told of a knight who travels far and wide with the image of his mistress in his heart. The knight's passion feeds on the pain of separation and leaves him pining with a love that will soon be fulfilled, and the song ends with a famous couplet:

> *Tanto è il bene ch'io aspetto,*
> *ch'ogni pena m'è diletto.*

This may be rendered:

> So great the good that I foresee,
> that every tribulation is joy to me.

Francis followed this performance with a warm and appealing sermon about the need for cheerfully enduring the discomforts and inconveniences of this life for the sake of life eternal; there was something of an antecedent in the gospel according to John. Speaking of their mission to proclaim the reign of God, Jesus told his disciples, "You will have pain, but your pain will turn into joy."

"He did this so devoutly," Leo recalled of that afternoon's sermon, "that the people stood there in rapt attention, as if listening to an angel."

And then an extraordinary thing occurred.

Count Orlando had heard of Francis, but this was the first time he had seen him. Touched by his message, he went up to Francis and said simply, "I would like to speak to you about the salvation of my soul."

But Francis, for whom courtesy to others was itself a cardinal virtue—even if it concerned only that of a host to his guests at a social gathering—gently replied, "My lord, go back and honor your friends, and after your meal we will talk as much as you wish." In those coarse, rude times, the novelty of Francis's politeness and consideration for others made him enormously attractive.

And so, after the feast, Orlando returned to Francis and announced, "Brother Francis, I have an abandoned and solitary mountain in Tuscany, called Mount La Verna. It is very suitable for those who wish to live a solitary life. If this mountain pleases you and your companions, I would very willingly give it to you for the salvation of my soul."

Because he had long wanted to have a place for prolonged retreats for himself and his fraternity, Francis said he would send two of his companions to inspect it. "You will show them this mountain, and if it seems suitable, I most willingly accept your charitable offer." The brothers made the trek, reported to Francis that the site was ideal, and a verbal agreement was sealed. From that time, the mountain became an important site in Francis's life, and it remains a major point of pilgrimage to this day.*

§

The gift of the mountain retreat was very welcome to Francis, for after his Eastertime recovery he fell back into something of a spiritual dilemma. Given his failure to accompany the poor people's Crusade to the Holy Land, he felt uncertain whether he should continue traveling and preaching, or whether in fact he would serve better by living apart from the world as a hermit, in contemplation—which in any case, as he told his closest companions, remained his greatest joy.

But he would not trust only his own instincts on so crucial a matter as a change of vocation; hence Francis sent Masseo to ask the advice of two trusted friends who had themselves withdrawn from the world—the priest Sylvester, who had been living alone in a hermit's cell at the *carceri* above Assisi; and Clare, at San Damiano. The reply from both friends was unequivocal, as Masseo reported to Francis: "You should go on preaching, because God did not call you only for yourself, but also for the good of others."

Francis's response to Masseo was instantaneous and enthusiastic: "Then in the name of God, let's go!" Soon afterward he planned a trip to Spain, choosing as his companion Bernard Quintavalle.

*Francis did not wish to receive a formal document of bequest, for he did not want the fraternity to own property; after his death, however, Orlando's sons drew up the required legal papers transferring Mount La Verna to the Order of Lesser Brothers. See the endnote on this matter.

After their defeat at Las Navas de Tolosa, the Muslims had retreated to North Africa. Still eager to convert them, Francis decided to go on foot to southern Spain, probably to avoid a repetition of his earlier debacle at sea, and from there to make the short boat crossing to Morocco.

He knew that this journey would almost certainly culminate in the martyrdom for which he so greatly longed. According to Islamic law, any preaching of Christianity in a Muslim country, any implicit attack on the Koran, any baptism of a Mohammedan was punishable by death; any Saracen who allowed himself to be baptized would likewise be executed.

He and Bernard left Assisi and took the traditional pilgrim's route: via Florence to Pisa, then north to Lyons, southwest across the Pyrenees and west toward that venerable place of devotion Santiago de Compostela. On horseback, pilgrims could travel from Assisi to Compostela in three weeks; walking, the journey would have required almost two months. "But Francis was so carried away with desire," according to Celano, "that he would sometimes leave behind his companion and hurry ahead, intoxicated in spirit, in order to carry out his purpose."

Francis made the long journey to Spain barefoot: he had not yet allowed himself even the luxury of sandals. Without money for lodging, he had to depend on the charity of others or find shelter in nature, and although the trip was made from June through September, frequent summer storms and squalls battered the route, especially in southern France and northern Spain. It is perhaps not surprising, then, that he was stricken with chronic illnesses that severely compromised his already delicate constitution.

In Compostela, he fell ill with a recurrence of malaria, by the pain and incapacity of what appears to have been a stomach ulcer, and perhaps also by a minor stroke. Francis himself left an accurate description of his malarial fever, which may well have flared up after he passed through the swampy waters that summer: "My head was spinning, my knees were giving way, and the whole framework of my body was shaking."

The ulcer, with its symptoms of severe gastric pain, dyspepsia and nausea, and shortness of breath, was probably the result of excessive fasting, poor hygiene, tainted water, inadequate nutrition and the abundance of viral infections. The possibility that he had a slight, transient stroke is suggested by the fact that for three days in Compostela, he lost the ability to speak or to understand what was said to him, although this may also have been caused by the delirium often associated with malarial fever. In any case, he seems to have made a gradual but complete recovery from his aphasia.

Greatly weakened, Francis, who turned 31 that September, had to abandon his plan to go to Morocco. But by now he was perhaps accustomed to finding strength in disappointment, and so, while recuperating, he decided that his fraternity ought not to be restricted to Italy. Spain was fertile soil for the brothers' preaching missions, their work for peace and reconciliation and their efforts on behalf of the poor.

Over the next three years, he supervised the dispatch of companions to villages and towns all over the Iberian Peninsula, where soon there were preaching centers and places to train recruits and host assemblies of friars; these were established mostly in abandoned hermitages, hospitals, an unused attic or cellar or an empty hut.

Eventually, he grew well enough for Bernard to take him back to Assisi. But the return journey completely exhausted him, and for the next four years—from September 1213 to November 1217—Francis was forced to restrict all his activities. In fact, he endured a series of ever more debilitating maladies, and for much of the time he was confined to his straw bed at Saint Mary's. Despite the imprecations of his companions, however, he insisted on preaching at least twice a week, although often the congregations had to be brought to him at Saint Mary's. He also visited the sick, despite his own infirmities.

"If people sent him tonics," recorded Celano,

he would give them to the others who were sick—even though he had greater need of them. He had great sympathy for all who were ill, and when he could not alleviate their pain, he offered words of compassion. He would eat on fast days so the weak would not be ashamed of eating, and he was not embarrassed to go through the city's public places to find some meat for a sick brother.

Some of his companions remarked that from this time, Francis endured "infirmities of the stomach, spleen and liver, over a long period, until the day of his death." Others did not hesitate to sound a more critical note: "He inflicted his flesh with such fasting that, whether he was healthy or ill, this excessively austere man hardly ever or never wanted to indulge his body. . . . He had become debilitated because of the excessive fasting and suffering he endured, and he became exhausted by his efforts."

§

All these practices were part of the medieval ascetical regime of penance and self-denial. The goal was to deaden the senses, to delight as little as possible in any bodily pleasure and thus to consider with as little distraction as possible the things of eternity; in extreme cases, however, people simply passed more quickly to eternity itself. "Francis lacked only one thing," according to Giles, who retired for two years to a hermitage in 1214, "and that was a strong body. If he had been robust like me, surely the whole world could never have been able to keep pace with his flaming spirit."

Francis also minimized the harshness of these penances, and he urged his brothers to do the same, and likewise urged them not to become obsessed with their sins and faults. "Why are you sad and sorrowful over your offenses?" his friends recall his asking one gloomy friar who was obsessed with examining and reexamining his conscience. "It is a matter between you and God. Pray to Him, and try to be joyful always around me and the others, because it is not fitting that a servant of God appear before his brothers with a sad and glum face!" Such an attitude was, for Francis, a matter of both common sense and courtesy.

But these difficult and debilitating years also marked the sealing of Francis's profound devotion to Jesus crucified. He looked to the cross as more than just a model of patience and submission to God's will, just as he regarded his own suffering as more than a means of penance for sin. He saw that those who suffer participate even more deeply in the lot of the poor and the castaways of the world. Most of all, in his passion to imitate Jesus the Christ in every way, he knew he could neither avoid nor despise the pain that was his master's lot and, in some way, the portion of everyone in the world.

In his self-inflicted mortifications, there was perhaps some element of neurotic or masochistic behavior. But that is not to claim that Francis was predominantly an unbalanced man. Psychoneurotics are not usually serene in the face of the pain they themselves do not select or control. When it came to the patient and uncomplaining endurance of the wretched health that would afflict him from the age of 31 until his death, at 44, Francis was psychologically and spiritually an extraordinarily balanced man—precisely because he looked to a frame of reference outside himself and beyond his pain to deal with it.

As we have seen since his epiphany before the crucifix at San Damiano in 1206, Francis had been drawn more and more to a contemplation of the sufferings of Jesus. For the rest of his life, he compiled and reworked psalms, antiphons and prayers for an Office of the Passion; he went into retreats to meditate on the sufferings and death of Jesus; and everywhere he went, he prayed with his companions the prayer that was on his lips at the end of his life: "We adore you, Lord Jesus Christ, in all your churches throughout the whole world, and we bless you, because by your holy cross you have redeemed the world"—the formula he had drawn from the ceremonies of Good Friday and the feast of the Exaltation of the Cross.

Francis did not reject suffering as something undeserved or offensive, he went *through* the pain to a consideration of God's inscrutable and mysterious love. He did not try to intellectualize or theologize, to explain it away or to find a rational means of dealing with suffering. His model in this, as in all things, was Christ his Lord, who abandoned himself to the unimaginable mercy of God—and who was finally vindicated and taken up forever into new life.

In proclaiming the mercy of God—not a common topic in the harsh worldview of medieval piety—Francis was steadfast. Having experienced divine mercy and pity in his own conversion, he made them the connective threads of the entire fabric of his teaching, from the first day to the last. Thus in a real way, suffering became for Francis a form of uninterrupted prayer, linking him wordlessly and therefore more directly to dependence on God.

§

By 1215, the Lesser Brothers were not only established in northern and central Italy, but were also found in France and Spain, and soon would move on to Germany and England. People met them on country roads and in village squares as they preached and nursed before retiring to their little hermitages in rural areas or in surrounding hillsides. They lived among the people, who provided their sustenance as voluntary alms for their preaching and their manual labor.

That autumn, Pope Innocent III convened the Fourth Lateran Council, which called both for major reforms in the Church and for a Fifth Crusade to begin in June 1217, with the goal of recapturing the holy sites of Palestine from the hands of infidels and freeing thousands of Christians languishing in Muslim prisons. He also set down an absolute prohibition against the foundation of any new religious Orders. Whether Francis was well enough to attend these sessions is not clear from the earliest sources.

Meantime, Archbishop Fulkes of Toulouse had sanctioned the work of the Order of Preachers (Dominicans), who were led by their charismatic firebrand and founder, the Spaniard Dominic Guzman, whose fraternity fiercely countered the Albigensian heresy. Fulkes brought Dominic to Rome for the pope's formal approval of his Order, but in light of the Council decree, the pope insisted that Dominic use the Rule of Saint Augustine as his model, and the Dominican Constitutions were eventually approved by Innocent's successor in 1217.

Although Innocent could not renege on the verbal approval he had already given Francis in 1209, Francis, too, had to draw up a formal Rule in order to be granted official status. That he would do, but reluctantly and sporadically; it was not finally approved by his fraternity or by Rome until 1223, by which time the Order of Lesser Brothers had become an organization very different from Francis's original intention.

§

By early 1216, Francis was so gravely ill with malaria that he had to accept the invitation of Guido to recuperate at the bishop's residence in Assisi. Francis's wandering and penitential life and the uncomfortable circumstances at Saint Mary's were simply inadequate for his recovery, and the brothers grew deeply concerned for his life. His emaciated body was bloated with fluid, fever raged every few days, his color was florid rather than ashen, he had upper right quadrant pain, and he could sustain no food—sure signs of quartan malaria or bilious remittent fever, probably complicated by enlargement of both his spleen and his liver. (These are also the symptoms of cholecystic jaundice, or liver and gallbladder disease, but it is unlikely that he would have been able to survive with such acute complications.)

Francis had also refused to take any more than the smallest amount of medication or painkiller (which were, granted, primitive and not very effective concoctions of plants and herbs). He feared indulging too much care on his body by defiling it with medicine, and recourse to treatments was, he believed, a short-circuiting of his desire never to place obstacles in the path of God's will. Choosing to take medicine would also have been an offense against poverty: ground-up precious stones were necessary ingredients in many medieval recipes that have come down to us, especially one for malarial fever—"To reduce the chills before the onset [of malaria], give the antidote with warm water mixed with one dram of powdered lapis lazuli." Only the wealthy could afford such remedies.

But even at the bishop's house, Francis would not rest. He insisted on welcoming his brothers for counsel and common prayer, and at the feast of Pentecost, in late spring, he convoked a Chapter, or general meeting, of all the friars, to discuss the Rule they knew they would have to formulate to satisfy Rome. They also had to make important decisions about which friars would be sent where: their numbers had increased to over 3,000, and Francis was ready to dispatch them all throughout Europe as missionaries.

For the first time, some disagreement arose among the friars about precisely how they were to lead a life of complete poverty. Francis, who could not stand for long periods, spoke to them from a chair. We do not have any transcripts of his words, but Celano's summaries and what has survived in the first draft of the Rule give us a clear idea of his intentions.

For Francis, the matter was simple: everything had to be seen in its proper place, and mere material realities were to be valued only insofar as they helped people to fulfill themselves before God. Possessions, he believed, fail in this function when they become so abundant that they constitute wealth, which can only distract from the life of the spirit. But he also recognized that degrading poverty could be equally destructive—hence his activities on behalf of the poor.

§

Among contemporary observers of the Franciscan missions that summer was the noted French historian, reformer and Church leader James of Vitry, a frequent visitor to Rome and traveler throughout Christendom; his writings and letters are invaluable guides through the thickets of 13th-century politics.

Vitry was blunt in his assessment of ecclesiastics, and after spending time among the cardinals and bishops who glided around the pope at the Lateran Palace, he wrote that he had "encountered a great deal that was repugnant to me. They were so occupied with worldly affairs, with rulers and kingdoms, with lawsuits and litigation, that they hardly let anyone speak of spiritual things."

But during his journeys in Italy, Vitry was deeply impressed by the Franciscans. In a letter he wrote to friends in Liège that summer, he called the fraternity his

> one source of consolation. They were called "Lesser Brothers" and "Lesser Sisters." They live according to the form of the primitive Church, about whom it was written, "the community of believers was of one heart and one mind" [Acts of the Apostles 4, 32]. During the day, they go into the cities and villages giving themselves over to the active life; at night, however, they return to their hermitage or solitary places to devote themselves to contemplation. The women [that is, Clare at San Damiano, and the nuns in other convents like hers] dwell together near the cities in various hospices, accepting nothing, but living by the work of their hands.

This literate and dedicated churchman concluded his letter with a signal observation about the Franciscans: God was accomplishing great good "through such simple and poor men, in order to put to shame our prelates, who are like dumb dogs not able to bark." Not the least reason for the Franciscans' success, he believed, was their ability to preach by example; when they spoke publicly, they were joyful and positive, never gloomy or pessimistic. In this aspect, they were unique among medieval preachers.

As it happened, Innocent had recently summoned Vitry to be consecrated as a bishop for the Holy Land. They were to meet that summer, during the pope's travels through northern Italy, where he was mustering support for the Crusades and negotiating the settlement of an intracity feud. In glowing health and with his usual irrepressible energy, the 56-year-old Innocent raced from town to town and finally arrived in Perugia. But on the night of July 15, he suddenly fell ill with a high fever, and by the next morning he was dead.

Before the funeral, according to Vitry, "some thieves stripped his body of all the precious vestments with which he was to be interred, and left it there in the church virtually naked and already decaying. I went into the church and saw how fleeting and empty is the deceitful glory of this world." The news of the pope's death and the pillaging of his corpse was a shock to everyone, and Francis summoned his brothers to a day of prayer. Then, after hasty political maneuvering on July 18, two Perugian cardinals appointed Cencio Savelli, an elderly man in poor health, to be the next pope; he took the name Honorius III and surprised everyone by surviving 11 years, passing away a year after the death of Francis.

§

At the Pentecost Chapter, held at Saint Mary's in May 1217, it was decided that friars would be sent out to Italy, Spain, Portugal, France, Germany, Hungary, Greece, Tunis, the Holy Land and England.

Generally, these missions failed—not the least reason being that the men went to their postings without any knowledge of the local language. A group of about 60 friars proceeded to Germany, for example, and when people asked if they needed food or a night's lodging, they cheerfully replied, *"Ja, ja!"*—which in their simplicity the men had come to believe was a kind of magical incantation. But when someone asked if they were heretics, and they cheerfully replied, *"Ja, ja!"* they were stripped and beaten, thrown into prison and almost starved. Released on condition they leave the country, the friars hastened back to Assisi, where they were asked if their mission had been successful. They may well have replied, *"Nein, nein!"*

The wily Elias, meanwhile, was appointed minister of the Holy Land, and a young man named Benedict went to Greece. Giles, who had returned from several years of retreat at his hermitage, left for Tunisia with a very frail teenage brother named Electus. This mission, too, was an immediate failure. Christians there, forced to remain anonymous because of Muslim restrictions and hostility, feared reprisals if the friars preached openly, and so Giles and his companion were forthwith put on a return vessel. But Electus, in a moment of enthusiasm, leaped back onto shore, crying that he would gladly die for his faith—which he soon did.

The Pentecost Chapter also decided that the fraternity would be divided into 11 provinces, with custodies within each of them. A general minister—not a superior, but one who was obliged to serve, or minister, to others—would be responsible for the entire organization worldwide; provincial ministers would supervise friars in specific countries or provinces; custodians would look after certain vital centers; and guardians would be responsible for local residences, hermitages and friaries. The words "superior" and "prior," typical designations in religious Orders, were never to be used among the Franciscans; their founder insisted that service, not control, was at the heart of these functions. He continually reminded his companions, "Let them remember what the Lord says: 'I have not come to be served, but to serve.' "

Francis remained as liberal as ever in accepting candidates: anyone willing to give up personal possessions was welcome, regardless of social status, background or level of education. He did not, as yet, even require aspirants to undergo a period of preparation and training for either the religious or secular aspects of their common life. Boncampagno had criticized the admission of "mere youths and boys" into the fraternity, and even the more sympathetic James of Vitry commented on this issue:

This Order is rapidly expanding throughout the world, but this is quite risky. They refuse no one entry into their Order (except those bound in marriage or to another Order). They send out, two by two throughout the world, not only formed religious, but also immature young men who should first be tested and subjected to discipline for a time. As it is, the Order is not a system for the weak and imperfect.

In time, Francis noted these problems as well, and in response dictated a series of general guidelines to establish a kind of probation in the society—a period of time called a novitiate. The ministers were given responsibility for looking after the welfare of the novices entrusted to their care and were urged to "spiritually help one who has sinned as best they can. . . . Let none of the brothers have power or control in this instance, and let no brother do or say anything evil to another."

The entire enterprise was to be characterized by mutual respect, unity in prayer and support by honest hard work. Francis was unwilling to provide any additional legislation beyond this, and when he was forced to do so a few years later, he resisted vehemently. He had an unregenerate faith in the goodwill of others and (like Jesus) refused to assume the role of a lawgiver, much less a martinet. It was precisely that spirit that enlivened the four short paragraphs that comprise the *Rule for Hermitages* he also composed in 1217: friars who choose to live an enclosed life (for a time or permanently) are bound to prayer, silence and contemplation, but they ought to alternate acting as custodians so that no one is ever tempted to act like a superior. Although he was very much aware of his position as the Order's spiritual guide, he was also quick to heed counsel, from either the youngest friars or the highest prelates.

§

In the summer of 1217, despite the pleading of his brothers, Francis insisted on walking to Florence (with Masseo as companion) to visit Cardinal Ugolino dei Conti di Segni, Innocent III's nephew, who was the bishop of Ostia and papal legate for Lombardy and Tuscany. Ugolino had considerable diplomatic skills, and—now under Honorius as before under Innocent—he worked to effect religious reform policies. At 62, Ugolino was a striking presence but not an egocentric cleric. He had heard of Francis's reputation for holiness and loyalty to the Church, and on meeting him that summer, was much impressed.

Francis told Ugolino that he wished to go on a preaching mission to his beloved France; he could not ask his companions to undertake arduous tasks in distant places and then exempt himself from those same duties. But the cardinal, perhaps seeing the wretched state of Francis's health (especially after his trek from Assisi in the summer heat), "advised him not to complete the journey he had begun, but rather to care for and protect those whom the Lord God had entrusted to him" back in Umbria.

Ugolino also believed that the structure of the fraternity was simply too weak to survive the absence of its spiritual leader at headquarters. He confided his fears remarkably frankly to Francis, which says something of the estimation in which he held him: "Brother, I do not want you to go beyond the mountains [of Italy], because there are many prelates in the Roman Curia who would willingly block the [fraternity's] interests. The other cardinals and I, who love your [fraternity], can protect and help it more willingly if you stay within the confines of this region."

Francis responded with equally remarkable candor: "Do you think that God cares only for Italy?" If Ugolino replied, his words have not been documented.

Whatever his reservations, Francis obeyed and, having decided that the minstrel Pacificus would be the most suitable candidate for France, sent "the king of the verses" on the mission he had hoped to perform himself.

Soon Ugolino became a constant presence in Francis's life as the cardinal protector of the friars—a guiding role created by the Roman machinery to accommodate religious groups within Church structures. But a question emerges at this point: what precisely was the nature of the relationship between the cardinal and the friar? Did Francis select Ugolino as protector and mediator with Rome because of the cardinal's support of the fraternity's ideals? Or did Rome impose the cardinal on Francis as a condition for the formal approval and acceptance of the fraternity into the institutional Church?

Up to now, we must remember, the official status of the friars was still unsettled. Innocent had given verbal consent to their way of life, but final approval awaited the drafting of a rule and the friars' formal pronunciation of Church-approved vows.

When all the early documents are studied and compared, several facts emerge quite clearly.

First, Ugolino seems to have had no particular agenda for the fraternity; he was always open to the suggestions of the friars themselves. Second, he sincerely admired Francis (whom he, as Pope Gregory IX, later canonized). Third, Ugolino was a cardinal and hence conscious of his obligation to ensure the smooth functioning of the ecclesiastical system.

But this was not simply the triumph of the bureaucratic mentality; it was precisely because he sincerely supported the goals of the Lesser Brothers that Ugolino tried to prevent Francis's lack of organizational skills and his refusal to impose his will on a group from leading him astray and effectively diminishing the potential strength of the fraternity.

If that brotherhood was to survive, then realistically it could do so only with the blessing of Rome. Francis was sufficiently savvy to realize that he had to accept Ugolino's guidance and mediation with the pope and his Curia, even though that meant a revision of his original plans—which were for the fraternity to remain essentially a lay movement without the bonds of institutional and clerical structures.

But there is a fourth point that becomes clear. Although Francis and Ugolino had to negotiate the waters of institutional bureaucracy, in the course of doing so they established a deep and permanent friendship based on mutual respect.

Thus, while it would be tempting to see the influence of Rome as nothing but a Machiavellian exercise in control, such an interpretation would be historically imprecise. Despite its many grave missteps, its sometimes blind imitation of the structures of worldly power and its frequently sad miscalculations about the way of authentic Christianity, the Church was also paradoxically but fiercely dedicated to a reform of spiritual life.

Ugolino and Francis represent two approaches to reality that are by their very nature in tension: the prophetic witness of the charismatic individual and the longer arm of the Church's tradition, which is able to foster and disseminate what is good by means of social structures not available to an individual. It is also important to keep in mind that Francis himself was a product of the Church: it was precisely the 1,000-year-old tradition of prayer, of proclaiming the Scriptures, of worshiping God—and the documentation of this tradition in books and manuscripts—that had fed his soul and had led him onto the path of sainthood. In other words, at every stage in its history, it is the Church itself that educates the very critics who will reform it. Those who are the Church's progressives, reformers, revolutionaries and saints can come from nowhere else but from within its ranks.

On his way back to Assisi, an incident took place that revealed both Francis's essential integrity and his political canniness. At Imola, a city in Romagna, Francis presented himself to the bishop, and for courtesy's sake, and in obedience to an ordinance of the recent Lateran Council, he asked for permission to preach in the local church. The bishop replied: "I preach to my people, and that is enough."

Francis bowed and departed. But an hour later he returned.

"What do you want now?" asked the bishop.

"My lord," replied Francis, "if a father throws his son out by one door, he should come back in by another!"

The next morning, with the bishop's blessing, Francis took his place in the prelate's pulpit.

§

During his travels, Francis noticed one aspect of clerical laxity that he could no longer tolerate, and he addressed the issue in a very brief document (*Exhortations to the Clergy*) composed sometime early in 1218. The Eucharistic bread and wine, he complained, were conveyed in "very dirty chalices and altar-linens . . . and kept in the open in many dirty places. . . . Let [the Eucharistic elements] be moved from there, placed in a precious place and locked up."

Several times during the remainder of 1218, Francis prepared to resume his travels around northern Italy, but he was repeatedly afflicted with incapacitating gastric pains and had to cancel his plans. During this time, news spread that the Muslim leader al-Malik al-Kamil, Saladin's nephew, had succeeded his father as *miramolin*, or sultan, of Egypt, Palestine and Syria.* Fiery preachers all over Europe stoked renewed enthusiasm for the Fifth Crusade, whose specific goal was to capture and command key Egyptian sites like the port of Damietta, thus severing Muslim supply lines from their strategic positions in Syria and preventing any return of the infidel from North Africa to Spain. Frederick II promised

*The name is variously transliterated as Malek-el-Kamil, al-Malek-el-Kamil and so forth. The text here follows the most recent linguistic usage. Henceforth, he will be identified simply as al-Kamil.

Pope Honorius that he and his imperial troops would join the Crusaders in Egypt; the emperor's long delay, however, would be a critical element in the campaign's failure.

As soon as he could rise from his pallet and sustain a little food, Francis announced to his companions that he would go to Egypt. Once again, he would risk martyrdom, this time in the cause of converting the new sultan. He was determined nothing would stop him—neither ill wind nor illness nor cardinal's command.

1219–1220

D URING MAY 1219, more than 3,000 friars gathered in the fields and forests near Saint Mary's for a general meeting. In groups of several dozens, they discussed many structural and managerial matters affecting the life of the growing fraternity: recruitment, prayer, the development of a formal Rule and the dispatch of missionary expeditions worldwide.

Pope Honorius III, despite age and infirmity, had energetically taken up his predecessor's call for the Fifth Crusade and had summoned clerics, monks, abbots and laymen to the task. To the vast assembly—most of whom had neither been trained by their spiritual leader nor even introduced to him—Francis announced his intention to respond to the pope's appeal by taking companions and heading for Egypt and the Holy Land. There were many loud objections to undertaking such a mission, which indicates how the increase in numbers had rendered the fraternity less homogeneous in its beliefs and freer in their criticism of what they considered Francis's unrealistic standards. Many of those present, for example, wanted the Lesser Brothers to be more like the great religious Orders: to engage in university studies and to learn foreign languages; to own churches; and to practice a less rigorous poverty, so that a broader range of work might be done in the world. In support of these arguments, the objectors pointed to the recent failure of various missions. The controversy would continue for several years and eventually split the fraternity into several divisions.

It is easy to understand the position of the new generation of friars, for the life Francis had established lacked any formal structure. A dozen men could maintain a simple community among themselves, but 3,000 (and perhaps 2,000 more who were not present at Saint Mary's that May) required organization if the Franciscan spirit was to be carried out in a viable fashion. But structure requires leaders, and management, perhaps inevitably, creates power struggles.

That Francis had become a much less venerable figure among his own followers was clear from an event that took place at that springtime gathering. While he was recuperating in Assisi (and perhaps, for a time, in a hut attached to San Damiano, where Clare and her companions could look after him), some friars had built a sturdy, large stone building near Saint Mary's; this would serve as a meeting hall and place for study. "He was annoyed," reported Celano tersely. "He complained, and not gently. Immediately, wanting to dismantle the building, he climbed up to the roof and started tearing out slates and tiles."

Saying that this building betokened a pretentious lack of poverty, Francis called for help in dismantling it. But some noblemen from the town were present, and they insisted that the building did not rightfully belong to the brothers—it was the property of the commune, which had supplied the material and owned the land. Faced with that argument, Francis had to stop at once. Among the loudest protestors that afternoon was none other than Angelo Bernardone, who then withdrew, never to reappear in his half brother's life.

But a more significant objection to his policies came a few days later. "We want you to persuade Brother Francis," some of the friars told Cardinal Ugolino, who was present at the meeting, "to follow the advice of wiser members and to adopt the Rule of Benedict or Augustine or Bernard."

Ugolino went at once to Francis with the request, and after their meeting, Francis addressed the group. The core of his discourse burned into the memories of several men that day, and his words have been substantially documented in an early source. Calling himself a new kind of jester or wandering minstrel for God, Francis said: "My brothers, God has called me by the way of simplicity and humility. Therefore, I do not want you to mention to me any Rule—whether of Saint Augustine, or of Saint Bernard, or of Saint Benedict—or any other form of life except the one that the Lord in His mercy has shown and given to me. And the Lord told me what He wanted: He wanted me to be a new kind of fool in this world.

God does not wish to lead us by any other way than this." And then his temper flared: "God will confound your knowledge and wisdom, and He will punish you, and you will return to [your former life] with your blame, like it or not."

The earliest source of this event coolly noted that "the cardinal was greatly shocked and said nothing, and all the brothers were very much shaken."

§

As it happened, this Pentecost Chapter did not adopt an existing canonical Rule, but clearly the winds of change were beginning to blow more strongly, and Francis may rightly have sensed that his leadership was drawing to a close. Most friars wanted a traditional, less arduous life; they and the Roman hierarchy were not comfortable with the classless and formless routine with which Francis had tried to practice his form of the lived Gospel.

Francis himself never wavered in his determined ambition to preserve the original simplicity of his fraternity. But in this effort, as in his desire to effect peace and reconciliation wherever he found disharmony, he would be resoundingly unsuccessful, and his collective failures in his fraternity and in the world would provoke the greatest spiritual disenchantment of his life.

But these apparent failures also forced him to rely ever more deeply and directly on his relationship with God, which was an attachment based on the absolute dependence that comes from spiritual poverty. "Who are you, my dearest God—and what am I, but Your useless servant?" was more and more insistently his prayer. It was an appeal characterized by complete abandonment to the ultimately mysterious Reality, which Francis perceived not as a philosopher's dilemma but as the Being behind all personality, the God Who infinitely and unconditionally loves humanity.

§

The world was in a confused, distracted and anarchic state that year of 1219, and it is no exaggeration to say that to some extent every member of what we now call Western society and the Middle East was somehow involved in and affected by preparations for the Fifth Crusade, to which Francis now turned. Now at last, as Celano wrote not long after the fact, "when bitter and long battles were being waged daily [in Egypt], Francis would not rest from carrying out fervently the holy impulse of his spirit." A man of his time, Francis could not (especially in the spring of 1219) escape sharing the stereotypical prejudices. Everyone who did not profess faith in Christ had to be converted, whether Jew or Muslim. But from the start, his approach was different: Francis wanted to convert by proclamation and example, not by force or threat.

Before he departed Umbria, however, Pope Honorius III sent him a letter of introduction on June 11 that would assure bishops and pastors that the Lesser Brothers belonged to an approved religious community (if not an Order). "We beseech and exhort all of you," Honorius wrote in the document known as *Cum dilecti* (its first two Latin words), "to receive the aforesaid brothers as true Catholic faithful."

§

On June 24 (the feast of his patron, John the Baptist) Francis took his companion Illuminatus, who had a rudimentary knowledge of Arabic, and boarded a ship sailing from Brindisi with reinforcements for the troops in Egypt. Their goal was the strategic port of Damietta, the focus of frequent naval raids, on the eastern arm of the Nile. It was a major commercial center and one of the wealthiest cities in Egypt.

John of Brienne had at first commanded the Crusade, but in late 1218, Rome replaced him with that formidable self-promoter the Spanish cardinal Pelagio Galvani. Imperious, vain, stubborn and inflexible, he refused to take into account the counsel of the most experienced commanders of the Crusades, and he virtually ignored John of Brienne, whom the pope asked to monitor the situation by frequent visits to Egypt from Acre. When John had led the Crusaders he had enjoyed some early victories, but the arrival of Pelagio as well as a brutal winter storm turned everything to the Saracen advantage.

Francis's journey took about six weeks, and his shipboard companions, numbering perhaps a thousand, included many brigands and murderers, hoping to earn clemency for their crimes by heeding the pope's call. Merchants jostled with monks for a few inches of sleeping space belowdecks; bishops and priests were shoulder to shoulder with mercenaries and the weary poor. Conditions were dreadful. Many died of hunger or dysentery en route or were killed when they were caught filching food or water.

The survivors disembarked in Egypt around the middle of August and pitched camp along the western bank of the Nile, joining almost 100,000 fighters who were already opposite Damietta and the Muslim fortifications; al-Kamil's camp was several miles to the south. The oppressive heat and humidity of midsummer on the Nile must have made the inconveniences of the journey seem pleasant in comparison. From the river rose the stench of rotting corpses, casualties of the yearlong siege. Everywhere were the signs of tropical diseases, made worse by the lack of pure water and sufficient food, by the general filth and decay, and by the ubiquity of insects and organisms to which the natives were immune but to which foreigners were most vulnerable.

The Muslim fortifications were formidable. Two high walls enclosed the city on the river side and three on the landward side. Chroniclers counted 22 gates, 110 towers, 42 castles and a navigable moat; iron chains were also strung across the Nile, to impede the passage of enemy vessels. The Saracens had successfully defended the fortress for a year, thanks to plentiful supplies from the East, and their archers and infantry had high morale. Things were not going as well for the Christian troops, who were doubtless depressed—as Francis was later impressed—by the fivefold Islamic call to prayer each day, when the muezzin cried out the *sâlat*. (The following year, Francis encouraged civil authorities in Italy to "foster honor to the Lord, that every evening an announcement may be made by a messenger or some other sign, that praise may be given by all people to the all-powerful Lord God.")

Still, Pelagio, with neither knowledge of strategy nor ability to organize and muster troops, took general command, rejecting all Muslim offers of a truce, often leading men into battle with his own banner and loud calls for victory. The Crusaders had eight projectile machines, and they hurled javelins and stones against the city walls and into the tower that controlled a major chain across the river, but these methods were ineffective against such massive defenses. Scaling ladders were even less so, and those brave men who climbed them were easily clubbed to death or doused with flaming oil.

Skirmishes alternated with weeks of tedium while discontented Crusaders waited for reinforcements, some dying of typhus on the squalid, sandy riverbanks. Almost a fifth of the army soon perished, and many of the men, disgusted and fearful, sailed back to Europe on the next supply ship. Among those who remained, tenacious class hatreds dominated, with knights arguing with infantrymen, and nobles disdaining the commoners.

As the siege was prolonged, al-Kamil again offered to negotiate a settlement—partly because he was an authentically devout man who wanted to avoid unnecessary bloodshed on both sides, and partly because he did not wish to risk diluting the strong Islamic presence in Egypt. His terms were generous: If hostilities ceased forthwith, he would turn over the relics of the true cross and the kingdom of Jerusalem, with the exception of areas commanding the desert roads to Egypt; he also offered a 30-year truce, by which time, he added, all other considerations could certainly be negotiated. In exchange, he asked the Crusaders to abandon Egypt.

John of Brienne wanted to accept the offer; with Jerusalem in Christian possession, the fundamental goal of the Crusades would be realized. But against John's counsel and the wishes of many warrior Crusaders and ordinary laymen, Pelagio flatly refused: the Crusaders, insisted the prelate, could win all those concessions and more by fighting on. Italian merchants, who did not want to give up their lucrative trade with Egypt, avidly supported this position.

§

A successful outcome for the Christians would have required a forceful and unified command, experienced military strategy, the continuous restocking of supplies and human reinforcements to replace those dispatched by disease or wounds. All these were lacking. Furthermore, the pope naïvely continued to presume that a common religious motive was sufficient to unite Crusaders of varying backgrounds and purpose. As one medieval historian persuasively concluded, Pelagio was immediately confronted with these [as well as] other distinctly materialistic questions. In order to maintain peace and unity and to further the authentic aims of the Crusade, he inevitably had to make military decisions. It was in such matters, requiring cool practical judgment, that his chief failure apparently lay, and in the final analysis, one may argue, this contributed to the disastrous ending of the Fifth Crusade.

Shortly after Francis arrived at the Christian camp, trying to lift morale by preaching and to ease suffering by nursing the sick and wounded, fresh atrocities occurred. A group of Saracen spies swam the Nile at night, carrying papers and homing pigeons, but a team of Christians on the lookout captured them when they reached the riverbank. They cut off the hapless Muslims' noses, lips and ears and then gouged out one of each man's eyes. Thus hideously mutilated, the victims were sent back to their own side. It was disheartening enough for Francis to find the Crusaders drunk, dissolute, greedy and availing themselves of the Sicilian harlots who wandered from tent to tent, but to see their worst murderous impulses freely indulged was revolting to the point of shock.

For revenge, the Muslims sent a swift galleon across the widest part of the river, catapulting the enemy camp with fire and tar; troops disembarked and raced onto the land, where they seized women and children and immediately impaled them on swords and pikes.

Francis at once sought some means of ending the carnage; never before had his message of peace been so necessary. Despite his familiarity with war in Perugia and campaigns elsewhere, nothing had prepared him for this degree of butchery. Within a week of his arrival, he learned that the Crusaders were planning a new assault on the Muslim walls, hastily constructing battering rams, towers and other siege mechanisms and also attempting tunneling operations to undermine the walls. This strategy was hopeless, as Francis rightly gauged.

Soon other friars arrived to join Francis and Illuminatus—Peter Catanio, Leonard, Barbaro and two former knights whose names have not come down to us. Francis gathered them at once, and his companions remembered his astonishing declaration: "This battle will not go well for the Christians, but if I say this, they will take me for a fool. If on the other hand I keep silent, my conscience will not leave me alone. What do you think I should do?"

One of the brothers spoke for all: "Do not consider how people will judge you. This would not be the first time people took you for a fool." (James of Vitry, who met Francis during the period in Egypt, described him as "a simple, uneducated person beloved by God and man.")

With that encouragement from his friends, Francis approached John of Brienne and many of the troops and garrison leaders; most of them agreed and wanted Pelagio to rescind the order to attack, but once again, the cardinal scarcely heeded them. The Crusaders, he said, were subjects not of the kingdom of Jerusalem, but of the Church of Rome. He was still obdurate when the Muslim legate returned with an additional cash offer of 30,000 bezants, a vast sum of money by any standard.

§

It began to seem to all reasonable men that Cardinal Pelagio may well have sought to go far beyond the Crusaders' original aims and attempt to conquer the entire Near East. Whatever his intentions, the attainable goal was supplanted as the result of his ambition. The liturgical calendar for August 29 commemorated the beheading of John the Baptist, and on that day, the Crusaders struck. At first, the Muslims pretended to take flight, but when the Christians began to look for freshwater, of which there had been none where their forces were camped, the Saracens raced to the attack. Over 6,000 Crusaders perished; Francis's forecast of defeat was tragically accurate.

Once again, al-Kamil offered to negotiate. He reinstated the previous terms and now also agreed to pay for the restoration of the walls of Jerusalem and all nearby fortifications. He also promised to send home all Christian hostages and to deliver 20 Muslim noblemen as hostages until all the reconstruction work could be completed. Pelagio's reiterated refusal to negotiate now seemed close to lunacy; he said he had been promised new Crusaders in September and that he was still awaiting the arrival of Frederick II.

Francis, more angry and disillusioned than ever with the conduct of Christians, charged into the presence of the cardinal and declared that if there was to be no negotiation, he wished to go to the sultan in person. He was convinced that this was no just war, and that introducing al-Kamil to Christian faith by nonviolent means was the only way to end the combat. "I wish only to show reverence to all," he explained, "and to convert everyone more by example than by word."

After an initial automatic denial, the cardinal relented and allowed Francis and Illuminatus to proceed on what Pelagio considered a suicide mission to the camp of Sultan al-Malik al-Kamil; Pelagio expected to receive their heads on poles or plates before nightfall. It was well known, after all, that Christians could practice their faith in Muslim lands, but if they tried actively to convert others from Islam, they were subject to capital punishment. Before the friars departed, Pelagio disavowed all responsibility for their welfare and with absolute gravity charged Francis not to compromise the name of Christian or the best interests of the Church.

§

Reports of Francis's sojourn to the Muslim sultan al-Malik al-Kamil are found not only in medieval French and Italian Crusade records and in Celano's account, but also in an Islamic chronicle. These documents tell how Francis and Illuminatus left the Christian camp in early September for the headquarters of al-Kamil. When the sultan's guards saw them approach, they took them either for messengers who had come to continue negotiations, or for holy men like their own Muslim *sufiyya* (Sufis), mystics who were also clothed in a rough garment tied with a rope and who also begged for their daily support. And so Francis and Illuminatus were hurried into the presence of the sultan.

The Muslim ruler of Egypt, Palestine and Syria was the same age as Francis, had ruled his empire's forces since 1218 and, also like Francis, was a man completely dedicated to the traditions of his faith and to its dissemination. Although he hated war and its violence, al-Kamil did not hesitate to engage in it as a last resort to achieve his religious-political goals. Trained by his uncle, the formidable Saladin, al-Kamil was proficient in the military arts; he much preferred, however, the disciplines of prayer. When, five times daily, he heard the call to adore Allah, he was the first to assume the humblest posture. In brief, Francis was now standing before a profoundly devout and pacific man who also believed in One God.

After Francis spoke through an interpreter—perhaps Illuminatus, perhaps an aide to the sultan—al-Kamil decided to summon his chief religious advisers. After listening to Francis's brief outline of Bible history and of faith in Christ, and his plea for peace in the name of God and His Son, Jesus, the counselors decreed that the visitors ought be decapitated on the spot for trying to convert them.

But the sultan was a man who appreciated true faith wherever he found it; he also admired Francis's character, his wholehearted commitment to his faith and his clear contempt for the luxuries of the world. "I am going to act against this advice," al-Kamil said to Francis when they were alone. "I will never condemn you to death—for that would indeed be an evil reward to bestow on you, who conscientiously risked death in order to save my life before God, as you believe."

So far as we know, the sojourn was unprecedented in the history of Muslim-Christian relations. For a week, Francis and Illuminatus were the sultan's guests. We have no details of the conversations and events of that period, but it is reasonable to infer from the record that each was respectful toward the other's religious traditions. Francis may have gone to the camp with the traditional desire to convert or to die trying, but as his writings over the next few years reveal, he departed with a far different attitude. We might even say that it was Francis's own conversion that progressed.

"He had no success," wrote James of Vitry *tout court*. "And when he saw that he was making no progress in converting these people and that he could not achieve his purpose, namely martyrdom, he went back," added Bonaventure. Their assessments are correct, and they state them tersely: Francis lost on every count—he failed to convert the sultan, he was not granted the martyrdom he so desired and he was unable to bring about a peaceful resolution to the bloodshed precisely because al-Kamil could not challenge the spiritual convictions that drove his men to battle. These were great disappointments that profoundly affected the rest of his life.

Finally, the sultan promised that he would provide Francis and Illuminatus safe conduct back to their camp—and even on to Jerusalem, where

Francis wished to venerate the Christian sites. He gave them food and wine for the return journey, but an additional offering of precious gifts Francis graciously refused, which only impressed al-Kamil all the more. After the departure of Francis and Illuminatus (and perhaps influenced by their visit), al-Kamil yet again extended his offering of a truce to Pelagio; again he received a negative reply.

Back in the Christian camp on the Nile, Francis found hordes of Christians just as needy of conversion as the Muslims—and just as unwilling to heed the call to a change of heart and commitment to peace. Francis's blessing and his prayer for the Lord's peace never went so unheeded as in that year of 1219, when his invocation and the invocation of the Arabic "salaam" fell on deaf ears among the rank and file.

He had attempted nothing less than the realization of peace amid the conflict with Islam—a goal supported by Pope Honorius III himself. Having accomplished nothing, and with every one of his plans and goals again come to naught, Francis departed for the Holy Land; at least there, he could follow literally in the footsteps of Jesus.

§

The Fifth Crusade continued on its disastrous course. After another siege, Damietta was taken on November 5 by the Crusaders, who found houses and streets filled with corpses half devoured by ravenous dogs while weeping children clung to their dead and dying parents, begging for food. Of 80,000 people in the city at the beginning of the siege, only 3,000 survived, and of these only 100 were not ill with fatal diseases. Many of the surviving children were kindly taken in by James of Vitry, and some of the adults were in fact treated with every consideration. Looters made off with the city's precious gems, silks, silver and gold ornaments. Cardinal Pelagio was triumphant.

But the victory was short-lived. When it was discovered that the treasure that had been amassed to pay for the Crusades had been filched by traitors, many Christian fighters left for home. The remaining troops spent all of 1220 awaiting the arrival of Emperor Frederick II, and that July, the armies headed toward Cairo, but because they were ignorant of Egyptian hydrography, they were forced to retreat by the Nile floods. They had 600 ships and 1,200 cavalry, 4,000 archers and 2,500 mercenaries, but the Egyptian forces, besides knowing the land and the habits of the Nile, had 40,000 troops. Crusaders seized what plunder they could, and by August 1221 their situation was precarious.

Once again, al-Kamil was merciful. Seeing that floods and famine could vanquish the Crusaders, he refused to engage in any further battle. (Unknown to Crusaders was the fact that the sultan's army was also weary and longed for peace, and that the larger Muslim world was in total disarray, fearful of the Mongol threat.) After he totally surrounded the Christian armies, they no longer had any alternative but to accept the truce. Al-Kamil graciously received Christian emissaries, showered upon them many fine gifts, food and other supplies and quickly negotiated a treaty. On August 30, 1221, an armistice was countersigned. A truce of eight years was proclaimed, and Christians agreed to abandon Damietta and all areas of Egypt conquered by them. There was to be a mutual exchange of prisoners and hostages, and the relics of the true cross were handed over to John of Brienne. So ended the Fifth Crusade, by any standard a failure for Christendom and for the world at large, and the last time a medieval pope launched a campaign to regain the Holy Land.

§

In the middle of November, Francis left for the Holy Land with Illuminatus, where he remained for about two months with Elias and with Cesare of Speyer, a noted preacher and gifted composer of sermons. We know little about his activities there—the sources are remarkably reticent, probably because Francis's whereabouts were difficult to trace—except for his likely visits to Bethlehem at Christmas and to Jerusalem, which lay ravaged and squalid. In both towns, Muslims allowed Christians to preach to their own people in small and quiet groups as long as they made no attempts to convert others.

During Francis's stay in the Holy Land, from December 1219 to perhaps early February 1220, he learned some tragic news: five brothers who had been sent to Morocco had been savagely martyred. That should have come as no surprise, for they had persistently and loudly provoked the Muslim leaders, who finally killed them.

Readiness to suffer for faith, in his view, no longer meant a reckless disregard for one's own life, much less a rush toward suicide. A preacher had to be plain and direct, to be sure; he should also be prudent, gentle and respectful—and the five friars in Morocco had shown none of these qualities. Francis had seen for himself that the Muslims were not the fierce monsters that they were invariably characterized as; he knew they had been deliberately provoked. The tragedy could have been avoided.

This sad report was soon followed by other disturbing developments, news of which was brought from Italy by a group of friars. Since the Pentecost Chapter of 1219, dissent among the Lesser Brothers had increased to the point that there were now distinct factions among them. One group wanted to retain the fraternity's original form, composed loosely and mostly of laymen, while the other wanted organization along the lines of a traditional religious Order, with many clergy, and stations in universities, dioceses and even the Roman Curia. Rome continued to urge the old fraternity to assume new conditions and forms substantially different from the former simplicity enjoined by Francis.

While it cannot be denied that structure had to be brought to the management of so vast a society if its stated goals were to be achieved, the threat to Franciscan simplicity was real, and Francis heard the news with increasing anxiety. Roman control, if and when the fraternity became an official Order, would not only subvert its fundamental poverty; it would also restrict the fraternity's freedom to go wherever it believed there was need. All sorts of major and minor superiors would have to be consulted, and all kinds of restrictions imposed to deal with so many members of an increasingly complex organization.

Francis's insistence on radical poverty, on simplicity of life and the fundamentally lay organization of his society were aspects of his thinking that were understood by neither the official Church nor by society at large. In fact, he caused considerable irritation and displeasure everywhere; his way of life contradicted much that was avidly supported by the Church and the culture.

But because he had no grandiose plans to revolutionize or even reform the Church, there was no evidence for heresy or insubordination that could be brought against him. He wished to change only the world's moral and spiritual perspective, primarily through the gentlest and most unobtrusive example, and through identification with all society's outcasts. As opposed to the fixed regulations and rhythms of the monastery, Francis had something both freer and more difficult in mind: the flexibility of the Gospel and the initiative of men of goodwill on the alert for the promptings of the Spirit rather than the letter of the law.

Relative to this Gospel flexibility, the friars who encountered Francis in the Holy Land were scandalized to find him dining with bishops and enjoying a hearty meal of meat, delicacies and fine wine. He was told that this sort of behavior was precisely what the rules of the new group wished to forbid forever, but Francis smiled, continued eating and reminded the brothers that Jesus had commanded the disciples on their missions to eat and drink what was set before them, without complaining and certainly without insult to their hosts.

In this case as always, his chivalric courtesy did not desert him, and he rightly saw no harm in suspending his lifelong habit of fasting to thank God for a fine meal—one he must greatly have enjoyed, for it was such an exception to his usual ascetical rigor. His life was increasingly defined by such spontaneity, and spontaneity threatens only those who believe every aspect of religion must be strictly legislated.

In preparing to return to Italy and deal with the conflicts of the Lesser Brothers, Francis had to face the fact he had no talent for administration. His fraternity had become a complex society, and he had neither the aptitude nor the emotional wherewithal to be its general. For example, he saw little need in his humble society of friars for formal academic learning— but he was not in principle opposed to it under suitable circumstances. Still, he wanted to avoid having monastic schools among the friars; he also discouraged others from the kind of mere intellectualism that was divorced from the spiritual life. The administrative ability to balance these issues in *ad hoc* situations was beyond him.

When the Portuguese canon Anthony of Lisbon joined the fraternity, for example, some of the brothers wanted him to teach theology at the university in Padua. Francis drafted a brief letter to Anthony, happily granting permission: "I am pleased that you teach sacred theology to the brothers—providing that you do not extinguish the spirit of prayer and devotion during study of this kind."

The salutation of this message reveals Francis's surprising and sophisticated sense of the real meaning of hierarchy: "Brother Francis sends greetings to Brother Anthony, my Bishop." The Latin word for bishop (*episcopus,* derived from the Greek *episkopos*) denotes an overseer or supervisor, and here Francis transfers the term to theologians, implying that when preachers or teachers receive permission to teach, they share the bishops' ministry. (Anthony did become a respected and influential Franciscan professor even during Francis's lifetime; he was canonized as Anthony of Padua in 1232.)

In his liberal acceptance of all classes of men, Francis attracted good and learned theologians and scholars, but a number of the newer candidates were also ambitious priests who wanted to become bishops and control dioceses, and eventually be awarded the red hat of a cardinal. This was completely contrary to his spirit, and it may well have made him want to start his work over again from the beginning; but of course it was too late for that. And even were it possible, it may not have been desirable. If the Franciscan spirit could somehow be kept alive, then (the new wave of friars argued) why could not some of their brothers be university professors, bishops—even pope?

Francis departed for home at the end of February or early in March 1220, aboard the first ship available, which was bound for Venice. With him were Illuminatus, Peter, Barbaro and Elias. Francis wanted all of them present at another General Chapter, at which the topic of discussion would be the future of the Lesser Brothers.

§

On the journey, which took many weeks due to strong winds, Francis became desperately ill. His malarial fever returned; he could neither eat nor drink from the pain in his upper right quadrant, which suggested a recurrence of his liver disease; and he suffered a frightening new malady when his vision became severely compromised. His eyes burned and teared, and sometimes he could not see at all; even when his vision cleared, shapes and forms were frequently blurry.

"From the time he was returning from overseas," according to two early sources, "he suffered from a very serious eye disease that caused severe pain. It started with the hardship and fatigue of travel and the extreme heat." A third source, Henry of Avranches, provided more details less than a decade after Francis's death. His vision was clouded as though by a veil, Henry wrote, and there was acute pain in the back of his eye. He at first endured almost constant tearing, and then the eyelids thickened with irritation and infection. Rubbing his eyes made things worse, and often there was generalized weakness and pain throughout his body.

Some recent scholars have misdiagnosed these symptoms as glaucoma, but in that case, Francis would have been violently ill and quickly lost his sight; and he certainly did not suffer from cataracts, for they would not have caused the other symptoms. The most likely diagnosis is that of a disease rampant in the dry, dusty climate of Egypt: trachomatous conjunctivitis, or more simply, trachoma.

Trachoma, which can be transmitted by hand-to-eye contact, by eye-seeking flies and even by sharing hand or face towels, is a highly contagious disease, caused by a microorganism closely related to bacteria. It depends for its transmission on poor hygiene, lack of freshwater and close contact with infected persons.

Its early symptoms include abundant teary secretions, swollen eyelids, progressive infection of both corneas and painful sensitivity to light; ultimately, impaired vision and even blindness result from corneal scarring. Even today it is rampant in poverty-stricken parts of North Africa, Central and South America and the Middle East, and it remains the most frequent cause of visual loss worldwide, producing about 146 million cases of blindness annually. Trachoma can be successfully treated with tetracycline or azithromycin, and a 10-minute surgical procedure can save the sight of those infected but not yet blind.

But Francis had spent a great deal of time in the Crusader camp, where proper hygiene was nonexistent and where innumerable diseases thrived along the fetid, humid Nile riverbanks. After nursing the sick there, he visited the Muslim court in Egypt. That Francis did not develop immediate symptoms of trachoma was not surprising: the disease has an incubation period of a month or even longer.

§

By the spring of 1220, after the many foiled aspirations and dashed hopes of his lifetime, Francis of Assisi had to come to terms with the most crushing disappointments of all—his inability to effect peace, to convert Crusaders or Muslims, and his failure to win the crown of martyrdom. What, indeed, was God asking of him?

With all its colorful sails unfurled, his ship approached the radiant light of Venice, torches lining the canals and guiding the way to safe harbor. Only with difficulty could Francis identify the faces of his old companions who welcomed him. They were a gray blur even in the brightness of a glorious evening in springtime.

THIRTEEN

1220–1222

I T IS IMPOSSIBLE to overstate the change that occurred in the life and spirit of Francis of Assisi in 1219. In one respect, in light of his failure to convert al-Malik al-Kamil, it was the most important year in the process of his own conversion; in another, it marked the onset of a deepening of his understanding of the true meaning of the cross in his life and of his own conversion.

It was precisely around this time that Francis gathered some verses from biblical psalms, ancient Jewish invocations for divine assistance in times of trial and trouble, words that were, in the Middle Ages, taken as apt references to the suffering of Jesus. These excerpts he shaped into an Office of the Passion, to be prayed privately as meditations on the meaning of Good Friday. Francis's only hope, as his eyesight failed, his general health worsened and the crisis in his fraternity grew, was to gaze at Jesus crucified.

And what sort of Jesus did Francis behold in these final years of his life, filled as they were with illness and a sense of futility, with suffering and disappointment? What kind of Jesus was a consolation for Francis as he saw many of his companions abandon him and give up his most cherished hopes for the simplicity of their lives? What Jesus could make sense to a man with such noble aspirations who had to face the fact that almost everything seemed unattainable?

He looked to the image of Jesus in the garden of Gethsemane, arrested and taken away on false charges of sedition and treason, while every one of his companions fled for safety and deserted him. He looked to Jesus outcast and alone.

§

As he returned from the Christian conflicts in Egypt to the friars' conflicts in Assisi, the conversion of Francis was continuing apace. The God he adored and to Whom he gave himself with such abandon was still revealing Himself as the God of all mankind, a God of astonishment Who overturned every expectation about what constituted His plan for Francis and for others.

Now the prayer Francis so often murmured became an act of total abandonment. "Who are You, my dearest God? And what am I, but Your useless servant?" In the face of his profound feelings of uselessness, failure and incompetence, he threw himself into the arms of God. It was not so far from the outcry of Jesus on the cross. Francis was sealing his alliance with and his fundamental trust in the God Who had not, after all, abandoned Jesus to death. This is as close to a definition of faith as anyone could seek.

§

Francis had been away nearly a year. Before he departed, he had left the fraternity in the stewardship of Matthew of Narni and Gregory of Naples. The former was a gentle soul who looked after the welfare of the friars at Saint Mary's; the latter strongly supported the broadening of the fraternity's work to include not only university studies but also the roles of bishop and cardinal—all of which Francis had staunchly opposed as dangerous to the ideal of poverty, and as an invitation to acquire individual power. Of these two temporary guardians, we know little else, except that Gregory (a good friend of Brother Elias, who liked to give orders) later became so cruelly authoritarian that he was released from the fraternity and placed in prison.

As the spring meeting of the friars began, Francis listened to the requests and complaints of ministers from every province in which the friars had a presence, and to the rank and file of brothers. At once, he knew that he had to confront four problem areas in the growth of the society.

The first was poverty. When the Lesser Brothers were few in number, they could live from day to day possessing nothing, dependent on their work and almsgiving to sustain them. Now that there were 5,000 friars and more joining every day, however, some degree of security had become necessary—even a minimal standard of living—so that everyone's needs could be met and the work of the fraternity properly carried out. These were perhaps reasonable expectations, but Francis saw dangers in legislating them. Some of the more liberal friars even said it should be acceptable for their communities to admit women, but men like Bernard, Giles and Peter agreed with Francis that this could lead only to chaos and charges of concubinage. Other friars were demanding more strict enclosure, a cloister away from the world, multiple fasts and a much tighter organization. Francis wanted to avoid both extremes.

There was also a call for the fraternity to own houses, but Francis profoundly distrusted even the notion of goods and property held in common—that is, as the possession of the community as a whole. If this attitude sounds rather like fanaticism, one must admit that there was always the element of the fanatic in Francis. Lovers are fanatics, after all, and they will often stop at nothing to defend the beloved. Harsher on himself than on anyone else, and quick to forgive all, he nonetheless continued to articulate a program of life that was perhaps becoming impossible for thousands to live out in increasingly diverse circumstances.

In fact, Francis had witnessed firsthand what had happened to monasteries and dioceses that owned property: wealth brought power; power diluted the presence of the Gospel. Bishop Guido, after all, owned half the real estate of Assisi, and he spent most of his time in litigation and little in the care of his people.

The second issue was one of authority. In Francis's absence, Gregory of Naples had visited many places where they were established, calling the brothers to account for what he considered to be instances of evil conduct, imposing appalling penances upon them, and forcing good men from the fraternity. Now that Francis had returned, many brothers begged him to compose at last a common Rule and asked that their advocate, Cardinal Ugolino, be allowed to serve formally as the fraternity's link with Rome. In fact, Ugolino had already accepted, after voice acclamation of the friars, the role of their representative before the papal Curia.

In May and September of that year 1220, for example, Pope Honorius III issued two documents—the first reminded French prelates that the Lesser Brothers were legitimate preachers; the second required a year's probation of all potential members of the fraternity, a correction to Francis's generous but indiscriminate welcome to everyone who wished to be part of his company.

Third, there was the matter of friar-priests, who were joining in significant numbers. They needed books, vestments and clerical paraphernalia, as well as assignment to a church or oratory. Francis always accepted priests, but he asked of them the same freedom from possessions that he requested from the humblest friars, and he granted them no special privileges.

This was not unrelated to the fourth problem, that of study. In addition to clerics, students and men of considerable intellectual sophistication were also joining the Lesser Brothers (among them, Thomas of Celano and Anthony of Padua). They were not happy about taking on a life that severed them from all academic pursuits, and they saw no reason why they ought to give up the studies necessary for first-rate preaching. This was not an argument that was easy to dismiss. Living as Francis did may have had a sublime and sublimely simple day-to-day style, but the lack of structure and legality made many friars unsure of their role in the Church. They understandably desired to follow the less risky, less free, but safer road traveled by traditional religious Orders.

How many members were in each faction in 1220 cannot be determined, but the progressives ultimately triumphed. Even before Francis's death, sufficient changes were made to the new Order of Friars Minor that it scarcely resembled the small band of wandering friars that had once lived in joyful simplicity at Rivo Torto. That way of life was quickly disintegrating.

Many in the opposition, it should be stressed, had no desire to do away with Francis's fundamental notion of good works that spring from faith; they simply regarded his system as too informal, too legally vague to enable them to maintain their identity in a rapidly transforming world. For them, Francis represented a level of idealism that was finally simply too impractical. On the other hand, many who disagreed with Francis simply ignored him, while others bluntly abused him.

Referring to the mistreatment to which Francis was often subjected from this time up to his death, a few faithful companions justly wrote: "We who were with him witnessed this often with our own eyes. Frequently, when some of the brothers did not provide for his increasing physical needs, or said something offensive to him, he would immediately go to prayer. On returning, he did not want to remember it by saying, 'Brother So-and-so did not provide for me,' or 'He said such-and-such to me.' " Instead, Francis sought no redress and, the better to serve as an example of charity and forgiveness, quietly endured what must have been among the most painful of his sufferings.

It was precisely at this time that Brother Giles returned from his hermitage to find Francis in a state of physical agony, confined to bed, shivering with malarial fever and all but ignored by a new group of brothers at Saint Mary's. One of the friars approached Giles and cheerfully recounted a dream of hell in which he saw not a single Franciscan. "You didn't go down deep enough," replied Giles, turning away and proceeding to the bedside of his beloved friend.

§

And so, with considerable anxiety, Francis began to draft the outlines of a formal way of life. But first, he made a surprising announcement: unwilling to impose his will on anyone and feeling overwhelmed by the burden of illness, he resigned from the leadership of the fraternity he had founded and guided for over a decade.

"From now on, I am dead to you," he said, and the words were sufficiently shocking that they have been recorded in several of the earliest Franciscan sources. He then pointed to one of his old friends and added: "But here you have Brother Peter Catanio: let us all, you and I, obey him."

With that, Francis led a prayer that was as heartfelt as it was instructive: "Lord, I give back to you the family which up until now you have entrusted to me. Now, sweetest Lord, because of my infirmities, which You know, I can no longer take care of them and I entrust them to the ministers." From that day, according to Thomas of Celano, Francis "remained subject [to the ministry and leadership of other friars] until his death, behaving more humbly than anyone else."

Later that year, Francis confided to a small group of friends that his resignation had been a relief, however concerned he was for the future direction of the friars:

> After I resigned the office among the brothers, because of my ill-
> nesses and for the greater good of my soul and those of all the broth-
> ers, from now on I am bound only to show good example. Even if my
> illnesses had not excused me, the greatest help I can render is to spend
> time in prayer to the Lord for the brothers every day. I have pledged
> myself to this, that if anyone perishes because of my bad example, I
> will be held to render an account to the Lord.

Francis resigned not because his own preferences had been dismissed, but
because he wished to forestall a permanent split in the fraternity or a violent power struggle among the friars. In all this, he depended on Ugolino to
be mediator and protector.

That same season, Francis dictated an exhortation to laymen and laywomen who could not join the fraternity because they were married or not
otherwise able to do so, but who wished to live in the spirit of the friars;
later, these individuals came to be known as members of the Third Order
of Saint Francis (the first being the friars, the second the enclosed nuns
eventually known as Poor Clares).

"I could not visit each one of you personally because of sickness and
the weakness of my body," he wrote, "so I decided to offer you in this letter the words of our Lord Jesus Christ." Citing, as usual, biblical texts, he
enjoined good works and deep prayer on all his new friends.

Francis may have resigned from his position as leader, but not from
daily vigilance. One day, the mother of two friars came to Saint Mary's
asking for help; she had no money, and owned nothing. "Have we anything
to give our mother?" Francis asked Peter, for he always called the mother
of any friar his own and that of every member of the community.

"We have nothing in the house we can give her," Peter replied, "and in
the church we have only one New Testament for reading the lessons." Such
books were, of course, very rare and expensive, and this particular volume
had been brought to the community years earlier.

Francis did not hesitate. "Give our mother the New Testament so she
can sell it for her needs," he advised Peter. "I firmly believe that the Lord
and *his* mother will be pleased more by giving it to her than if we read

from it." The woman went away with the book and sold it for enough money to live for two years.

His friends recalled a similar incident, when Francis gave an order that must have been somewhat shocking. To provide alms when they had none, he told Peter, "Strip the Virgin's altar and take its adornments when you can't care for the needy in any other way. Believe me, she would be happier to have her altar stripped and the Gospel of her son kept, than to have her altar decorated and her son despised."

§

For more than two years from the summer of 1220, Francis worked on several versions of a Rule, but the fraternity at large rejected each. In the midst of this crisis, his old friend Peter Catanio died suddenly, in March 1221, and was replaced not by his own choice but by Ugolino's. The leadership fell to none other than Elias Bombarone, who had become more of a somewhat condescending escort to Francis than the once-loyal longtime friend; Elias was, as one of the Order's great modern historians has unequivocally stated, "the least Franciscan of men." Indeed, his high-handed, deceitful and self-important attitude soon became evident after Francis had delivered one of his revisions; the document had been accidentally lost, Elias untruthfully reported to a gathering of friars, and so Francis would have to begin again.

By the end of 1221, Francis had completed a Rule he believed reflected the general meeting of friars; it has come down to us as the Earlier Rule. Like the lost brief regulations of 1209, this document is composed mostly of biblical citations and exhortations to the virtuous life. The friars who wanted a document with finely tuned rules, ordinances, schedules and statutes were dissatisfied; most of all, Francis had refused to provide what every religious Rule had had since the days of Saint Benedict: chastisements, punishments and the primacy of authority rather than love. Francis wanted the fraternity to survive and grow by encouragement and example, not by threats or sanctions. Fraternal love, in other words, should always take precedence over juridical considerations.

Basing his Rule on the simple statements of 1209 that he had set before Innocent III, Francis described the way of the Lesser Brothers as a life spent "in obedience, in chastity and without anything of their own," for the sake of "following the teachings and footprints of our Lord Jesus Christ." Anyone willing to give up possessions could come to the fraternity, be clothed in the simple garb that identified them and begin a period of probation. That was all he had to say on that matter, but in deference to many who asked him, Francis had, however, compromised on the minor issues of the schedule for common prayers and the days for fasting.

He continued to insist that ministers were servants of all, and that no one should be designated as superior or prior—another point that irritated many. Work and service were to be the hallmark of their life, in return for which the brothers "can receive whatever is necessary excepting money." He did allow them to have "whatever tools and instruments are suitable for their trades."

The sick were to be tended and sinners gently corrected; to prevent the Lesser Brothers from slipping into concubinage, Francis also stipulated that friars guilty of fornication be forthwith dismissed—and encouraged to do penance. He never pronounced damnation on such men, but neither would he sustain a scandalous breach of promise.

And then Francis inserted a section based on his recent experience in Egypt:

> Let any brother who desires go among the Saracens and other nonbelievers. They can live spiritually among the Saracens and nonbelievers in two ways. One way is not to engage in arguments or disputes, but to be subject to every human creature for God's sake, and to simply acknowledge that they [the friars] are Christians. The other way is to announce the Word of God. But wherever they may be, let all my brothers remember that they have given themselves and abandoned their bodies to the Lord Jesus Christ. For love of him, they must make themselves vulnerable to their enemies.

Most of the principles drafted by Francis were regarded by his rank and file as too strict or too vague or as lacking in sufficient specific regulations:

> I command all my brothers, both cleric and lay, that when they go through the world or dwell in places, they in no way keep any animals

either with them, in the care of another, or in any other way. Let it not be lawful for them to ride horseback unless they are compelled by sickness or a great need.

Why this injunction against pets and horses? Because at that time only wealthy people could afford to keep and feed animals.

The brothers who know how to read the Psalter [Book of Psalms] may have one. Those who do not know how to read, however, may not be permitted to have any book.

Francis still believed that studies were unnecessary for genuine piety, and he wanted to ensure that the fraternity did not collect books, however sacred the content.

Wherever the brothers may be, either in hermitages or other locations, let them be careful not to make any place their own or contend with anyone for it.

This regulation made it virtually impossible for the friars to form any kind of stable community life. But the gentler side of Francis appears in the next sentence: "Whoever comes to them, friend or foe, thief or robber, let him be received with kindness."

In the end, the Earlier Rule was never approved. When Elias and other members of the community read it, they saw that Francis had retained the severity of his primitive customs but had not supported them with adequate disciplinary codes. They noticed, too, the gaps and the lack of precision. And so the Rule was handed back to him with the charge to rewrite it yet again—first with the assistance of Caesar of Speyer, a learned German friar, later with the direct collaboration of Cardinal Ugolino.

"Who are these people?" Francis complained when another draft of the Rule was brought back to him for revisions. "They have already snatched my religious congregation out of my hands. What more do they want? Well, when I go to the General Chapter, then I will show them what my will is!" But as he soon learned, his will was more and more disregarded.

In desperation, Francis one day confronted Elias: "What do these brothers want?"

"They heard that you are making a new Rule," Elias replied coolly. "They fear that you are making it very harsh, and they say—and say publicly—that they refuse to be bound by it." And then Elias, abandoning all discretion and rudimentary courtesy, stared directly at Francis and said sarcastically, "Make a new Rule for yourself, not for them."

§

It was only a matter of time until the friars, as one modern Franciscan scholar has written, "acted just like the other non-monastic religious. . . . Posts of responsibility were originally regarded as being opportunities to serve, but now they were seen as personal attainments to be used to dominate others and exercise power over them." The trend developed swiftly. Beginning that year, the Lesser Brothers were more than ever a group with heterogeneous interests and aims; in a short time, there would be quite distinct factions of Franciscans—as there are to this day.

Can Francis be legitimately criticized as an intractable literalist who refused to see the necessity of his Order's adapting to the demands of growth? Was he overly protective of his own prerogative as spiritual leader of the brothers?

In certain respects, he was—as founders tend to be. But as he might argue, the religious world of his time was lax to the point of decadence. His months among the Crusaders had shown him that to call oneself Christian was no guarantee that one was faithful to the Gospel of Jesus. Everywhere, he saw signs of indifference, everywhere the grasping for power that subverted the Church and veiled the face of Christ from the world. What alternative did he see but to insist on the form of life that had worked so well for himself and a few brothers for so long? Francis was a prophetic personality—not a legal theoretician. He was a witness to the wholeness of the life of faith—not a manager. Were he indeed a literalist or fundamentalist, moored only to the past, his writings would certainly have included punishments and penances.

Nor was he a mere literalist in the matter of poverty, as some of his friars believed. Being poor was not a question of being without possessions merely for the sake of being without possessions. Rather, the condition was to be freely chosen as a sign of one's essential poverty of spirit—total reliance on God in every aspect of life. And for Francis, dependence on God was impossible unless one regarded oneself as a mere steward, and not an owner, of one's own being. For Francis, this was wonderfully liberating, not a deprivation: he was free, and he wished others to share his joy at the freedom from the obsession with money and things, with what is visible, tangible, profitable.

After his hopes for the retention of the original Rule were not realized, many began to regard him (at 39) as a churlish old man, the venerable but antiquated founder. As for his original companions, many agreed with him and remained loyal, while some took to hermitages, disgusted with what they saw as the corruption of the Lesser Brothers.

§

In 1223, a so-called Later Rule was finally deemed acceptable, and was submitted to Rome and approved by Pope Honorius III on November 29. The Franciscans were now a formal Order within the Church: the Order of Friars Minor. As finally drafted, the document is shorter, better organized, more precise than the Earlier Rule—and obviously written by someone other than Francis, for in place of the simple, often awkward, meandering and repetitious style of the 1221 document, the approved Rule was smooth, literate and polished. And everywhere may be detected the modulating, moderating hand of Cardinal Ugolino, who later acknowledged that he had collaborated on it. In the new formulation principles became laws, positive exhortations were altered to read like juridical regulations, and the frequent referral to Scripture and the life of Jesus was minimized. The 24 chapters filling as many pages in the earlier document were reduced to 12 chapters and seven pages.

To cite one major excision: Essential to Francis's practice and Earlier Rule was the directive "When the brothers go through the world, let them take nothing for the journey, neither knapsack, nor purse, nor bread, nor money, nor walking stick"—an injunction drawn directly from the gospel passages Francis and his companions took for their standard in 1208. This passage was removed from the Rule of 1223 by the opposition, and Francis expressed his profound dismay. "The brother ministers think they can deceive God and me," he remarked; for his part, he observed his original form of life to the end.

This is not to say, however, that the final Rule was a complete corruption of Francis's basic intention. Instead, it marked a new stage in the evolution of a Franciscan spirit that had begun with the founder's guidelines of 1209 and 1221—norms from which a spiritual sensibility could indeed be extracted and adapted to different circumstances. Thus his vision was not completely abandoned, although the newer forms of Franciscan life certainly diminished the original vitality of the founder's vision.

But it is perhaps a proven principle of history that radical movements arise, develop and then with time must be altered if their goals are to be constantly pursued and freshly realized. It is equally true that entrenched institutions—ecclesiastical or otherwise—are hesitant to endorse a revolutionary movement and are suspicious of its members. The principal figures in the hierarchy of the Church, struggling to retain its identity against the tide of Muslims and heretics, simultaneously admired and feared Francis of Assisi.

In the end, as institutions will do, the Church—with the eager collaboration of the new group of intellectuals within the fraternity—did away with everything that identified the friars with the poor. Pope Honorius III and Ugolino realized that the Order could be a powerful instrument for realizing reforms, and they constantly intervened to direct its growth to this end. Very soon, the itinerant lay movement once known simply as the Lesser Brothers became a clerical Order of men who abandoned their small huts and rural hermitages, settling in urban residences, where they performed priestly duties. The observance of poverty was more and more relaxed by the popes—Gregory IX most of all—and some of the friars became distinguished philosophers and theologians.

§

Even before the new Rule was approved, and while he and others were rephrasing it, Francis began to withdraw more and more from the daily workings of the fraternity; in fact, the last five years of his life were increasingly lonely. Of his closest companions from the early days, only

Giles and Leo were willing to attend him. Once the new Rule was approved, Francis responded to inquiries about this or that aspect of the friars' life by saying, "The brothers have their *Rule* now and have sworn to it. Since they already know what they should do and what to avoid, the only thing left for me to do is teach them by actions, because this is why I have been given to them during my life and after my death."

One instance of that occurred around this time, when Clare and her sisters finally prevailed on Francis to come to San Damiano and deliver a sermon. The women had been offered some property that Clare wanted to refuse but some of the nuns felt should be accepted, and she asked her old mentor to preach to them.

Frail, sickly and in spiritual darkness over the future of his fraternity, Francis entered the convent and took a seat amid the nuns. Clare, who had rarely seen him in recent years, was stricken by his appearance: his color was waxen, his limbs rail-thin, and his abdomen swollen. The malarial microbe had enlarged his liver and spleen, and now barely a day passed without severe abdominal pain and dyspepsia that made eating extremely difficult. His vision had become worse, and he required the help of a friar to find a place for him to sit.

Francis had brought a bowl of ashes, which he sprinkled on his head and in a circle around him. Then, without having uttered a word, he bowed to the nuns and departed. That was his sermon by gesture: a clear and immediately comprehensible reminder of mortality, drawn from the ceremony of Ash Wednesday ("Remember that you are dust and will return to dust"). The following day, not one sister voted to alter their life of radical poverty by accepting the gift of land.

Despite his sickly constitution, Francis did preach in public when he could—as he did on at least one important occasion in Bologna, during the summer of 1222. The city was riven by conflicts between various classes of citizens and between political factions, and so on August 15—with the main piazza crowded for the feast of the Assumption—he came to beg for peace. Thomas of Split, a Croatian law student at the university, recalled that Francis employed a type of rhetoric typical of assemblies in the Italian communes; he was certainly referring to the *ars concionandi:*

This unlettered man's sermon became the source of not a little amazement for the many educated people who were present. He did not, however, hold to the usual manner of preaching, but spoke like a political orator. The whole tenor of his words concerned itself with abolishing hostilities and renewing peace agreements. God gave his words such efficacy that many factions of the nobility were led to negotiate peace. There was such great popular reverence and devotion towards him that a mob of men and women crowded in upon him.

The consensus of the crowd, one of his companions said that evening, was that Francis was a living saint. Nonsense, he replied, adding (perhaps with a sly smile), "Don't praise me—after all, I'm still not sure that I won't have sons and daughters!"

He was not speaking from false humility. Dismayed at the new direction his fraternity was taking and afflicted with a deep sense of futility, Francis considered abandoning everything—and at such moments, nothing seemed more attractive than finding a woman, perhaps marrying, raising a family. Thomas of Celano described his condition bluntly: Francis endured temptations to "violent lust."

One winter day, however, he went out into the woods near Saint Mary's and piled seven figures in the snow. One of the friars asked him what he was doing; as Francis explained, he was preaching a sermon to himself. "Here," he muttered, "this large one is my wife, and those four over there are my two sons and two daughters—the other two are my servant and maid, who are needed to look after us. So hurry—get all of them some clothes, because they're freezing to death!" He smiled at his companion, who at once understood the meaning: for Francis, celibacy was perhaps not so bad an option after all.

FOURTEEN

1223–1224

FOR ALMOST TWO YEARS, from the time of the first conflicts within the fraternity and the worsening of his health and eyesight, Francis of Assisi was pitched into a profound spiritual crisis. Nothing seemed to bring him happiness or contentment; he was haunted by a dread of evil and a fear of death and consumed by a sense of failure. He was, according to Thomas of Celano, "filled with anguish."

The lives of saints are often composed by those who offer them and us a grave distortion when they fashion literary halos over their lives, effectively diminishing or even erasing the humanity God assumed and has given us, and which He uses to bring us to Himself. Sanitized stories of holy men and women too often describe them as essentially perfect, always pious, suffering without complaint, ever clear about their commitment and their destiny. In no way would such a description suit the life and character of Jesus of Nazareth, who fully shared our frail humanity.

How much more credible and moving are the truer accounts of those who endured daily struggles, to remain true to their beliefs—those who constantly had to battle temptations to discouragement and despair; those who suffered physically, emotionally and psychologically; those who felt betrayed and abandoned. Whatever one takes it to mean, saintliness is not a position one attains or state of life one achieves, the way one is called a doctor after receiving a medical certificate, or a parent after bringing forth a child. However we choose to discuss it, holiness is certainly (like conversion) a lifelong process, and genuine saints probably never think about it. Their energies are directed toward God, not toward a consideration of their own merits or excellence. Most of all, their lives proclaim to the world the existence of a reality that transcends it.

Francis of Assisi had to deal not only with his physical decline but also with the psychological torment of ugly temptations to self-loathing, and with the emotional torment of believing that he was ultimately a failure. In no aspect of his life could he find any grand or tangible accomplishment; even his brotherhood was being transformed daily before his eyes. Nowhere was there any visible sign of glory; his spirit was crushed under the burden of his own impotence in the face of life.

Sometimes he tried to cope by undertaking more rigorous acts of penance and self-denial (to the horror of friends like Leo and Giles), but these practices were of no help. Prayer, likewise, brought him little serenity, and his thoughts were often eerily morose, as when he said to his companions that an obedient religious man "is like a corpse you take and place wherever you want. He doesn't argue about why he's being moved; he doesn't care where he's placed; he doesn't pester you to transfer him." He was obviously speaking of himself when he concluded the analogy to a dead body: "The more he's honored, the more he considers himself unworthy."

At other times, he erupted with furious outbursts about the new ways of some of the friars. "A time is coming when this Order will have such a bad reputation because of bad example that it will be embarrassing to go out in public! Woe to those who congratulate themselves over the appearance of a religious way of living, those numbed by idleness, those who do not firmly resist temptations."

Occasionally, he did not refrain from indulging in the ancient Italian custom of the *malocchio* (the evil eye) against his detractors, even in the context of a public prayer he led one day: "By You, Most Holy Lord, and by me, Your little one, may they be cursed who break up and destroy by their bad example what You earlier built up." Later, he confided to his friends that "the bad ones are stabbing me with a sharp sword, twisting it in my bowels all day long." And so Francis withdrew more and more often to one hermitage or another. There, he wept for his impatience, prayed for forgiveness and hurried back to ask pardon for his foul moods. No one who knew of his increasing physical sufferings and the anguish of encroaching blindness could have justly reproached him.

Uncertain about his past and confused for his future, he feared that his own fraternity would expel him. "Suppose they all come and shout at me,

'You are not as eloquent as you should be, and you are too simple and illiterate. We are very ashamed to have such a contemptible man.' Then what? Suppose they throw me out?" His friends tried to reassure him. "Well," he replied, "maybe I should rejoice if they throw me out in shame—perhaps it would profit my soul."

From a gentle soul who was ordinarily a model of courtesy and patience, these were in fact exceptional moments. One day a friend asked Francis if he went so often into retreat because he no longer loved his religious brothers. "Oh," he replied with tears in his eyes, "I do love them—but I would love them still more and not be such a stranger among them if they would follow in my footsteps and stop citing examples of what the other Orders do!"

When questioned about the meaning of following in his footsteps, Francis referred to the last sections of the Rule he had drafted in 1220 and 1221—the document rejected and diluted by the fraternity. The sense of his words was clear:

- God is the absolute good and must have priority in our lives.
- Our lives themselves manifest the praise of God.
- We give thanks for the beauty of the world.
- We long to believe fully in the triune God, Who created, redeemed and will finally act in love to save us forever.
- We long to desire nothing but God, on Whom we depend and in Whom we hope.
- We want to love God because He has first loved us.
- Doing penance means constantly turning to God.
- We are poor because God alone is rich, and everything good belongs to Him. Therefore, we need not be concerned about ourselves, our honor, our earthly goals. We can abandon ourselves and leave ourselves open to Him Who gives us everything. He is not unfeeling or indifferent, but He constantly draws near to us, speaks to us, saves us.
- For all these reasons, we are also concerned for the well-being and salvation of all mankind.
- We prefer the celebration and the living out of faith rather than disputing about it—hence we go among unbelievers and preach to others mostly by example.

It would be difficult to find, then or now, a better outline for a good life.

§

In mid-December 1223, Francis traveled to a hermitage near Greccio, about 35 miles south of Assisi. While staying with friars, he sent a message to a devout nobleman of the town, asking his help in preparing a Christmas memorial.

According to the Lukan account in the New Testament, Jesus was born rudely, in a barn. Francis reasoned that there must have been animals present, and a verse from the Old Testament came to him: "The ox knows its owner, and the donkey knows the manger of its master." And so Francis asked that livestock be brought in and carefully tethered next to a local husband and wife with their infant, who stood in for the Holy Family. The gospels also told of a number of astrologers (magi) and shepherds, so Francis asked some of the friars to represent them, as well.

Candles and torches lit up the night sky that Christmas Eve, and the *tableau vivant*—a liturgical drama or medieval mystery play—made of Greccio a new Bethlehem. At midnight Mass, Francis preached on the humility of God's entrance into time, and on the poverty of Jesus. Countering the severity of most medieval preaching, Francis spoke of the mercy and tenderness of God, whose ingenuity chose neither violence nor cataclysm to approach man, but instead arrived in the form of a helpless infant. After the service, he helped the nobleman serve a feast to the guests, and he asked that a double portion of hay and oats be given to the animals, and grain scattered outside for the birds.

For Francis, the celebration was not a piece of sentimental theater but a symbolic representation of an everyday occurrence—Christ being reborn in the hearts of all who would have him. The evening's festival was therefore a kind of experiential mysticism of what the Eucharistic celebration offered—the presence of Emmanuel, God-with-us.

Building on the earlier Cistercian emphasis on the humanity of Jesus (particularly as expressed in the sermons of Bernard of Clairvaux and Aelred of Rievaulx), Francis brought to ordinary people the meaning and message of the drama of salvation history. His Christmas crib was thus the high point of the *ars concionandi*, and it offered a new kind of preaching by which he focused on the events of Christ's birth, sufferings and death. In

Francis's representation, the Jesus of Christian faith was not the fantasy or visiting angel of the Cathar heretics, who denied the humanity of Jesus. Nor was he the remote founder of a great religion. Nor did he enter a world that was fundamentally evil. God had embraced time and matter, and creation was good.

Francis was not the inventor of the Christmas crib; it was already part of the holiday customs at the cathedrals in Rome and elsewhere. But he took the event out of the past and linked it the present—not only by using ordinary people in ordinary places and in their own garb, but by linking the birth of Jesus to the present mystery of God's drawing near in the liturgy. The tradition of the Christmas crèche, or crib, would come to be one of the most widely recognized religious images in the world, being depicted countless times over the centuries on canvas, in plaster and in wood, printed or engraved, skillfully or crudely.

§

Francis remained at the Greccio hermitage for the first five months of 1224; in almost constant prayer, he saw his companions only for worship and an occasional meal. For part of the summer, he returned to Umbria, but the heat was oppressive. After he expressed a wish to make a 40-day retreat from mid-August to the end of September, Francis agreed to go to the coolness of Mount La Verna with four of his most faithful companions—Leo, Angelo, Rufino and Masseo. On the way, he and Leo had several intense conversations, for he saw how dismayed his friend was over the state of the Order, Leo's future in it and Francis's health.

Composed of vast rocks with caves and chasms in unusual formations, La Verna rises 4,200 feet in the middle Appenines. Its fresh, pure air, dark trees and remote location made it ideal for a summer retreat, and since the bequest of La Verna by Count Orlando in 1213, the friars had constructed a simple hermitage with small cell-like huts for privacy and a modest meeting room with refectory. Francis chose a rough stone chamber fashioned in one of the mountainside fissures. A log was placed over the chasm below so that Leo could cross to bring Francis food and see to his physical needs.

Francis had to cover his head with a hood, for both bright daylight and nighttime fire were intolerable to him. In addition, he was now covered with sores and skin ulcers. These may have been the result of years of self-inflicted penance, severe malnutrition and cell breakdown—and were very likely also the signs of leprosy, the result of having cared for lepers for years, most recently in Egypt.

We have very few details of this long solitude, and in his final *Testament,* dictated not long before his death, Francis told us nothing of his inner life and nothing of the events of 1224. We can gauge his state of mind only by assessing the attitude with which he bore acute suffering, and by appreciating how the final stages of his conversion were now beginning: in other words, how he was to be transformed in the last two years of his life. Engulfed in profound spiritual darkness, certain only of his failures, Francis "longed to know what in him and about him could be most acceptable [to God] . . . in what manner and with what desire could he cling more perfectly to the Lord"—so his companions told the compiler of a very early source.

This is perhaps the deepest form of prayer: a silent turning of the self toward God in acknowledgment of one's emptiness and impotence—the realization that one is helpless to effect one's own enlightenment or salvation. This is perhaps also the deepest form of poverty: the conviction that one is completely contingent, dependent in the core of one's being on God, Who acts only mercifully, only on our behalf.

Because prayer is never for oneself alone, because the entire enterprise of finding oneself before God inevitably turns us outward, Francis was not unaware of the spiritual distress felt by Leo, nor was he unwilling to respond to it. He could offer only the fruits of his prayer, and so he summoned his friend, asked him to bring parchment and dictated these verses for Leo's meditation:

You are the holy Lord God Who does wonderful things.
   You are strong, You are great. You are the most high. You are the almighty king. You are three and one, the Lord God of gods. You are the good—all good, the highest good, Lord God living and true.
   You are love, charity. You are wisdom, humility, patience, beauty, meekness, security, rest, gladness and joy—our hope and justice— You are all the riches we need.

You are beauty, the protector, our custodian and defender. You are strength, refreshment—and You are our hope, faith and charity. You are all our sweetness. You are our eternal life, great and wonderful Lord, almighty God and merciful Savior.

On the reverse, Francis wrote in his own hand a blessing for Leo, based on the venerable ancient benediction in the Hebrew Scriptures' Book of Numbers:

> May the Lord bless you and keep you.
> May He show His face to you and be merciful to you.
> May He turn His countenance to you and give you peace.
> May the Lord bless you, Brother Leo.

And for his signature, Francis marked the parchment with the sign of the tau—his own seal, the biblical sign of salvation and the blessing he always placed on the brow of his friars, now inscribed by Francis by placing it on a small outline of a forehead between the second and third letters of Leo's name.

Months later, even as Francis's health declined further, he continued to make himself available to friars who needed his guidance. A letter to Leo has survived in which Francis insists that Leo's own goodwill and conscience must be his guide as he looks to the future:

> Brother Leo: health and peace from your brother Francis!
> I am speaking, my son, in this way—as a mother would—because I am putting everything we said on the road in this brief message and advice. In whatever way it seems better to you to please the Lord God and to follow His footprint and poverty, do it with the blessing of the Lord God and my permission. And if you need and want to come to me for the sake of your soul or for some consolation, Leo, do come.

The recipient must have been consoled from the first words, for Francis used his nickname, indicating familiarity: he spelled his name francis-sco. (The early Italian nickname for Francisco or Francesco was Sco.) The

blessing of Leo and the subsequent letter are the only two surviving documents in Francis's own hand.

§

During his retreat, probably in mid-September, Francis had a dream he
took for an important revelation—indeed, he apparently told it to his companions in the form of a vision that synthesized and disclosed the meaning
of his life and sufferings. The earliest source for this vision simply states:
"Among many other graces which the Lord bestowed upon him, there is
the vision of the seraph [an angel] that filled his soul with consolation and
united him closely to God for the rest of his life. When his companions
brought him his meal that day, he told them what had happened."

Like his experience before the crucifix at San Damiano 19 years earlier,
the vision was not an external apparition perceivable to the senses but an
internal, spiritual experience, though none the less real for that. Francis had
a knowledge of angels, as did everyone in medieval Europe, and he had
prayed long and deeply over the sufferings and death of Jesus, which were
the most common themes in the piety of the Middle Ages. Hence the depths
of his soul transmitted the image of a crucified angel to his inner sight.
Only later, in prayerful reflection, could Francis realize the full meaning of
the interior vision—when, little by little, as we read in the early sources,
wounds covered his body. An angel had looked kindly on him and come to
comfort him, just as an angel comforted Jesus during the agony in the garden of Gethsemane the night before His death. From now through the last
two years of his life, Francis knew, his dedication to God would be lived
out in keeping with the patience of Christ crucified.

All his life, he had prayed to know who God was. The answer came in
the dream vision: his God was the God of the abandoned, dying Jesus—
and he, Francis, was now united in the dying of Jesus, to whom he had
given his life. With Saint Paul, he could say of his sufferings, "I have been
crucified with Christ"—faith alone gave meaning to his agony and
redeemed him from the crushing burden of absurdity. "It is no longer I
who live," Paul continued; "it is Christ who lives in me. And the life I now
live in the flesh, I live by faith in the Son of God, who loved me and gave
himself for me."

At last Francis knew the meaning of conformity to Christ in absolute poverty—to accept his own limitations, his own complete reliance on God. If he was not to be a merchant, not to join the world's struggle for material success, then he had to follow this refusal to its logical term: there were to be no visible signs of spiritual success—neither converted infidels, nor a baptized sultan, nor a fraternity that remained as he had planned and formed it. He had tried to imitate the life of Jesus; now, in his decline and death, in his frustrations and failures, he would follow that path all the way to the cross.

But it was not Jesus' cross Francis was to take up—it was his own. "If any want to become my followers," Jesus had said, "let them deny themselves and take up their cross and follow me." He did not say, "Take up *my* cross," but "*their* cross," the specific burden given to each in this world.

"I carry the marks of Jesus branded on my body," Paul wrote in the same letter, referring to all the sufferings, diseases and illnesses he had to endure in his constant life as an itinerant preacher in the service of the Gospel. Those "marks"—*stigmata* in the biblical Greek—included "great endurance in afflictions, hardships, calamities, beatings, imprisonments, riots, labors, sleepless nights, hunger . . . in ill repute and good repute." Paul spoke for all who proclaim Jesus by word and example: "We are treated as impostors, yet are true; as dying, and see—we are alive; as punished, and yet not killed; as sorrowful, yet always rejoicing; as poor, yet making many rich; as having nothing, and yet possessing everything."

&

During his 40 days, Francis received his epiphany in a cave on a mountain—just like Moses and the prophet Elijah, who spent 40 days on Mount Sinai, and like Jesus, who fasted 40 days before he gave the Sermon on the Mount.

How could the early Franciscan sources convey the sense of these final stages, of his awareness during intense prayer of his deepest vocation as a follower of Jesus? They knew only that he was wracked by suffering of all kinds, and that was their clue: Francis was indeed a participant in the agony of Christ. But the only way the medieval artist and commentator could make that idea concrete was in the brilliant symbol of the stigmata—the miraculous piercing of Francis's hands, feet and side, as if by nails, replicating the wounds of Jesus crucified.

For centuries, very many people of goodwill took the description of these wounds literally, as have most artists when depicting Francis of Assisi. Because this was the first time in history for which such a claim was made by someone's partisans, it may be helpful to reflect on what may be the far richer and deeper significance of the stigmata.

First, it is important to consider the reliability of the early sources on this matter.

In fact, the existence of the stigmata was denied by those interviewed for Francis's canonization, and even his good friend Ugolino—who became Pope Gregory IX in 1227—flatly disbelieved the report for a decade. His proclamation of Francis's canonization (*Mira circa nos,* July 1228) makes no reference to the stigmata, and it is unlikely that an element so dramatic would have been omitted, for this alone might have made the extraordinary holiness of the man a self-evident truth.

But later, in 1237, Gregory IX mentioned the stigmata in no less than three proclamations; the shift in his thinking, however, was due to political rather than religious considerations. The Dominican friars, who had become very much a rival Order to the Franciscans, were widely discounting and even mocking Francis's supposed stigmata. Because Gregory needed the prestige and support of the Franciscans in Church reform, he moved to end the rivalry and to secure Franciscan loyalty by writing to the Dominicans to affirm the truth of the alleged miracle. At the same time, there seemed to be a race to balance canonizations from each Order: Anthony of Padua was canonized in 1232, Dominic in 1234—and so it continued. Not to be outdone, the Dominicans eventually presented their competition: Catherine of Siena, undeniably a great saint and an important woman in Church history. She was reputed to have invisible stigmata, whatever that term is taken to mean.

But we must also consider the influence of medieval art on the tradition—specifically, a kind of religious art in which symbol was soon naïvely equated with literal reality. The earliest painting of Francis that depicts him with the stigmata was by Berlinghieri, in 1235: round black circles were visible on the saint's hands and feet. Twenty years later, an anonymous painter added the wound in the side. Later still, in his paintings of Francis's dream vision at La Verna (completed over a period of three decades), Giotto based his images on the only biography of Francis authorized by the Order—the volumes composed by Saint Bonaventure, who drew parallels to the life of Jesus in almost every facet of the founder's life. Almost 40 years after Francis's death, Bonaventure identified the angel with Christ, and Christ with Francis.

One early written source for the idea of a miraculous impression of wounds was believed to have been the testimony of Brother Elias in a letter to Pope Gregory IX, supposedly written immediately after Francis died: "Not long before his death, our brother and father appeared crucified, bearing in his body the five wounds which are truly the marks of Christ. His hands and feet had, as it were, the openings of the nails and were pierced front and back revealing the scars and showing the nails' blackness. His side, moreover, seemed opened by a lance and often emitted blood."

Unfortunately, no original manuscript of this letter exists; in fact, it was not published until 1620, and it may have been written at that time. Such a late appearance alone would perhaps not be probative of its illegitimacy, for authentic manuscripts often turn up centuries after their composition—the first-century Dead Sea Scrolls were not discovered until 1947, for example, and *Dyskolos,* a Greek comedy by Menander, turned up in a papyrus manuscript in 1957, more than 2,000 years after it was thought lost forever.

The problem lies in the fact that this alleged letter of Elias is couched in religious, biblical and theological concepts unknown to Francis's time, and it refers to Franciscan practices that had not been developed in the 13th century. To cite but one example from the excerpt above: Elias supposedly presents Francis as another Christ—an idea, as one scholar has rightly noted, that would have been almost blasphemous at the time of its alleged composition.

According to Jordan of Giano, a contemporary of Francis, Elias did indeed write some sort of letter referring to the stigmata and other miracles, but it is not the document published in the 17th century—and we cannot be

certain that even Jordan took the description of the stigmata literally. Whatever he believed, it is crucial to recall that to the medieval mind, everything
in the life of a saint was transparently the work of God: after Francis's swift
canonization (21 months after his death), it was presumed that every aspect
of his life revealed direct divine intervention. And it is unsurprising that
Franciscans, especially, used all the resources available to them (the talents
of Bonaventure, for example) to promote their cause.

In addition, all the early sources contain numerous variations and con-
tradictions about the appearance of wounds. Thomas of Celano, Francis's
first biographer, stresses that the marks were "formed by his own flesh,"
and he calls them "signs of martyrdom." This sober description, entirely
consistent with the understanding that suffering may be endured in imitation of Christ, was 40 years later far exceeded by Bonaventure's highly
interpretive account—itself dependent on a document written in 1255 by
Pope Alexander IV.

A 20th-century Franciscan scholar, author of the most thorough academic analysis of primary texts, rightly concluded, "No early source worthy of credibility reports bloody wounds in the hands and feet [of Francis]."
Instead, the marks—which were observed only by two or three people during Francis's lifetime and not subjected to any thorough examination after
his death—were described in all the earliest accounts as blackened excres-
cences, which are not inconsistent with diseases such as leprosy.

Diagnoses based on accurate readings of symptoms are a fine art;
even in modern medicine, highly refined skills are required. Also, in an
era of primitive therapies and even more imprecise methods of analysis,
the sufferings of Jesus were the primary coping mechanism for the sick—
people looked to the cross for strength, for the ultimate promise of deliv-
erance. It would not be surprising, therefore, if Francis's companions,
after his death, quite logically interpreted his leprosy as a sharing in the
sufferings of Christ. Lepers were the pariahs of the Middle Ages, forced
to be outcasts and regarded only as reprehensible sinners to be avoided at
all cost. Because Francis, in imitation of Jesus, had been unafraid to touch
and nurse them even in their worst state, would not Francis's own leprosy
have been a form of crucifixion? Was not this terrible illness a kind of
stigmata?

§

There is no doubt that wounds and sores covered the spent body of 42-year-old Francis, and the sources are unanimous that he always tried to hide them. But what did they mean to him?

First, it is essential to stress that Francis never claimed he had received an impression of the wounds of Christ, nor did he ever utter the word "stigmata." An argument from silence is never entirely persuasive, of course: humility may have silenced him. But he always forestalled any discussion that seemed to identify his sufferings with Christ's.

"What is this, Brother?" asked a companion, seeing marks on Francis's feet.

"Mind your own business!" was his response—hardly the reply one would have expected if Francis knew the lesions to be a gift of God. (In the source, the medieval Latin is in fact quite rude: *Curam habe de facto tuo!*) On the other hand, the tone of the remark may be more comprehensible if we understand that he did not wish the signs of morbid illness to frighten his brothers; in this regard, he always tried to hide the marks with gloves or bandages—also a habit of lepers.

On another occasion, Francis was asked to hand over his tunic for washing; on returning it, a friar asked him, "Whose blood stained your habit?"

This time, the reply was a gesture. Pointing a finger to his eye, Francis said, "Ask what *this* is—if you don't know it's an eye!" Whose blood could it be but his own? With the gesture, he may have gone a step further and implied the familiar Italian motion for the *malocchio*.

After Francis's death, people saw his bruised and wounded body, and after he was canonized, reports of miracles were needlessly multiplied. Not surprisingly, those who believed that Francis's commitment to Gospel living repeated the life of Christ were inclined to interpret his last years as a new Passion. In time, the enormous spiritual suffering of this flesh-and-blood saint was diminished in light of his physical torments—a natural development, perhaps, in light of the terrible diseases and general misery of life at the time. The same medieval religious spirit that was the foundation for the artistic rendering in excruciating detail the twisted features of

Christ on the cross and elaborating the poignancy of his suffering—an emphasis that had begun with Saint Bernard and monastic (specifically Cistercian) piety—came to see Francis primarily as a bearer of the Lord's agony.

§

It is not difficult, then, to understand how devout people, amazed by the enormity of Francis's suffering, were inclined to turn his pains into a reminder of Christ's; thus the stigmata were soon taken as externally imposed insignia rather than for what they really were—signs of illness and disease resulting from a lifetime of dedication to others. It took only a century for the Franciscans, who were given responsibility for the Holy Land shrines in 1342, to spread the practice of the Stations of the Cross— a series of pious pictorial tableaux that concludes with the burial of the dead Jesus.

With that sort of iconography, the Resurrection, which is at the heart of Christian faith, was effectively ignored. With attention deflected to the suffering of Jesus in the past, the Risen Christ of the present—who suffers no longer and lives forever—began to fade from the Church's ordinary proclamation of the fundamentals of faith.

§

Viewed as a miracle and not as the result of suffering patiently endured, the stigmata of Francis of Assisi must also be assessed in the context of a seismic shift in the spiritual climate of Europe. People had come to long for a less remote God and a more warmly human religion that took their sufferings into account. Because Francis had lived the imitation of Christ with revolutionary and unusual intensity and demonstrated a positive, loving concern for everyone, it was natural that the Friars Minor be eager to present him as uniquely similar to Christ. But it is important to recall that there were large numbers of the clergy who, while regarding Francis as unquestionably a saint, vigorously denied that the marks on his body were miraculous impressions of the wounds of Jesus on the cross.

Of equal significance is the fact that among the more than 300 cases of reported stigmata since Francis, the Church has never officially pronounced on the origin, nature or authenticity of any of them, including Francis's. To the contrary, the Church has insisted that there can be physical, psychological or preternatural explanations for the phenomenon. Even if miraculous, these extraordinary signs are no guarantee of holiness, and people are not canonized merely because of such oddities.

Unfortunately, a kind of materialistic piety that emphasizes the extraordinary has come to prevail even more tenaciously since the Enlightenment of the 18th century. This attitude is the best ally rationalists have, for it is easy to discount a religious sensibility that effectively reduces great and symbolic visions to the level of a pious sideshow. Paradoxically, in stressing the mystery of the stigmata, his supporters do not elevate Francis of Assisi: he becomes instead a kind of religious freak, completely alienated from our experience.

The true Francis is the man whose prayer was always, "Who are You, my dearest Lord—and what am I but Your useless servant?" Despite darkness and disappointment, he remained faithful, knowing that his own life was utterly insignificant without reference to God. "I am a useless man," he said at this time, and he blamed his own "negligence and weakness, because I am ignorant and stupid." This was not pride masquerading as humility, nor was it a desire to have his sentiments corrected by admirers. He knew the truth of it: only in relationship to the immensity of God could he find any meaning in himself.

Popular piety often finds no room for this sense of mystery, this incessant hunger for the Infinite that was at the root of his character and his charm. The truest sign of his humanity was in his wounded, scarred body, used up at 40 after years of service. It is this aspect of his life that has the most to say to us—more than the fact that he devoted himself to poverty or became a fool for Christ. Faced with the suffering of others, Francis had fixed his gaze on Jesus crucified since the day he sat before the crucifix at San Damiano; since the time he took chalk and sketched the cross on his tunic; since the day he took the tau as his hallmark.

At Mount La Verna in 1224, Francis came at last to understand that the martyrdom he had so avidly sought was to come in the most unexpected form—in his willing abandonment of self to God, his acceptance of diminishment and pain and in the dissolution of his dreams for his companions.

When he and they descended at the end of September, he understood the true term of his search for knightly glory and chivalric honor, his quest for martyrdom and his longing to baptize others.

Until the end of November, Francis remained quietly at Saint Mary's, and then he went to preach in the countryside. When his companions objected to his making such efforts as winter approached, he smiled. "Let us begin, brothers, to serve the Lord God—for up until now, we have done little or nothing."

FIFTEEN

1225–1226

AT WINTER'S END 1225, Leo, Rufino and a few others feared Francis was about to die. "Only skin clung to his bones," they told an early chronicler, and when one of them remarked to Francis that a quick martyrdom would have been easier, he had to agree. "To suffer this illness, even for three days, is harder for me than any martyrdom would be."

Francis asked to be moved to a small hut sometimes used by priests who came to celebrate Mass at the convent of San Damiano, and there his companions delivered him toward the end of March. He was returning to the place of his first conversion, but now he could no longer see the crucifix whose serene gaze had so moved him, nor the contours of the little church he had so lovingly renovated.

For two months, his friends recalled, "he stayed inside, in that dark little cell. He was unable to bear the light of the sun during the day or the light of a fire at night. He had constant and severe pains in his eyes, and at night he could scarcely rest or sleep." Clare and her nuns brought him food, but he could sustain very little; most of it he left for the mice that scurried around the room at all hours. There is no record of any private conversations between Francis and Clare, but—to the eternal disappointment of romantics—it is unlikely that they occurred. It would have been highly irregular for a medieval nun to be alone with a man, even a friar who had been her spiritual mentor.

Francis was aware of the hardship his incapacity caused the friars and nuns, and he sensed the frustration and even annoyance of some of them. "My dearest brothers," he said quietly one evening when a few had gathered round him, "do not grow weary or burdened because of my illness. The Lord will return to you all the fruit of the good work that you are

unable to do because of your care for me. You should tell me, 'We're paying your expenses, but the Lord will be our debtor!' " He had lost neither
his courage, his sensitivity to others nor his humor.

   After one particularly painful and exhausting night, he called for one of
the friars and said excitedly that he wished to compose a new song. "I want
to write a new *Praise of the Lord* for his creatures, which we use every day,
and without which we cannot live. Through them, the human race greatly
offends the Creator, and we are continually ungrateful for such great
graces and good gifts, not praising, as we should, our Lord the Creator and
the Giver of all good."

   As the friar hastened to transcribe his words, Francis poured out one of
the great hymns to come down to us from medieval civilization—a song
centuries ahead of its time in its mystical and, we might say, its ecological
sensibility. We have no record of the tune he improvised, but the original
Umbrian dialect has been preserved with all its verbal melody intact:

> *Altissimu, omnipotente, bonsignore,*
>   *tue sono le laude,*
>   *la gloria elhonore*
>   *et omne benedictione.*

> Most High, all-powerful, good Lord:
>   Yours are the praises, the glory
>   and the honor, and all blessing.

> *Ad te solo, Altissimo, se konfano*
>   *et nullu homo enne dignu*
>   *te mentovare.*

> To You alone, Most High, do they belong,
>   and no human is worthy to mention Your name.

> *Laudato sie, misignore, cum tucte le tue creature,*
>   *spetialmente messor lo frate sole,*
>   *loquale iorno et allumini noi par loi.*

> Praised be You, my Lord, with all Your creatures,
>   especially Sir Brother Sun,
>   who is the day, and through whom You give us light.

Et ellu ebellu eradiante cum grande splendore:
    de te, Altissimo, porta significatione.

And he is beautiful and radiant with great splendor,
    and bears a likeness of You, Most High One.

Laudato si, misignore, per sora luna ele stele:
    in celu lai formate clarite
    et pretiose et belle.

Praised be You, my Lord, through Sister Moon and the stars:
    in heaven You formed them, clear, precious and beautiful.

Laudato si, misignore, per frate vento,
    et per aere et nubilo
    et sereno et omne tempo
    per loquale a le tue creature
    da sustentamento.

Praised be You, my Lord, through Brother Wind,
    and through the air cloudy and serene,
    and every kind of weather,
    through whom You give sustenance to Your creatures.

Laudato si, misignore, per sor aqua,
    laquale et multo utile et humile
    et pretiose et casta.

Praised be You, my Lord, through Sister Water,
    who is very useful and humble, precious and pure.

Laudato si, misignore, per frate focu,
    per loquale ennalumini la nocte:
    edello ebello et iocundo
    et robusto et forte.

Praised be You, my Lord, through Brother Fire,
    through Whom You light the night,
    and he is beautiful and playful, robust and strong.

Laudato si, misignore, per sora nostra matre terra,
    laquale ne sustenta et governa,
    et produce diversi fructi
    con coloriti flori et herba.

Praised be You, my Lord, through our Sister, Mother Earth,
      who sustains and governs us, and
      who produces various fruits with colored flowers and herbs.

❧

Exhausted but radiantly happy, Francis sat down and leaned against a wall.
He had just composed the first example of poetry in vernacular Italian,
then emerging out of its Latin chrysalis; the romantic young troubadour
had at last become the mystic minstrel of God.

He sent for Pacificus, his old friend and king of the verses, and
together they sang the words. Gathering a few more friars, Francis told
them how he wished the song to be presented—after the sermons they
preached. "We are minstrels of the Lord," he wanted his friars to say.
"What are the servants of God if not His minstrels, who must move people's hearts and lift them up to spiritual joy?"

Instead of yielding to bitterness and withdrawing from the world,
Francis was beginning to enter into a closer union with God through everything God created; instead of weeping over his own darkness, he thanked
God for the light of sun and fire. He was familiar with both the great biblical song of the three young men in the fiery furnace (in the Book of
Daniel) and Psalm 148, which certainly provided inspiration and influence
for the "Canticle," as did an 11th-century Advent hymn called "Jubilemus
Omnes," which urged all people to rejoice in God's creation, and which
specifically mentioned the sun, moon, stars, air, wind and flowers.

But perhaps, as he was searching for the right phrases, Francis's memory also went back to the "Litany of Love," the song from his teens he had
once known and sung so well:

> So pleases me the gentle season,
> And pleases me the gentle summer weather,
> And please me the birds, singing so much,
> And please me the flowers in bud—
> So pleases me all that pleases the courtly,
> And most of all please me deeds of chivalry:
> I undertake them joyfully
> Bending all my heart and mind to them right willingly.

§

It was the unique genius of Francis to proclaim—contrary to the teachings of the Cathari and Albigensians—that creation was not only beautiful but also good. And it was good precisely because it reflected a Creator who was Goodness right through. But what good is it to praise God? What need, in fact, has God of our praise? The Psalms disclose the meaning: to praise God is to render to Him what He has made, to consecrate everything in the world to Him by using everything properly.

But this is abstract language, and Francis is concerned with the concrete: he does not love "nature"—he loves the sun, moon and stars; the wind, air and water; fire and all that grows and comes from the earth. Francis is no nature mystic, no philosophical transcendentalist, no romantic, pantheistic poet. Everything beautiful reminds him of Beauty itself.

At this point we are at the sign and seal of Francis's conversion, and the guarantee, if ever he or we doubted it, that his life was a radiant model. Out of the lowest depths of illness, misery and rejection, the man who had so loved to sing—who drew an imaginary bow across a twig and sang for his friends as they made their way along rural roads—recognized everything in creation as his sister and brother and friend.

Francis speaks from blindness and pain; he can no longer see the sun or moon, stars, water or earth. The colors of flowers are only dim memories now. We do his point no harm, in fact, if we turn it about: Francis has known the One Who is Beauty, and so he is reminded of all that is beautiful in the world. Against every current of his time, he loves everything created to the extent that he sees himself as connected with God's world.

For years, a scholarly debate has been waged over the proper understanding of the word *per* in the "Canticle": is God to be praised *for* (on account of) these things, or praised *by* them (through their agency) or praised *through* them (by means of them)? In other words, the word *per* may be translated "for," suggesting thanksgiving; "by," in the sense of instrumentality; or "through," insofar as God is really present in but also beyond all creation. In the early 13th century, *per* was used in Italy as the equivalent of both the French *par* and *pour;* in fact, Dante uses *per* in both these senses.

Francis would not hold with the idea that the things of creation in and of themselves could praise God, but that He is to be praised for and through them was self-evident. Since the Italian itself has a rich ambiguity, it may not be necessary for us to choose between the other two meanings: we consecrate creation to God because we are grateful for it; we dedicate and use creation rightly because God Himself is found within and beyond everything. Francis's fraternity extended beyond persons to things; everything, after all, comes from God, is related to God and finds its meaning in God.

Francis's perception of the world and everything in it had become completely God-centered, and to deny or diminish this by proclaiming him a kind of patron of the cosmos is quite simply to miss his point. He did not love an impersonal universal force, nor did he salute a vague rhythm of life. He was drawn to the divine; he was in love with God. Apart from the Creator, nature for him was empty and worthless—in fact, Francis would have no comprehension of the word "nature." God was *misignore*—"my Lord"—and Francis was His true and faithful knight, the steward of all the beauty in the world he had known. At the beginning of his conversion, Francis saw people in their specific, unique situations: lepers and beggars, poor and sick, wealthy and powerful. Now he had a sense of something deeper: the unity in God of all that is.

§

In early spring 1225, Cardinal Ugolino and Elias (who was then acting as unofficial general minister) prevailed on Francis—now virtually blind and enduring constant headaches—to be transported to the hermitage at Fonte Columbo. This was near Rieti, where they had found a physician respected for his treatment of eye diseases. The doctor had devised a revolutionary approach, he explained, and was eager to see its results in his famous new patient. The early sources record this futile procedure in all its gruesome details: "The doctor arrived with the iron instrument used for cauterizing in eye diseases. He had a fire lit to heat the iron, and when the fire was lit, he placed the iron in it."

The friends who had accompanied him told Francis what the doctor was about to do: when red hot, the irons would be applied to burn the flesh on both sides of Francis's head, from his cheeks to his eyebrows, and the veins in his temples would be cut open. The hope was that the infection that caused blindness would thus be drained away.

As the irons glowed in the fire and the doctor prepared for his task, Francis astounded everyone. "My brother Fire," he said in his weak and certainly anxious voice, "you are noble and useful among all the creatures the Most High has created. Be courteous to me in this hour. For a long time I have loved you. I pray our Creator who made you, to temper your heat now, so that I may bear it." He then made the sign of the cross over the fire.

This was a moment his companions never forgot: overwhelmed with terror and revulsion, "we who were with him all ran away, and he remained alone with the doctor."

And then the surgeon took the instruments from the fire, "and applied the hissing irons into the flesh"—the burn was extended slowly, straight from the ear to the eyebrow. "His head was cauterized, his veins were cut open, poultices applied and drops [of egg yolks mixed with rock salt] poured into his blind eyes."

The eyewitnesses returned to a room filled with the stench of burning flesh, but the patient was remarkably calm and uncomplaining. "The doctor thought it well thus to treat him," his friends recalled, "but other doctors who were opposed to this procedure considered the operation inadvisable—and this proved to be correct, for it brought him no relief. He kept getting steadily worse."

As if this were not enough, Francis was taken six months later to a physician in Siena, who declared that the only way to stop the infection (and by then the constant oozing of pus from the poor man's eyes) was to insert red-hot irons into his ears—this, too, was accomplished one dreadful afternoon, and also to no effect except the patient's agony.

§

By early 1226, Francis endured his most debilitating attack of malaria to date. His organs were now permanently enlarged with lesions and became virtual reservoirs for malaria parasites; the earliest sources record all the symptoms of that disease—enlarged liver and spleen with profuse and frequent vomiting; anemia (which gave his skin a gray-blue color); profound weakness and dramatic weight loss; shortness of breath; "and then the swelling began in his abdomen, his legs and his feet," at which point Francis began to vomit blood.

His companions feared that death was imminent, and they summoned Elias. Desperate to find some remedy for his friend's agony, the general minister asked if Francis could sustain any bit of food or drink. "I do not wish to be concerned about eating or drinking," Francis replied. "I entrust myself to you. If you give me something, I'll take it. If you don't, I will not ask for it." But he lingered through the spring, until he became so feeble that the brothers decided to lodge him at the bishop's residence in Assisi, where friars from surrounding communities could alternate their care and vigil.

As it happened, Francis's hometown was once again at war with Perugia—just as it had been in the robust enthusiasm of his youth. A man named Oportulo Bernardo, who was Assisi's podestà (essentially the mayor), had signed an alliance of mutual aid with Perugian nobles; Bishop Guido, following the decree of Pope Honorius, forthwith excommunicated Oportulo, who countered with a decree that any merchant in Assisi who transacted business with the bishop was liable to imprisonment. And so the absurd recriminations and violence in the commune worsened. "There was a savage hatred between them," one contemporary wrote of the bishop and the podestà, "and no one could be found to reestablish peace and concord."

Francis, ignoring his incapacity, asked that the two warring leaders assemble in the courtyard of the bishop's palace. Doubtless because of his fame, they could not ignore the summons, and when all were gathered in the presence of a vast crowd of citizens, Francis was carried in on a pallet.

By this time, the repetition of his "Canticle of the Creatures" (as it is often called) had familiarized many people with its verses, and its melody was heard throughout Umbria. As quiet came upon a nervous crowd that spring morning, Francis lifted himself up and with great effort improvised an additional verse, his voice floating the tune over the cloister:

> *Laudate si, misignore, per quelli ke perdonano,*
> *per lo tuo amore*
> *et sostengo infirmitate et tribulatione.*

Beati quelli kel sosterranno in pace,
    ka da te, Altissimo,
    sirano incoronati.

Praised be You, my Lord, through those who grant pardon
    for Your love and bear infirmity and tribulation.
Blessed are those who endure in peace, for by You, Most High,
    shall they be crowned.

On that day, the bishop and the podestà, who could scarcely disregard the prayerful pleading of a dying man so well known and loved, asked forgiveness of each other and agreed on terms of a peace treaty. Although the hostilities were not completely ended, for a long time at least, open conflict was allayed and concord restored to Assisi. Francis had at last succeeded, in his own home and bowed by weakness, in bringing two individuals to dialogue; it was the small but not negligible victory of peacemaking he had sought on a much grander scale in Egypt. "May the Lord give you peace," Francis had said so often; now, through his efforts, his prayer was answered.

§

In midsummer, it was clear to everyone that Francis was indeed dying. Francis wanted to be brought to Saint Mary's, and so he was carried down from Assisi. On the way, he told his friends to stop and set him down for a moment. Raising himself up slightly, he turned and blessed the city, and his prayer disclosed not only his love for his hometown but also the shift in his attitude about it: "Lord, just as I believe that at an earlier time this city was the abode of wicked and evil men, so now I realize that, because of Your abundant mercy and in Your own time, You have shown an abundance of mercies to it."

Clare, who was confined to her bed with illness (but survived another 27 years), sent word that she grieved at being prevented from seeing her old friend at such a time. "Go and tell Lady Clare to put aside all her grief and sorrow over not being able to see me now," Francis replied, adding enigmatically, "Let her be assured that before her death, both she and her sisters will see me." His statement was fulfilled when his body, transferred for burial, was taken to San Damiano and briefly lifted to a convent window.

But another old friend, also a woman but healthy and capable of traveling, received an invitation to Saint Mary's that astonished Francis's companions, for his Rule strongly enjoined the friars from allowing a woman to enter their residences. "You know how faithful and devoted Lady Jacoba was and is to me," he explained to them. "I believe she would consider it a great favor and consolation if you notified her about my condition." He sent a friar to ask her to bring some cloth for a tunic. "Have her also send some of that almond cake she often made for me."

Several hours later, there was a knock at the door of Saint Mary's, and a friar opened to find Jacoba herself, who had perhaps already heard of her friend's desperate condition. "What shall we do?" asked the friar, going to Francis's bedside. "Shall we allow her to enter and come in here?"

"The command against it need not be observed in the case of this lady whose faith and devotion made her come here from so far away," Francis replied. Ever the courtly knight, Francis believed that kindness and gratitude superseded mere human prescriptions.

"When I was praying," Jacoba told the friar as he was escorting her to Francis's bedside, "a voice within me said, 'Go, visit your father, blessed Francis, without delay. And hurry, because if you delay, you will not find him alive. Moreover, take such and such for his tunic, as well as the ingredients for making that particular confection.' "

She must have been shocked at his appearance. Francis at the age of 44 seemed much older, his small frame shrunken to the point of emaciation, his face drained of all color, his blind eyes covered with bandages because the light he loved so much was inexpressibly painful. Jacoba at once began to make the little dessert Francis so loved. "He ate only a little of it," according to an eyewitness, "because he was so near death."

Throughout his ordeal he offered no complaint, and he told his companions that he was much cheered each evening at dusk, when he heard the flights of larks, winging low around the eaves of Saint Mary's. "They are birds that are friends of light and dread the shadows of dusk, when they circle about noisily for a long while," a medieval source commented. The evening flights and high chirping of larks and swifts may be heard in this region even today. The larks were like his very own choir, Francis said; later, his companions recalled that he "dearly loved and freely contemplated them."

During the final days of September 1226, a doctor visited, at the request of Guido. "Tell me," Francis asked, "how do I seem to you?"

The doctor tried to prevaricate: "It will be well with you"—an answer given, his friends recalled, "because he did not want to tell him that he would die in a little while."

But Francis was not to be so easily put off. "Tell me the truth. How does it look to you? Do not be afraid, for by the grace of God, I am not a coward who fears death. With God's help and by His mercy and grace, I am so united with my Lord that I will not be sad over dying nor rejoice over living longer."

The doctor spoke frankly. "Your illness is incurable, and you will probably die at either the end of the month or early in October."

And with that, Francis asked Leo, Angelo and Rufino to come to his bedside and to sing for him his "Canticle."

But when they had finished, Francis whispered that he had one last verse to add:

> *Laudato si, misignore, per sora nostra, morte corporale,*
>   *da laquale nullu homo vivente poskappare.*
> *Gai acqueli ke morrano ne le peccata mortali!*
> *Beati quelli ke trovarane le tue sanctissime voluntati,*
>   *ka la morte secunda nol farra male.*
> *Laudate et benedicite, misignore,*
>   *et rengratiate et serviate li cum grande humilitate.*

> Praised be You, my Lord, through our Sister Bodily Death,
>   from whom no one living can escape.
> Woe to those who die in mortal sin!
> Blessed are those whom death will find in Your most holy will,
>   for the second death shall do them no harm.
> Praise and bless my Lord and give Him thanks,
>   and serve Him with great humility.

With one last burst of energy, Francis then dictated a brief *Testament*, devoted mostly to final admonitions to his friars about their manner of life. But as he lay dying, perhaps thinking of his own leprosy, his mind went back to the first lepers he had tended—the work that had marked the first stage of his penance, or conversion toward God. He allowed himself a brief personal statement at the outset:

> The Lord gave me, Brother Francis, thus to begin doing penance in this way: for when I was in sin, it seemed too bitter for me to see lepers. And the Lord Himself led me among them, and I showed mercy to them. And when I left them, what had seemed bitter to me was turned into sweetness of soul and body.

§

The life of Francis of Assisi and the journey of his progress toward God had meant accepting a series of corrections and simplifications, a refining of his understanding about what God had wanted of him. We might even say that Francis had constantly to revise what he believed would honor God. Hence Francis's conversion was the work of a lifetime, with all its autumns and winters; it was not the achievement of an afternoon in springtime.

Like Jesus, Francis had been a seeker in the world. He had not fled to the desert or a monastery but rather believed that God could be found in the crowd. As God's knight, he had been willing to sacrifice his life; now, his share in the cross was the illnesses contracted in the service of him who had been nailed to the cross once and for all, and who now lived beyond death forever.

His life was not based only on a single moment in a ruined church, for this did not do away with his frail humanity and replace it with extreme piety and instant achievement. On the contrary, Francis learned that he had nothing he could call his own except his utter dependence on unimaginable mercy. The daily process of turning to God, of allowing himself to belong to God, reveals the deepest logic of Francis's ever more serious insistence on poverty—which did not primarily mean having no possessions but rather not being possessive about anything or anyone, not acting as if he were the proprietor of anyone or anything.

Every day, he tried to have no single thing as his own property so that he could rely on nothing, so that nothing would become a wedge between himself and God. Hence he could paradoxically sing—quietly in his troubadour heart, and aloud in the songs he composed and sang—that everything in creation belonged to him: the sun, moon and stars, the water and wind and fire, the earth and trees, birds and meadows. Everything was his sister and brother.

The divine paradox was that poverty had enriched him, for it was just as Saint Paul had written: "All things are yours—yes, everything belongs to you, and you belong to Christ, and Christ belongs to God." Untouched by monastic discipline and uncorrupted by sterile academism, he was a supreme spiritual realist whose only literary influence was the New Testament. With him, as Evelyn Underhill wrote, "mysticism comes into the open air, seeks to transform the stuff of daily life, speaks the vernacular, turns the songs of the troubadours to the purposes of divine love."

The paradox was deepened by the fact that suffering was to be endured—not mutely accepted but *endured*—in the belief that God finally acts in love. This made possible Francis's joy in creation at the end of his life, even as his pain increased and his sight failed. Creation was no longer an obstacle, or something lost to him and mourned in the losing.

Across the centuries, Francis insists that we exist only in relation to Him Who is. What we do and what we have is ultimately of such little importance; what matters is that we decide what we do and how much we have in light of Him to Whom we belong. Everything follows from this. It was a lesson followed, in their own times, by the likes of Vincent de Paul, Dorothy Day and Mother Teresa—all of whom gave their lives to the poor, the defenseless, the lonely, the disenfranchised.

In one important respect of course Francis was indeed a pioneer: he was the first to cross territorial borders—and not only regarding his Lesser Brothers, whom Ugolino wanted to remain in Italy. He was also the first person from the West to travel to another continent with the revolutionary idea of peacemaking. This he did as he had rejected the economic system of calculated wealth: without the anger of a protester, and without condemning a single soul. If we had only this one aspect of his character, it might well mark him for heroic sanctity—the complete absence of anathemas in his sayings and writings. Unlike so many devout people, he knew not how to condemn. Neither aggressive nor intolerant, he was a peacemaker and reconciler who open-mindedly admitted almost everyone who came to join the Lesser Brothers.

It has to be acknowledged that Francis was also an eccentric, as saints tend to be. As much as we might prefer them to be polite traditionalists who never upset our certainties or challenge our mediocrities, they are resoundingly not normal people, for how indeed does one remain somnolently normal after being shaken to the roots by an encounter with God, however imperfectly perceived? Of course, eccentricity can degenerate into self-regard, but when (as in the case of Francis) we witness untiring service to others, then the eccentricity may be a sign of the presence of God. Anyone firmly on the road to conversion will sometimes not act "normally"; our worship services and prayer books might well benefit from the addition of formal requests to God that He deliver us from the limitations of normality.

The most challenging aspect of Francis of Assisi, finally, is the utter seriousness of his life. He risked everything to gain more than just some thing: as his life became more problematic, more complicated and more painful, he kept his focus not on himself but on God. He did not use people and things to climb up to God; he began with God, and there he found the truth of everyone and everything. That, after all, is the deepest logic of his "Canticle," from its praise of things and of those who forgive to its acceptance of Sister Death.

Facing suffering with the utmost gravity, Francis saw the world as steeped in tragedy but also embraced and ultimately redeemed by God. He perceived that the world could be understood as either divine or diabolical—either it belonged to God or everything was meaningless. In that regard, he was a medieval man. But his faith was based (and here we are at a crucial point) on his experience. In his youth, riches and pleasure were diverting for a time but could not finally bring him any peace. He did not analyze his restlessness; he felt it and sought a remedy for it.

Only silence before the cross of San Damiano could bring him to an initial sense of peace—that and the surprise that he no longer fled from lepers. With that, he began to see that he would never find what he was looking for in the world of things; later, he also learned that he would not even find it in a religious Order, the foundations of which he insistently tried to avoid. Nor would he find God in any standard by which the world judged success.

And here we come very close to the true meaning of holiness. It is, at its deepest level, a condition of spiritual integrity that always upsets public presumptions and counters the selfishness and madness of power that strangle so much peace in the world. Faith certainly professes that God continues to disclose Himself in all the intricate beauty of the world and its ongoing evolution, but perhaps God reveals Himself most of all in that sudden and unexpected radiance of extraordinary human goodness that we call sanctity.

Holiness does not, we should stress, necessarily depend on fidelity to an institution, or on allegiance to a particular juridical tradition. The true mark of holiness is the character of a life that gives to others, that extends beyond the narrow frontiers of itself, its own comfort and concerns—a life that furthers the humanizing process. Whether one uses the specific vocabulary of religion or not, this is the core: living close to God—a habit of being that (at least according to the great Hebrew prophets of old and the insistent message of Jesus of Nazareth) is seen concretely in loving service, a hunger for peace and justice and an active longing for concord among nations, groups and individuals.

The Hebrew prophets provided fair signs of holiness: "Cease to do evil, learn to do good; seek justice, rescue the oppressed, defend the orphan, plead for the widow. . . . Do justice, love kindness, walk humbly with your God." Jesus summed it up as love of God, made evident in love of neighbor—and the habit of forgiveness as the required standard of our love of God and of God's embrace of us. By forgiveness we do not mean that something wicked is to be forgotten, much less that it is not so wicked after all; forgiveness means the refusal to seek vengeance, to wish or to wreak pain, suffering or death on the offending enemy. Godliness, in other words, is about peace in all its ramifications.

Perhaps there is no clearer sign of Francis's journey and achievement than in the question he asked so often: "Who are You, my dearest God? And what am I but Your useless servant?" This is a sublime prayer, not the expression of a philosophical inquiry about the nature of God and the self.

It faces with absolute gravity the idea that God is utterly unknowable—as is the deepest truth of one's own life. But it is also, by the very fact of being addressed to God, a statement of unreserved conviction about the supreme reality of God, Who brings sense out of Francis's own emptiness and absurdity, his uselessness.

Such words can be uttered only by one who somehow knows through direct experience (not by concepts or ideas) that ultimately only God fills the gap, makes up all the difference. It was for Francis as it had been for another who had been surprised by grace, eight centuries earlier: "This alone I know," Augustine said to God in his *Confessions*, "that apart from You it is evil with me, not only outside myself but also in my self, and that for me all abundance that is not my God is but want." At first, Augustine too had resisted.

In Francis of Assisi, the world has taken to its heart a man whose life was about peace. It was also a chain of disappointments and failures. But the abandonment of his plans and goals brought him to the profoundest identification with Jesus, who died outcast, alone and rejected. His illnesses were but the external sign of his identification with the one who confounded the world. But at the end he was confident. "I am not ashamed," he could confidently say with Saint Paul. "I know whom I have trusted."

❦

On September 30, Francis summoned a few old friends to his tiny chamber—Bernard, Giles, Leo and perhaps Angelo and Rufino. They had cared for him in recent weeks, sparing no effort to provide what few comforts were still possible. He blessed them all, and when they asked if he wanted anything, he replied that he would like to have had more time to serve lepers. "Goodbye," he said in a thin voice. "I am hurrying to the Lord, and I am confident that I am going to my God, Whom I have served in my spirit."

The next day he slept, and his breathing was so shallow that the friars often thought he had left them. On late Friday evening, he stirred and surprised everyone by saying that he was hungry and would like to have a little parsley from the garden, which was often taken to fight an upset stomach, to enable him to chew a morsel of bread. But he could keep nothing down.

On Saturday morning, October 3, 1226, Francis told his caregivers, "When you see that I have come to the end, put me out naked on the ground, and allow me to lie there for as long as it takes to walk a leisurely mile." That afternoon, they heard him whisper the opening verses of Psalm 141: "I call upon You, O Lord: come quickly to me. . . . Give ear to my voice when I call upon You. . . . In You I seek refuge: do not leave me defenseless."

His friends followed his instruction, and placed him stripped on the floor of his cell—it was the full realization of the dramatic moment before Bishop Guido so many years earlier. Thus, as he lay dying and the afternoon began to fade, Francis's final prayer was a sublime gesture, his ultimate *ars concionandi*—the action by which he expressed what he was and Whose child he was, about to be born again in eternity. In the core of his being, Francis was at last utterly dependent on God alone. His poverty was absolute: there was now nothing between him and God. After a brief time, he was clothed in his tunic again and gently lifted back on his straw bed.

Bernard and Giles, his companions for 18 years, took his hands. "I have done what is mine," Francis whispered. "May Christ teach you what is yours to do."

The radiant blue light of evening shone over the valley and covered the hills above Assisi. In describing his last moments, Francis's friends never forgot one detail: "Many birds, called larks, flew low above the roof of the house where he lay, wheeling in a circle and singing."

Notes

These abbreviations are used in the notes:

AC: The Assisi Compilation (1244–1260)
AF: Arnaldo Fortini (see Bibliography)
AP: The Anonymous of Perugia (1240–1241)
FA: Francis of Assisi
FA:ED I, II, III: *Francis of Assisi: Early Documents,* 3 vols. (see Bibliography)
LP: The Legend of Perugia (1245?)
L3C: The Legend of the Three Companions (1241–1247)
GR: Greyfriars Review, a quarterly publication of the Franciscan Institute, St. Bonaventure University
1C: Celano, *The Life of Saint Francis*
2C: Celano, *The Remembrance of the Desire of a Soul*
3C: Celano, *The Treatise on the Miracles*

INTRODUCTION

xiv. On the establishment of methods for measuring time, see Blaise.

xvi. "Bonaventure's general untrustworthiness": Octavian Schmucki, O.F.M. Cap. (trans. Ignatius McCormick, O.F.M. Cap.), "The Passion of Christ in the Life of St. Francis of Assisi," *GR* 4, supplement (1990): 43.

xviii. The Prayer of Saint Francis was very likely composed by the French aristocrat the Marquis de la Rochetulon. He sent Pope Benedict XV some prayers for peace during World War I, and one of them was published in *L'Osservatore Romano* in December 1916, at the height of the conflict. A French Franciscan circulated the prayer even more widely among Franciscans when it was published in *La Croix* (a French Catholic newspaper), and so began its popularity. See Boff.

CHAPTER ONE

1. The name Assisi (from the Latin *Asisium*) may derive from the old orthography *Açu,* meaning east—i.e., east of the commune of Perugia. Very often, medieval towns took names used by neighboring citizens; see AF, p. 90n.

3. The dreadful famine of 1182–1187 was first noted by an anonymous Bene-dictine monk in the *Annales Casinenses*, the chronicles of the abbey of Monte Cassino; see, e.g., AF, pp. 82–83. Fortini's massive, multivolume original study, comprising 2,000 pages of daunting historical scholarship, clearly reflects his posi-tion as longtime mayor of Assisi: no detail of the place seems to have escaped his investigation. Moak's one-volume English distillation has been used here.

4. The location of the Bernardone house has been a matter of some contro-versy, although AF (p. 89) and the current guardians of Assisi are confident of this location near the Piazza del Comune. AF based his conclusion on the fact that in 1228, two years after the death of FA, the central piazza of Assisi was enlarged, the enterprise paid for by taxes levied against those who owned houses facing it. According to documents still preserved in Assisi, FA's brother (or half brother), Angelo, was among those so taxed; he had apparently inherited the family business and residence. Still, the precise site of the house is unknown, AF and the tour guides to the contrary notwithstanding. Engelbert (pp. 418–19), following an 18th-century chronicler, persuasively argues that during FA's youth the family relocated to another house in Assisi; hence there is no necessity to choose between the two places that lay claim to being the saint's home.

5. We cannot know for certain whether FA was born in 1181 or 1182, although modern scholarship prefers the later year; see Engelbert, pp. 364–73. In fact, let it be stated at the outset that (as with most ancient and medieval biographies) very few dates in the life of FA can be firmly established. "The chronology of the life of St. Francis of Assisi is enough to make one despair," according to an unnamed col-league of Engelbert's (p. 364). Quite apart from the general disinterest medieval hagiography took in factual details, there is the problem of the two medieval Italian methods of reckoning the calendar year. The Pisan calendar began the year on March 25 *before* Christmas, while the Florentine calendar began the year on March 25 *after* Christmas. To further complicate matters, the first and last of the years are taken when counting according to the Pisan way—hence, three years after 1206 is 1208, and two years before 1226 is 1225. With this caveat, we should add that many important civic and ecclesiastical events can in fact be dated, since they have the additional checks of the years of the reigns of both pope and emperor. As for the life of FA, I do provide many dates throughout this book. These dates are based on the findings of contemporary scholarship, which has only recently filled in many gaps from philological studies as well as from the comparison of the dates in Franciscan sources with the dates of contemporaneous events.

5. Regarding the Bernardones, some early Franciscan sources contain anec-dotes implying that Pica was a sweet-tempered and devout mother and Peter a ruth-less and dyspeptic father, but these accounts are not always reliable and cannot be verified. Their context suggests that they were created to support the drama of FA's conversion and the concomitant break from his father.

5. There is no record of the christening and naming of FA; baptismal records were not required until legislation set down by the Council of Trent (1545–1563). As for the place of baptism, this was very likely Santa Maria del Vescovado, since the Cathedral of San Rufino was being repaired that season, and Santa Maria was the procathedral. The baptismal font was later transferred to San Rufino, where it remains to this day; see *FA:ED* II, p. 241. (This is the second of a recent three-volume series running to more than 2,360 pages of translated early sources, the result of many years of serious scholarship.) See also Engelbert, pp. 405–6.

5. On the garb and diet of John the Baptist, see Mark 1, 6; the tradition behind this description casts John as a prophet in the mold of Elijah (2 Kings 1, 8), an understanding attributed in the synoptic gospels (Mark, Matthew and Luke) to Jesus himself.

5–6. The change of name to (as we now say) Francis may also reflect Pietro Bernardone's own nickname, "the Frenchman," in light of his many trips to his beloved France; such was stated as early as 1345 in a sermon delivered in Paris by the Franciscan priest James of Padua; see *Archivum Franciscanum Historicum* 44 (1951): 472. In addition, it was not at all unusual to name infants after the place of their father's business; see M. Bihl, "De nomine Sancti Francisci," *Archivum Franciscanum Historicum* 19 (1926): 469–529.

6. Regarding FA's grandparents, we know nothing. Trexler (p. 10) states that FA "deprecate[s] his grandfather Bernardone as having been *rusticum, mercenarium, et inutilem,* a characterization whose closest translation might be 'a useless country worker.' " Alas, Trexler misreads the text to which he refers; it is FA who describes *himself* with these words—"That," says FA, "is what the son of Peter Bernardone needs to hear." And so, "speaking in this fashion, he called to mind the humble origins of his birth." (The source to which Trexler refers has no mention of a grandfather.)

8. On the history of the papacy with special reference to Gregory VII, see, e.g., Küng, pp. 92–93.

10. On Alexander III, Saint Hippolytus and the *Annuario Pontificio,* and the popes during FA's lifetime, see, e.g., McBrien, *Lives of the Popes,* pp. 203ff. and 398.

11. Regarding Francis's religious upbringing, the story of the piety of FA's mother, much embellished over the centuries, began with a brief, religious introduction to the second of four works by FA's contemporary the Franciscan friar Thomas of Celano, who joined the fraternity about 1213 and who certainly knew FA; he was the first to write about the saint and the early days of his followers. Before proceeding to a brief observation on Celano's treatments of FA's mother, some historico-critical remarks are in order concerning Celano.

Celano's writings are valuable and fascinating, but even a cursory reading of them reveals that they cannot be considered biography or history in our modern sense. The (supposedly objective) goals of 21st-century biography were unknown to the medieval writer; the purpose, in this case, was to celebrate a man who was regarded as a saint even during his lifetime. Hence Celano used eyewitness and secondhand accounts, interweaving them with literary and liturgical sources and the didactic traditions of writings about the saints. His work, in other words, has a deliberately moral and instructional sensibility and purpose.

With that understood, it is critical to add that Celano certainly includes important and accurate facts, deeds and events that situate FA in concrete historical circumstances. But the principles of meticulous literary, linguistic, archaeological and historical scholarship (as well as comparison and contrast with other early Franciscan writings) must be applied to any consideration of these valuable writings of a gifted, devout Franciscan, in order to distinguish (so far as may be possible) actual deeds and words from the flights of devout embellishment commonly exploited by those who loved their subject.

Celano composed four works on FA.

The Life of Saint Francis was commissioned by FA's friend Pope Gregory IX, just before the canonization, in July 1228, and at the same time Gregory called for the construction of a basilica in FA's honor. *The Life* was completed in about six months and approved by the pope in early 1229. It is a work of its time and place, written in the style of contemporary hagiography—to praise the subject and to edify the reader, to justify the maintenance and growth of the Franciscan Order and its superiors and to portray FA as a prophet, the perfect imitator of Jesus, the ideal founder of a new religious Order and, of course, a great saint.

Celano brilliantly composes poetic passages that link FA to both the ancient Christian traditions of the saints and to the Church of his time. *The Life of Saint Francis* will be cited in this book as 1C, with the numbered section following. It has been newly translated from the medieval Latin and published in *FA:ED* I, pp. 171–308.

Celano's second work, *The Legend for Use in the Choir*, an abbreviated version of 1C divided into nine brief paragraph selections, was completed in 1230. A legend, in the medieval ecclesiastical and monastic sense, was literally *legenda:* something that was *to be read* aloud—in this case, when the friars sang and prayed the psalms and prayers of the Divine Office on the saint's feast day and during the ensuing week. It may be found in *FA:ED* I, pp. 319–26.

In 1244, Celano was asked by his Franciscan brothers to compile a third book, and the result was a collection of anecdotes and stories that were circulating about FA that had not been included in 1C. The result was *The Remembrance of the Desire of a Soul,* which depends not only on 1C but also on other early sources such as *AP, LP* and *L3C,* also important documents to be cited in this book. Celano's title was inspired by Isaiah 26, 8: "Your name and your remembrance are the desire of my soul." This work, completed before the summer of 1247, may be found in *FA:ED* II, pp. 233–393; it is cited in this book as 2C, with the number of the chapter following. Its editors rightly identify it as "a piece of spiritual literature . . . [that] must be read in the context of the historical milieu of the middle of the thirteenth century" (p. 237).

Celano's fourth and final work on FA was *The Treatise on the Miracles,* a schematic, inspirational account of 157 wonders supposedly worked by FA during his life and after his death. One-third of it is drawn from Celano's three earlier works. It was completed by 1252, but the complete work was never published until 1995; the translation may be found in *FA:ED* II, pp. 397–468. It is designated herein as 3C.

Brother Thomas of Celano died in 1260, at about the age of 70—on October 4, the feast of FA. He is widely held as the author of another famous work, the anthem "Dies Irae," that terrifyingly picturesque meditation on the end of the world and the last judgment. For centuries, the "Dies Irae" was part of the Requiem Mass and was often set to music—by Mozart and Verdi, among others. It is not likely that many people mourn its absence at funerals today.

Regarding Pica (whom Celano does not name), she is described in 2C-1 in the traditional style of a saint's mother—she has, for example, "a prophetic spirit" and foresees her son's glorious destiny (*FA:ED* II, p. 243). It should be noted that this much softens the picture of the mother given in 1C, where—although she is not as harsh with FA as her husband—there is no mention of maternal piety, only of maternal instinct; both parents "reared him to arrogance . . . indulgently and carelessly" (1C-1, *FA:ED* I, p. 183).

CHAPTER TWO

16. "It is difficult to grasp": From the entry for August 20, the feast of Saint Bernard, *Butler's Lives of the Saints,* vol. 8/August, p. 199.

18. On FA's early education, see, e.g., Octavian Schmucki, O.F.M. Cap. (trans. Ignatius McCormick, O.F.M. Cap.), "Divine Praise and Meditation According to the Teaching and Example of St. Francis of Assisi," *GR* 4, no. 1 (n.d.): 25–26; Marino Bigaroni, O.F.M. (trans. Lori Pieper, S.F.O.), "The Church of San Giorgio in Assisi and the First Expansion of the Medieval City Walls," *GR* 8, no. 1 (1994): 96–98.

18. On the level of FA's Latin, see Leonhard Lehmann, O.F.M. Cap., "The Man Francis as Seen in His Letters," *GR* 5, no. 2 (1991): 159. It is not irrelevant to add that Francis's mistakes in grammar, spelling and syntax help to authenticate his writings; they are valuable criteria for establishing the original wording of his writings.

18. "written in bad Latin" (*per litteram, in qua fuit falsum Latinum*): Laureilhe, cited in Micò, "The Spirituality of St. Francis: The Gospel Life," p. 284; see also the Hermann translation of Eccleston.

18. "a man of very little education" (*homo valde parum litteratus*): Quoted in Oktavian [sic] Schmucki, O.F.M. Cap., "St. Francis's Level of Education," *GR* 10, no. 2 (1996): 168.

19. On the Bible in the Middle Ages, see Micò, "The Spirituality of St. Francis: The Gospel Life," p. 284; Cook and Herzman, pp. 3–28.

20. "A soldier who": Hippolytus of Rome, *The Apostolic Tradition*, in Deiss, p. 53.

20. The life of Martin of Tours is compelling summarized in *Butler's*, November/vol. 11, pp. 83–87.

20. "I was naked": Matthew 25, 36.

20. "Saul, Saul": Acts 9, 4.

22. On FA's first contact with troubadours during his childhood visits to France, see Lázaro Iriarte, O.F.M. Cap., "Francis of Assisi and the Evangelical Movements of His Time, *GR* 12, no. 2 (1998): 170. The article was originally a lecture delivered at the symposium "Movimenti evangelici nel Medioevo: Pietro Valdo e Francesco d'Assisi," sponsored by the Institute of Historical and Theological Studies of Caserta on December 15, 1995.

24. "vastly different": *The Legend of the Three Companions* (hereafter *L3C*) dates from 1241–1247. The trio identify themselves as Brothers Leo, Angelo and Rufino, who were close companions of FA. This and the *Assisi Compilation* and *The Anonymous of Perugia* provide facts and insights not found in Celano and other early accounts, and are lively, indispensable sources. Despite scholarly disputes over the dating of the earliest incomplete manuscripts of these works, it becomes clearer each year that they are invaluable complements to our knowledge. See the introduction to *L3C* in *FA:ED* II, pp. 61–65; the selections at this point in the text are from *L3C*-2, p. 68.

25. The height of FA was gauged when his tomb was opened and his skeleton examined in 1978; see, e.g., Giandomenico, pp. 40–41. Celano's description is in 1C-81; see *FA:ED* I, p. 253.

CHAPTER THREE

27. "in sin": The Latin is clear: *cum essem in peccatis* ("when I was in a state of sin"). The short *Testamentum* of FA, as it has been called, was probably dictated at different times during his last agonizing weeks. The sense of "testament" is probably not that of a last will, for he had no material goods to leave; rather, it is the old Latin idea of *testamentum* as a covenant, which FA believed he had received from God and shared with his companions. The text may be found in *FA:ED* I, pp. 124–27.

27. "the seductions of the world": Pope Gregory IX, *Mira circa nos*—the document promulgating the canonization of FA in July 1228. See *FA:ED* I, pp. 565–69.

27. "indulgently and carelessly": 1C-1, in *FA:ED* I, pp. 182–84. The editors comment that "the literary tradition of the Middle Ages and the strong influence of [the converted sinner] Saint Augustine of Hippo [who died in 430] on medieval hagiography prompted Thomas to stress the power of evil operative upon the young Francis." This argument, reiterated by Franciscan partisans, often implies Francis's innocence of the charges enumerated by his companions and may be too subtle to be credible. Francis's louche life is described in every one of the oldest sources—and in the hymns his own friars sang soon after his death. It is probably better to accept Celano at his word; he would not have found it easy to write these things of a saint (especially with some of the Bernardones still alive), but neither could he omit what was obviously common knowledge.

27. "steeped in luxury": *Satiatus erat deliciis mundi et delectationibus carnis . . . fuit enim magnus peccator.* These phrases are found in the fifth and eighth sermons of Cardinal Eudes, who delivered 10 on FA; they have been published in "Sermons franciscains du Cardinal Eudes de Châteauroux," *Études franciscaines* 29 and 30 (1913).

27. "a deceitful huckster": Henry of Avranches, *The Versified Life of Saint Francis*, a dramatic poem written between 1230 and 1235; it recasts and supplements much of the information of 1C. Published in *FA:ED* I, pp. 423–520.

27. *"Hic vir in vanitatibus"*: These lines were composed for a liturgical Office of FA by Julian of Speyer between 1228 and 1232. See *Analecta Franciscana* 10 (1941): 379. For the bowdlerized version, a few lines later, see O. Oliger, O.F.M., "De ultima mutatione officii Sancti Francisci," *Archivum Franciscanum Historicum* 1 (1908): 45–49.

28. The *legenda* (documents to be read aloud) and sermons of Saint Bonaventure (general minister, or superior, of the Franciscans from 1257 to 1273) were composed between 1255 and 1267. See *FA:ED* II, pp. 495–765. Bonaventure's writings are interpretive theological and mystical works that recast earlier sources so that everything in FA's life has a religious, didactic and biblical purpose. As Octavian Schmucki has written, we must beware of "Bonaventure's general untrustworthiness in handling historical data" ("The Passion of Christ in the Life of St. Francis of Assisi," *GR* 4, supplement [n.d.]: 43).

29. "Because of the senseless waste": Julian of Speyer, *The Life of Saint Francis*, was completed by 1235; he died at about the age of 60 in 1250. Although he became a Franciscan, the German-born Julian never met Francis. In addition to the *Life* he composed a liturgical Office (see above, the last note for p. 27 above). Inspired by, but not a mere repetition of, Celano's text, Speyer's *Life* provided a clear and direct account aimed at the religious formation of young friars. It has been published in *FA:ED* I, pp. 363–420; this excerpt appears on p. 370.

29. On the *tripudianti*, see, e.g., AF, pp. 131–36; Allen and Allen, p. 16. On Francis's role as leader, AF is confident but bases his conclusion *tout court* on "some of the documents in the Assisi archives." Because AF devoted virtually his entire adult life to a study of those archives (he was mayor for many years), he can be trusted; in this case, however, one wishes for more detail.

29. On the feast of Saint Nicholas, see Melchiore Roberti, "La cerimonia dell'Episcopello a Padova," *Archivio delle storie italiane* 31 (1903): 172–75, and, e.g., AF, pp. 98–99.

30. "So pleases me": From *The Litany of Love* by Vidal of Toulouse; see John Holland Smith, p. 25.

31. "Time for gladness": From the *Carmina Burana;* see Bishop, p. 292.

31. The tale of the nightingale, written before 1190, has been translated by Patricia Terry; see Bishop, pp. 298–99.

32. On the spread of the legend of Roland into Italy, see Heywood, pp. 6–13, and G. Vitaletti, "Tradizioni carolingie e leggende ascetiche raccolte presso Fonte Avellana," *Archivum Romanicum* 3 (1919): 409–510, and 5 (1921): 313–89.

32. "the emperor Charles, Roland and Oliver": see *FA:ED* III, p. 257. The early-14th-century manuscript of the *Mirror of Perfection* (hereafter, *MP*) exists in two forms, today referred to as the Lemmens and the Sabatier editions, the work of those two scholars in, respectively, 1901 and 1928. It is composed of materials taken from *AC,* Celano and other sources. See *FA:ED* III, pp. 207–13.

33. "my Knights of the Round Table": *LP*-71; see Habig, p. 1047. This work is most likely a redaction of *L3C* and was essentially a written collection of originally oral anecdotes about FA that, although codified only in 1311, had obviously been one of Celano's sources. The English translation of 1991 (in Habig) is the work of Paul Oligny.

33. "If that poor man": 1C-17 (see *FA:ED* I, p. 195); see the parallels in *L3C*-3 (*FA:ED* II, p. 69) and *AP* (*FA:ED* II, pp. 34–35). The last work, from the city whose name it bears, dates from 1240–1241; discovered in 1671, it has been seriously studied only since the 1970's. This work stresses the growth of the early Franciscan fraternity. As the editors of *FA:ED* have indicated, less than half of the material is found in 1C; the remainder is new, evidently based on the shared recollections of FA's friends and religious brothers. In English, it is included in *FA:ED* II, pp. 31–58.

34. On the concept of chivalry, see Huizinga, pp. 56ff. His translator (Hopman) neatly found the right phrase when he defined chivalry as "an aesthetic ideal assuming the appearance of an ethical ideal" (p. 58). For general historical treatment of the Assisi uprising of 1198, see, e.g., AF, pp. 2ff., 18–19, 23–31, 53–55, 66ff.; and Brown, *The Roots of St. Francis,* pp. 137–45. Engelbert provides important corrective summaries in Appendix VI, pp. 420–26.

36. "Nothing cheers my soul": A few lines of the original are provided by AF, p. 140.

36. On the battle of Collestrada, see AF, pp. 153–57.

36. On the prison, see Bonazzi, pp. 261ff. *L3C* was the first to state that FA was imprisoned with knights, not with ordinary citizens, but there is no evidence for class distinctions in the Perugian prison. The place in which FA was held was probably on the site of the present Palazzo del Capitano del Popolo.

37. Regarding the medical detective work and the conclusion that FA endured lifelong consequences of malaria contracted in 1203, see the array of international studies cited by Octavian Schmucki, O.F.M. Cap. (trans. Sergius Wroblewski, O.F.M.), "The Illnesses of St. Francis of Assisi Before His Stigmatization," *GR* 4, no. 3 (1990): 31–61. The reader will note that Professor Schmucki sometimes writes as Octavian and sometimes as Oktavian. What remains constant, however, is his unfailingly meticulous and significant scholarship, always translated by a team of equally gifted colleagues.

37. "would not have been possible": Küng, p. 91.

38. "Many priests": The excerpt from the decree of the Fourth Lateran Council (1215) may be found, e.g., in AF, p. 254.

38. "When he had recovered": 1C-4; see *FA:ED* I, p. 185.

39. "I was very frail": *LP*-76; see Habig, p. 1051.

39. "began to regard himself ": 1C-4, see *FA:ED* I, p. 185.

39. "It is difficult": Ibid.

39. "prepared clothing": *L3C*-5; see *FA:ED* II, p. 70. The identity of the nobleman is unknown to us, although *L3C* understood the word "gentile" as a proper name; the original source, probably represented in *AP*-5, is simply a designation of a gentleman: *unde disposuit ad comitem gentilem:* "he arranged to join up with a noble [or gentle] count."

40. "I know that I will become": *FA:ED* II, p. 71.

40. "My soul to God": AF, p. 180.

40. "Who can do more good": The dialogue is cited in *L3C*-6; see *FA:ED* II, p. 71; see also *AP*-6.

41. The dialogue with a voice that Francis recalled from his time of illness in Spoleto is shaped by the earliest sources to reflect the beginning of Saint Paul's conversion. Thrown to the ground on the way to Damascus, Paul hears a voice: "Get up and enter the city, and you will be told what to do" (Acts 9, 6).

41. On dreams in the Bible, see, e.g., McKenzie, pp. 204–05, and Janet Meyer Everts, "Dreams in the NT and Greco-Roman Literature," in Freedman, vol. 2, pp. 231–32.

41. FA's return from Spoleto to Assisi must have occurred before June 1205, for that was the date of the death of the leader of the Apulian troops, Walter of Brienne, whom FA and the nobleman were going to join.

42. "What were you thinking about": *L3C*-7; see *FA:ED* II, p. 72. FA's response is interpreted by 1C-7 and *L3C*-7 and 13 (and many Franciscans later) to be a prophetic statement: FA will espouse poverty as his noble lady. This is a good example of *post hoc ergo propter hoc:* in light of his subsequent life, a flippant remark was retrojected and interpreted on a deeper level. Surely FA had no such symbolic or prophetic intent when he replied to his tormentor.

CHAPTER FOUR

44. For the history and description of the church of San Damiano, see AF, pp. 29, 213–16. The crucifix has been preserved to this day, and may be seen in the Basilica of Saint Clare in Assisi.

44. "different from when": 2C-10; see *FA:ED* II, p. 249. The event is also described in *L3C*-13; see *FA:ED* II, p. 76.

45. On FA at San Damiano, there are many thoughtful commentaries. See, e.g., Leonard Lehmann, O.F.M. Cap. (trans. Paul Barrett, O.F.M. Cap.), "Prayer Before the Crucifix," *GR* 11, no. 1 (1997), esp. 2–5; Julio Micò (trans. Paul Barrett, O.F.M. Cap.), "The Spirituality of St. Francis: Francis's Image of God," *GR* 7, no. 2 (1993): 129–49; and Octavian Schmucki, O.F.M. Cap. (trans. Ignatius McCormick, O.F.M. Cap.), "The Passion of Christ in the Life of St. Francis of Assisi: A Comparative Study of the Sources in the Light of Devotion to the Passion Practiced in His Time," *GR* 4, supplement (1990).

47. "Most High": See *FA:ED* I, p. 40. It is not known for certain how soon after the San Damiano experience FA composed the Prayer Before a Crucifix. Two of the oldest manuscripts of *L3C* place it just a moment before the crucifix speaks to him (*L3C*-13, see *FA:ED* II, p. 76). But the prayer does not exist as an autograph (in his own hand); it was dictated, and so it may come from some time after his first companions joined him.

47. On the subject of conversion, see, e.g., the excellent articles on the subject by Karl Rahner in Rahner, ed.; by Fragomeni in Downey, ed.; by Walter in Komonchak, Collins and Lane, eds.; and by Miller in McBrien, *Encyclopedia of Catholicism*.

48. "He went about doing good": Acts 10, 38.

49. "I beg you": *L3C*-13; see *FA:ED* II, p. 76.

49. "living outrageously": 1C-9; see *FA:ED* I, p. 189.

50. "on pressing family business": 1C-13; see *FA:ED* I, p. 192.

CHAPTER FIVE

51. Regarding Pica's love for Francis, one source refers in this context to her "other children" (*L3C*-9; see *FA:ED* II, p. 73). Some (e.g., Trexler) believe that she had been a widow when Peter married her and that there were children from that first marriage. Only one other son, Angelo, makes a single appearance in FA's later life: whether his father was indeed Peter or another cannot be known.

52. "He no longer falls": *L3C*-19; see *FA:ED* II, p. 79.

53. "all the goods": AF, p. 254.

53. On Guido, bishop of Assisi, see M. Robson, "Assisi, Guido II and Saint Francis," *GR* 12, no. 3 (1998): 255–87.

53. "Your father": *L3C*-19; see *FA:ED* II, p. 80. This famous event is also described in 1C-15 (*FA:ED* I, pp. 193–94) and *AP*-8 (*FA:ED* II, p. 37).

54. On Francis's rejection of worldly things, see, e.g., Cook, p. 41.

54. On the *ars concionandi,* see Raoul Manselli (trans. Patrick Colbourne, O.F.M. Cap, and Edward Hagman, O.F.M. Cap.), "Gesture as Sermon in St. Francis of Assisi," *GR* 6, no. 1 (1992): 37–48. Manselli provides a detailed annotated bibliography on the forms of oratory and on the Italian commune at the time of FA.

57. On conspicuous consumption, see Veblen.

57. There is considerable debate about the time of FA's first journey to Rome. After the final rupture with his family, however, he did place himself for a time under the spiritual direction of the bishop of Assisi, and because the visit to Rome occurred some time between the end of 1205 and early 1206, I have placed the event here; likewise, the incident with the leper. On lepers and leprosy in Europe during the 12th and 13th centuries, see, e.g., G. G. Merlo, "Esperienze religiose e opere assistenziali in un' area di ponte tra XII e XIII secolo," *Annuali di storia pavese* 16–17 (1988): 72–74.

58. The NT account of Jesus healing the leper is found in Mark 1, 40–42; Matthew 8, 2–3; Luke 5, 12–13.

59. "For God's sake": 1C-17; see *FA:ED* I, p. 195.

59. "The Lord gave me": *Testament,* in *FA:ED* I, p. 124. On the importance of caring for lepers in the early Franciscan tradition, see Luciano Canonici (trans. Anthony M. Carrozzo, O.F.M.), "Leper, Leprosarium," *GR* 9, no. 3 (1995): 247–58.

59. "I choose the poverty": Mother Teresa of Calcutta, in her speech accepting the Nobel Peace Prize in Oslo on December 10, 1979.

61. According to *AC*-60 (see *FA:ED* II, pp. 162–62), FA "used to go through the villages and churches in the area around the city of Assisi, proclaiming and preaching to the people that they should do penance. And he would carry a broom to sweep the churches. For blessed Francis was very sad when he entered some church and saw that it was not clean," and he urged the priests to "exercise care and concern in keeping churches clean, as well as altars and everything that pertained to the celebration of the divine mysteries."

61. On FA's labor to restore the three churches, see also *L3C*-21 (*FA:ED* II, p. 81).

61. "You might tell Francis": *L3C*-23; see *FA:ED* II, p. 83.

61. "I left the world": *Testament,* 3; see *FA:ED* I, p. 124.

62. On FA's garb at this time, see 1C-21 (*FA:ED* I, p. 201), *L3C*-25 (*FA:ED* II, p. 84).

62. On the eremitical tradition, see J. Micò, "The Spirituality of St. Francis," *GR* 7, no. 1 (1993), esp. 12–13.

62. "He favored the sign": 3C-3; see *FA:ED* II, p. 402. On the mark of the **T**, see Ezekiel 9, 4 and Revelation, 7, 3. When Pope Innocent III opened the Fourth Lateran Council in 1215, he proclaimed, "We are called to reform our lives, to stand in the presence of God as righteous people. God will know us by the sign of the TAU marked on our foreheads." See also Octavian Schmucki, O.F.M. Cap. (trans. Ignatius McCormick, O.F.M. Cap.), "The Passion of Christ in the Life of St. Francis of Assisi: A Comparative Study of the Sources in the Light of Devotion to the Passion Practiced in His Time," *GR* 4, supplement (1990): 13–17.

63. "Blessed are the poor": Matthew 5, 3.

64. "He inflicted": *L3C*-14; see *FA:ED* II, p. 76.

64. "He rarely or hardly ever": 1C-51; see *FA:ED* I, p. 227; see also pp. 219, 221.

66. The incident with the highwaymen and the attendant dialogue is found in 1C-16, *FA:ED* I, p. 194.

CHAPTER SIX

67. On the history of Saint Mary of the Angels, the Porziuncula, see, e.g., *FA:ED* I, p. 201n; also Brown, *Franciscan Mystic,* p. 20.

67. The feast of Saint Matthias was celebrated on February 24 until 1969, when the Church calendar transferred it to May 14. The account of FA at the Porziuncula on this date is found in 1C-22 and *L3C*-25; see *FA:ED* I, pp. 201–2, and II, p. 84. It should be noted that the gospel reading assigned for this day in 1208, the Matthean account of Jesus sending out the first disciples, was later changed to another reading when the *Ordo Missae* (the order or schedule of readings for Mass) was revised in the 16th and again in the 20th centuries.

67. "As you go": Matthew 10, 7. 9.

68. "He was no deaf hearer": 1C-22, in *FA:ED* I, pp. 201–2.

68. There is considerable dispute about the original Franciscan habit, how closely it matched FA's own garb, and how it developed over the next century. A fair summary and assessment appears in Octavian Schmucki, O.F.M. Cap. (trans. Ignatius McCormick, O.F.M. Cap.), "The Passion of Christ in the Life of St. Francis of Assisi," *GR* 4, supplement (1990): 60–67.

68. On FA living the Gospel, see, e.g., Julio Micò, O.F.M. Cap., "The Spirituality of St. Francis: The Gospel Life," *GR* 7, no. 3 (1993): 271–99; see also the same author's essay "The Spirituality of St. Francis: Francis's Image of God," *GR* 7, no. 2 (1993): 129–49.

69. "His words were neither": *L3C*-25; see *FA:ED* II, p. 84.

69. "he inspired his listeners . . . preached penance": 1C-23; see *FA:ED* I, p. 202.

69. "May the Lord": 2 Thessalonians 3, 16; compare 1 Thessalonians 5, 22, 24: "May the God of peace himself sanctify you entirely. . . . The one who calls you is faithful, and he will do this."

69. "must be careful": *Later Rule* (1223); see *FA:ED* I, p. 104. On FA at the home of Bernard Quintavalle, the earliest account is probably that of *L3C*-28; see *FA:ED* II, p. 85. But a fuller treatment appears in 2C-15; see *FA:ED* II, pp. 253–54.

72. Despite a lack of scholarly consensus, there is a strong possibility that the missal used by FA and his companions at the Church of San Nicolò is in the collection of the Walters Art Museum, Baltimore.

72. "Go, sell": Mark 10, 21.

72. "Take nothing": Luke 9, 3.

72. "If any want": Matthew 16, 24.

73. "Some declared": *L3C*-34, 35; see *FA:ED* II, pp. 88–89.

73. "You did not pay me": *AP*-12 and 13; see *FA:ED* II, p. 39.

74. "not to look down": *Later Rule* (1223), 11–17; see *FA:ED* I, p. 101.

74. "As you announce": *L3C*-58; *FA:ED* I, p. 102.

74. On the eremitical and cenobitic vocation, see Julio Micò, "Franciscan Poverty," *GR* 11, no. 3 (1997): 269.

76. "It seems to me": *L3C*-35, in *FA:ED* II, p. 89; see also *AP*-17 in *FA:ED* II, p. 41.

76. "After the Lord": *Testament* (1226), 14–19; see *FA:ED* I, p. 125.

76. On the poverty of FA and its relationship to Christian life, see Smith, *Francis of Assisi*, pp. 64–66. Smith's is an odd book with a curiously condescending and even occasionally downright negative view of FA.

77. "I worked with my hands": *Testament*, 20–21; see *FA:ED* I, p. 125.

77. "Go on your way": *AC*-97; see *FA:ED* II, pp. 201–2.

78. "Some people willingly": *AP*-19, 20; see *FA:ED* II, pp. 43, 45.

79. We know very little about FA's early companions—just as the gospels tell us hardly anything of the 12 apostles. Engelbert (pp. 427–40) has synthesized the scholarship on the first friends of FA.

79. "He instructed": 1C-42; see *FA:ED* I, p. 220—compare 1 John 3, 18: "Let us love—not in word or speech, but in truth and action."

CHAPTER SEVEN

81. "We adore You": *Testament*, 5; see *FA:ED* I, pp. 124–25; see also *L3C*-37 and 1C-45.

83. "not in the usual manner of preaching": Thomas of Split, *Historia pontificia Salonitanorum et Spalatensium*, in *Monumenta Germaniae historica*, 29; see *FA:ED* II, pp. 807–8. See also the second note for p. 54 on p. 226.

83. On the nature of Francis's group, cf. Raoul Manselli: "Francis wanted at most a *fraternitas*." See his essay "Francis of Assisi and Lay People Living in the World: Beginning of the Third Order?" *GR* 11, no. 1 (1997): 46.

84. On the history of monasticism there is, of course, an enormous bibliography. With special relevance to the rise of the Franciscan movement, see Jean Leclercq, "Women's Monasticism in the 12th and 13th Centuries," *GR* 7, no. 2 (1993), esp. 178–81.

84. "other times": 2C-127; see *FA:ED* II, p. 331. See also *AC*-38, in *FA:ED* II, p. 142. Compare *MP*-93, in *FA:ED* III, p. 340. *MP*, dating from 1318, is composed of materials taken from what is now known as the *AC* and other early sources.

85. There is a wide literature on the Cathari. In addition to the standard works on medieval heresy, see, e.g., Brooke and Brooke, pp. 100–103, and Julio Micò, "The Spirituality of St. Francis: The Franciscan Apostolate," *GR* 10, no. 1 (1996): 6–8. An excellent book on the subject is by Lambert (see Bibliography).

88. "Unfortunately, the extremists": Micò, "The Spirituality of St. Francis: The Franciscan Apostolate," p. 8.

88. On Pope Innnocent III, see, e.g., McBrien, *Lives of the Popes,* pp. 209–11, and von Galli, pp. 67–81.

88. On Boniface VIII, McBrien is succinct: "Other popes were more inept and more corrupt, but none made claims for the papacy that were further removed from the spirit of the Apostle Peter, not to mention the Lord himself. . . . Historically naïve and theologically uninformed Catholics continue to cite him today as if his exaggerated claims of papal authority, even over the political realm, are, in fact, consistent with the will of Christ" (*Lives of the Popes,* pp. 232, 435). Visitors to Rome even today can hardly escape the name and image of the imperial Boniface VIII: he set up his likeness everywhere—so ubiquitously, indeed, that some Romans quietly accused him of idolatry.

90. "they did as he said": *AP*-31; *FA:ED* II, p. 48.

90. "and I had this": *Testament,* 15; see *FA:ED* I, p. 125.

91. "Detailed practical guidance": Brooke, *The Coming of the Friars,* p. 34.

91. Cardinal John Colonna's full name was Giovanni Colonna di San Paolo; he was a Benedictine monk attached to the monastery of the Roman Basilica of Saint Paul's Outside the Walls (hence his name).

92. "But Francis refused": 1C-33; *FA:ED* I, p. 212.

92. "If we refuse": Bonaventure, *The Major Legend of Saint Francis* (completed by 1263), 3.9; see *FA:ED* II, p. 547. This is an instance of Bonaventure's inclusion of a precious historical detail.

92. "Your life is too hard": *AP*-34; *FA:ED* II, p. 49. See also *L3C*-46 through 53; *FA:ED* II, pp. 95–99. The accounts of Francis's interviews with John Colonna and Pope Innocent III were much embellished with dreams and visions in subsequent *legenda.* The description here follows the best recent scholarship; see, e.g., AF, von Galli, Schmucki, Micò and Lehmann.

93. "What need have you": O'Sullivan, pp. 19–20.

CHAPTER EIGHT

95. tonsure: In 1972, Pope Paul VI, as part of the sensible liturgical streamlining he supervised, eliminated the tonsure and the ceremonies for all minor orders (porter, lector, exorcist and acolyte). The revised Code of Canon Law of 1983 invites women as well as men to fulfill certain functions of ministry. Some consider this a vague first step toward the inevitable and appropriate priestly ordination of women.

96. On the contrast of FA with Innocent III, see Küng, pp. 99–101.

96. "I want this fraternity": 1C-38; see *FA:ED* I, p. 217.

97. "We were simple": *Testament,* 19; *FA:ED* I, p. 125.

97. On the form and content of FA's early preaching, see Julio Micò, "The Spirituality of St. Francis: The Franciscan Apostolate," *GR* 10, no. 1 (1996): 1–25.

97. "the benefit and edification": *Later Rule* (1223), 9.3; see *FA:ED* I, p. 105.

97. "What we do not completely forgive": From "A Prayer Inspired by the Our Father" which is difficult to date; see *FA:ED* I, p. 159.

98. "Do penance": *Earlier Rule* (1221), 21.3–6; see *FA:ED* I, p. 78. The exhortations bring together texts from Matthew 3, 2 and 6, 14; Luke 3, 8 and 6, 38; and Mark 11, 25.

99. On monastic culture compared to the Franciscan revolution, see, e.g., Regis J. Armstrong, O.F.M. Cap., "Clare of Assisi, the Poor Ladies, and Their Ecclesial Mission in the *First Life* of Thomas of Celano," *GR* 5, no. 3 (1991): 389–424, esp. 419–20; also Dawson, pp. 154–77, and Leclercq.

99. There are considerable problems in attempting to date the origins of the Third Order of Franciscans, those laymen and laywomen who commit to a life of Franciscan values in the world, without vows, ordination or friaries. The most likely thesis is that of a gradual formation of the Third Order, which seems not to have been founded in a specific place or time, and certainly not directly by FA. See Octavian Schmucki, O.F.M. Cap. (trans. Nancy Celaschi, O.S.F.), "The Third Order in the Biographies of St. Francis," *GR* 6, no. 1 (1992): 81–107.

100. "There was a great multitude": This and the following account of FA and the birds may be found in 1C-58 and 59; see *FA:ED* I, pp. 234–35. Julian of Speyer also mentioned it in his *Life of Saint Francis* (about 1235); *FA:ED* I, pp. 396–97, 400–402. The version by the English chronicler Roger Wendover, written very soon after FA's death, is quite different. In his *Flores historiarum* (about 1235), Wendover wrote that the people of Rome "would not listen to him or even be present at his holy exhortations." Francis left the city and on the outskirts found birds of prey which, commanded by FA, listened to him for many hours. This occurred consecutively for three days, and when they heard of it, the Romans brought him back to the city and listened to him again, "and their hearts were softened and changed for the better" (see *FA:ED* I, pp. 599–600).

101. "The wild beasts": Celano, *The Legend for Use in the Choir* (1232); also 2C-166 and 165: see *FA:ED* I, p. 322, and II, p. 354. On the rabbit caught in a trap, the captured fish, the lambs destined for slaughter, the worms and bees, see 1C-60, 61, 77, 79, 80; *FA:ED* I, pp. 235–51.

102. "he dwelt securely": On Saint Aventin of Troyes, William of Malavalle, Saint Girard of Saint-Aubin d'Angers, Caesarius of Heisterbach et al., see William J. Short, O.F.M., "Hagiographical Method in Reading Franciscan Sources: Stories of Francis and Creatures in Thomas of Celano's *First Life* (58–61)," *GR* 4, no. 3 (1990): 63–89. On the desert fathers and the symbol of tamed nature, see, e.g., Daniélou, p. 9.

103. Frugoni, p. 82, suggests *Les Livres du roy Modus et de la royne Ratio* as a parallel for the animal stories in Celano et al.

103. Clark, *Civilization*, discusses the iconography of birds, their symbolism and use in heraldry on pp. 71–72.

103. On FA's association with the poor, see Byrne, pp. 10–11.

104. On the time at Rivo Torto, see, e.g., 1C-42 to 44 and *L3C*-55; *FA:ED* I, pp. 220–22, and *FA:ED* II, p. 98. Engelbert (p. 468, n. 1) summarizes the debate over whether FA moved to Rivo Torto before or (more likely) after his sojourn in Rome.

104. "Well, it's easier to get": 1C-42; *FA:ED* I, p. 220.

104. "Woe to those": From *The Admonitions*, which is difficult to date; see *FA:ED* I, p. 136.

105. "I'm dying of hunger": *AC*-50; *FA:ED* II, pp. 149–50; for a fresh English rendering and extended commentary, see Raoul Manselli, "We Who Were with Him: A Contribution to the Franciscan Question," *GR* 14, supplement (2000): 58–65.

105. "My brothers": *FA:ED* II, pp. 149–50.

106. "If he could eat": *AC*-53; *FA:ED* II, p. 152. According to this text, Francis picked the fruit himself and shared it with the sick brother.

106. "Our brother the body": *LP*-96, in Habig, vol. 2, p. 1073. The translation is from Engelbert, pp. 132–33.

106. "He insisted that it was": 2C-22; *FA:ED* II, p. 259.

106. "Listen, do not be troubled": 1C-50; *FA:ED* I, p. 226.

107. "unorganized and unruly tramps": de la Bedoyere, p. 104.

109. "Go on": 1C-44 and L3C-55; see *FA:ED* I, pp. 221–22, and II, pp. 99–100.

CHAPTER NINE

111. "Dear brothers": *The Deeds of Blessed Francis and His Companions,* 5–20 (hereafter cited as *Deeds*). This work, attributed to the friar Ugolino Boniscambi, is also called (after its Italian title) *The Little Flowers of Saint Francis;* it dates, in its original form, from about 1328–1337. See *FA:ED* III, p. 447.

111. "Let's give this": 2C-190; see *FA:ED* II, pp. 368–69; see also *AC*-61.

112. "Why you": *Deeds*, 10–11; see *FA:ED* III, p. 458.

113. "Murderers like you": The event is variously recorded: see *FA:ED* III, p. 66, and the parallels to *MP*-66 found in *AC*-115 and *LP*-90. There is some variation in the accounts, especially regarding Angelo Tarlati, but Engelbert (pp. 140–42) is convinced of that friar's primary role in the incident.

114. Juniper and Giles are two of the most colorful figures among the early Franciscans; their exploits exist in various literary forms (*AP*, for example) and have been compiled in the *Analecta Franciscana* series, vols. III and IV (1885–1926). See also Engelbert, pp. 144–52, and his secondary references on pp. 434–35.

116. On Rufino, see *Little Flowers*, chaps. 29–31; *FA:ED* III, pp. 617–22. Until this accurate new translation (the work of Franciscan scholars), editors have ignored this text or used coy Victorian euphemisms for the verb "to shit." But in fact FA used the Italian verb *cacare*, borrowed from the same word in Latin (a derivation from the Greek verb *kakkao*), which means "to shit" (hence the modern "caca"), and so it is rightly translated on p. 618.

117. The circular letter FA dictated to Leo in the spring of 1211 is the *Earlier Exhortation to the Brothers and Sisters of Penance* (formerly designated the *First Version of the Letter to the Faithful*); it was certainly composed between 1209 and 1215, but the most likely date may be after FA's Lenten retreat in 1211. For the text, see *FA:ED* I, pp. 41–44.

CHAPTER TEN

121. On the Children's Crusade, which was very likely nothing of the sort, see the important article by Peter Raedts (trans. David Nicholas), "The Children's Crusade of 1212," *Journal of Medieval History* 3 (1977): 279–324. See also G. Miccoli, "La crociata dei fanciulli," *Studi medievali,* third series, no. 2 (1961): 407–43.

122. For background on Clare, there are extended bibliographies in, e.g., Armstrong and Brady; Fortini; Habig; and *Butler's,* vol. 8, p. 89. The most thorough contemporary source is *The Legend of Saint Clare,* probably written by Thomas of Celano shortly after her death; it is in the 64-volume *Acta sanctorum* (begun in 1643) and has been edited and translated by Brady, *Legend.* The best modern texts are by Carney and Peterson.

123. "lovely to look at": Thomas of Celano, *The Legend of Saint Clare,* p. 4; cited in AF, p. 337.

123. "wanted her to make": Ibid.

123. "She saved the food": *Process of Canonization,* XX, 3, cited in "St. Clare: The Eight Hundredth Anniversary of Her Death," *GR* 6, no. 2 (1992): 151. (The title contains an error: the article clearly commemorates the 800th anniversary of Clare's *birth,* in 1193, not her death; she died in 1253.)

123. "to enlighten my heart": Clare of Assisi, *Testament,* in Armstrong and Brady, p. 228.

125. "must not be left": Idung of Prüfening, in Leclercq, "Women's Monasticism."

125. For FA on the sin of Adam, see *The Admonitions–*II, in *FA:ED* I, p. 129.

126. It is unlikely that Clare's profession of vows and subsequent enclosure could have occurred without the approval of Bishop Guido, or that FA would have unilaterally assumed the privilege of so directing her. Not only was the Offreduccio family highly placed in Assisi; the matter also concerned Guido's jurisdiction. Had FA not turned to the bishop, Clare's family would have been all the more convinced they were right to demand her return. Furthermore, there is the detail of Guido coming down to Clare in the cathedral on Palm Sunday morning and placing a palm branch in her hand—a gesture that may indeed have implied his approval of what FA was about to do. Finally, we should note that it was Guido who put San Damiano at the disposal of Clare and her companions. See Michael Robson, "Assisi, Guido II and Saint Francis," *GR* 12, no. 3 (1998): 255–87, esp. 278–79, and A. P. Tini, "La culla delle Damianite e Guido vescovo," *Miscellanea Franciscana* 14 (1912): 33–37. There are, as we might expect, discrepancies in the early sources; much of this has been sorted out by Luigi Padovese, O.F.M. Cap. (trans. Madonna Balestrieri, O.S.F.), "Clare's Tonsure: Act of Consecration or Sign of Penance?" *GR* 6, no. 1 (1992): 67–80.

126. On the Rules gradually constructed by the Friars Minor and the Poor Ladies, see Pierre Brunette, O.F.M. (trans. Edward Hagman, O.F.M. Cap.), "Clare and Francis: A Saintly Friendship," *GR* 11, no. 2 (1997): 185–227, esp. 195.

127. On the difficulties Clare faced in establishing her own Rule for her nuns, see Moorman, pp. 38–39. In 1219, Cardinal Ugolino drafted a Rule that was intended to supercede FA's basic guidelines. Ugolino's Rule was essentially the Benedictine one, and Clare was deeply distressed, for there was nothing specifically Franciscan about it: private possessions were forbidden as inconsistent with the vow of poverty, but community property (as in the Benedictine tradition) was not prohibited. Furthermore, the strict rule of cloister put an end to Clare's hopes for an active ministry among the poor. Clare's anguish was all the more poignant because at this time FA was in Egypt and Syria. She finally prevailed, however, and in 1253 Ugolino (by then Pope Gregory IX) allowed her own Rule, with the so-called privilege of poverty that was more in keeping with Franciscanism—just before her death. The Rule became, however, the norm for Poor Clare convents worldwide.

129. On Jacoba Settisoli, see *FA:ED* II, p. 122n.

130. On FA's desire for martyrdom, see, e.g., Octavian Schmucki, O.F.M. Cap. (trans. Ignatius McCormick, O.F.M. Cap.), "The Passion of Christ in the Life of St. Francis of Assisi," *GR* 4, supplement (1990): 72–73.

131. "Always eager": 1C-55; see *FA:ED* I, p. 229.

132. Regarding the food and wine FA received as he was returning to Italy, Celano reworked the basic, simple oral tradition. He joined the biblical account of both the seafaring Jonah and the miracle Jesus wrought with loaves and fishes, and thus wrote that FA's food and wine were miraculously multiplied for the entire shipboard population, and the ship was saved from destruction through his mere presence. See 1C-55, ibid.

CHAPTER ELEVEN

133. "in part mere youths": Boncampagno of Signa, *Rhetorica antiqua,* cited in *FA:ED* I, p. 590.

134. "the ambivalence felt": Ibid. In addition to the three editors of this three-volume series (see Bibliography), there were 13 translators, contributors and consultants on the project; their names appear in each volume.

134. "Those brothers of mine": 2C-195; see *FA:ED* II, p. 372.

134. "We must honor all theologians": *Testament,* 13; see *FA:ED* I, p. 125.

134. "he considered doctors of sacred theology": 2C-163; see see *FA:ED* II, p. 352.

135. "He sought out": 2C-94; see *FA:ED* II, p. 309.

135. "He made himself insensible": 1C-91, 71, 103; *FA:ED* I, pp. 243, 261, 273.

136. "He did this so devoutly": The entire report of this event and the Italian lyric were presented (probably based on an eyewitness telling by Leo) in *Deeds*, IX; see *FA:ED* III, p. 453. The Johannine text is 16, 20.

137. The original, Latin text of the legal document transferring ownership of Mount La Verna (in Latin, Alverna) contains this key sentence: *Orlandus Clusii, comes inter milites Imperatoris strenuissimus miles, et doctorum pater, oretenus dederit, donaverit atque concesserit libere et absque nulla exceptione Fratri Francisco, ejusque sociis fratribus, tam prasentibus quam futuris, Alvernae montem, ita ut praedictus Pater Franciscus, ejusque fratres ibi habitare possint.* The complete document, which was drawn up for the Order on July 9, 1274, by Orlando's sons, has been reprinted in Jörgensen, pp. 313–14; an English translation appears in *FA:ED* III, pp. 801–3. It is dated May 8, 1213—*anno Domino MCCXIII, die octava Maji,* in the medieval Latin.

137. "You should go on": *Fioretti*, 16, and *Deeds*, 16; see *FA:ED* III, pp. 592, 468–69.

138. On Islamic laws against preaching Christianity, see, e.g., Kajetan Esser, "Melius catholice observemus," *Werkbuch zur Regel des hl. Franziskus* (Wurl: Franziskanischer Geistigkeit, 1955).

138. "But Francis was so carried away": 1C-56; see *FA:ED* I, p. 230.

138. "My head was spinning": 2C-64; *FA:ED* I, p. 289. On this subject, see Octavian Schmucki, O.F.M. Cap. (trans. Sergius Wroblewski, O.F.M.), "The Illnesses of St. Francis of Assisi Before His Stigmatization," *GR* 4, no. 3 (1990): 31–61.

139. "If people sent him": 2C-175; see *FA:ED* II, p. 359.

140. "infirmities of the stomach": 2C-96; see *FA:ED* II, p. 311. There are dozens of references in *AC* to Francis's lifelong frailty and his various illnesses.

140. "He inflicted": *L3C*-14 and 22; see *FA:ED* II, pp. 76 and 81. See also *A Mirror of the Perfection* (Sabatier edition), 18; *FA:ED* III, p. 269.

140. "Francis lacked only": Giles of Assisi, quoted in O'Sullivan, p. 134.

140. "Why are you sad": *AC*-120; see *FA:ED* II, p. 230.

141. "We adore you": *Testament*, 5; *FA:ED* I, p. 125. The Latin text is: *Adoramus, te, Domine Jesu Christe, et ad omnes ecclesias tuas, quae sunt in toto mundo, et benedicimus tibi, quia per sanctam crucem tuam redimisti mundum.*

141. On the importance of mercy in the life and teaching of FA, see C. Bazarra, O.F.M. Cap., "Francis the Teacher," *Cuadernos franciscanos* 26 (1992): 130–36.

142. *AC*-49 and 2C-148 to 150 mention that FA and Dominic Guzman met at the Fourth Lateran Council, praised each other and outdid each other in acting humbly. These anecdotes are repeated in *The Lives of the Brethren* by the Dominican friar Gerard de Frachet (about 1257–1260) and in the *Golden Legend* of Jacopo de Voragine (1255–1267). A lively scholarly debate continues over whether the meeting between the two founders actually occurred or is a sort of moral fable call-ing for unity between Franciscans and Dominicans, who were much in conflict after the deaths of Dominic, in 1221, and of Francis, five years later. Moreover, *AC* pre-sented Dominic as telling bystanders, "Other religious should follow this man Francis, as his holiness is so perfect"—an endorsement much needed when *AC* was composed.

143. "To reduce the chills": Cited in a monograph by A. Pazzini, *Le pietre preziose nella storia della medicina et nella leggenda* (Rome, 1939). Also of interest is Thomas of Cantimpré, *Liber de natura rerum*, book 1, no. 33.

144. "encountered a great deal": James of Vitry, *Letter I,* cited in *FA:ED* I, pp. 579–80.

145. According to the English chronicler Thomas of Eccleston (writing, from about 1232 to 1258, a history of Franciscans in Britain), FA was present at the deathbed of Innocent III in Perugia (Eccleston, p. 95). This detail is found nowhere else and is of doubtful authenticity, especially in light of FA's poor health that year and the suddenness of the pope's demise.

145. On the sending of friars outside Italy, see Jordan of Giano's *Chronicle* (1262), in Hermann.

145. The account of the friars' linguistic fiasco in Germany is found in Jordan of Giano's *Chronicle,* translated in Hermann.

146. "Let them remember": *Earlier Rule,* IV. This document was written in 1220–1221 but was based on principles articulated in the (now lost) proposal FA made to Innocent III in 1209 at the Lateran. See *FA:ED* I, p. 66.

146. "This Order is rapidly": Jacques de Vitry, *Letter VI* (1220) and *Historia occi-dentalis* (1221/1225); see *FA:ED* I, pp. 580–85.

147. "spiritually help one": *Earlier Rule,* IV; *FA:ED* I, pp. 67ff. *The Rule for Her-mitages* is translated in *FA:ED* I, pp. 61–62.

148. "advised him": 1C-75; *FA:ED* I, p. 247.

148. "Brother, I do not want": *MP*-65; see *FA:ED* III, p. 310.

150. "I preach to my people": 2C-147; see *FA:ED* II, p. 342.

150. "very dirty chalices": *Exhortations to the Clergy* (written before 1219), 5.11; see *FA:ED* I, pp. 52–53.

CHAPTER TWELVE

153. "He was annoyed": 2C-57; see *FA:ED* II, pp. 285–86. It is not possible to confirm the claims of some later and less reliable sources that Dominic Guzman (later Saint Dominic), founder of the Order of Preachers, came to this Pentecost Chapter to meet and honor FA.

153. "We want you": This and FA's speech following are cited, e.g., in *MP*-68; see *FA:ED* III, pp. 313–14.

154. "Who are you": *Deeds,* IX; see *FA:ED* III, p. 455.

155. On the Fifth Crusade, see Powell; see also Bernard McGinn, "*Iter Sancti Sepulchri:* The Piety of the First Crusaders," in Lackner and Philip, esp. pp. 38–41, and Thomas C. Van Cleve, "The Fifth Crusade," in Setton, pp. 377–428.

155. "when bitter and long battles": 1C-57; see *FA:ED* I, p. 231.

155. "We beseech and exhort": From the papal document *Cum dilecti, FA:ED* I, p. 558.

155. On the siege of Damietta, see, e.g., AF, pp. 395–439; Van Cleve, "The Fifth Crusade," pp. 397–428; and Powell, pp. 157–73.

155. On the historical significance of Pelagio Galvani and his policies, see, e.g., Grousset, vol. III, pp. 235ff.

156. "foster honor": *A Letter to the Rulers of the People* (1220); see *FA:ED* I, p. 59.

157. "was immediately confronted": Van Cleve, "The Fifth Crusade," p. 403.

158. "This battle will not go well": 2C-30; see *FA:ED* II, p. 265.

159. "a simple, uneducated": James of Vitry, *Historia occidentalis,* cited in *FA:ED* I, p. 584.

160. "I wish only": Recalled by FA's companions and included in *AC*-20; see *FA:ED* II, p. 134.

160. On Francis's visit to al-Malik al-Kamil, see 1C-57, in *FA:ED* I, p. 231; *Deeds,* 27, in *FA:ED* III, pp. 490–92; the *Chronicle of Ernoul* (c. 1227), cited in *FA:ED* III, pp. 605–7; and Pipino of Bologna's edition of the chronicle of Bernard the Treasurer (1229/1230), *FA:ED* III, pp. 607–8. James of Vitry is a particularly valuable witness, for he was present at Damietta from 1218 to 1221; he praised the Lesser Brothers but, perhaps because he was not a Franciscan friar, did not easily or indulgently dismiss their faults or miscalculations; see his *Epistolae,* pp. 228ff. Recent translations may also be consulted of his *Letter VI* (1220, the year following the event) in *FA:ED* I, pp. 580–81, and his *Historia occidentalis* (1221–1225, during FA's lifetime), *FA:ED* I, pp. 581–85. See also the *History of the Emperor Eracles* (1229/1231), *FA:ED* I, p. 609; Bonaventure, *The Major Legend* (1260–1263), *FA:ED* II, pp. 603–4; and Basetti-Sani, p. 263, no. 13. For important periodical literature with references, see Golubovich, pp. 1–84, and Martiniano Roncaglia, "Fonte Arabo-Musulmana su S. Francesco in Oriente?" in *Studi franciscani,* third series, vol. 25, no. 50 (1953): 97–106, and his bibliography in n. 207. Also important: Leonard Lemmens, "De S. Francisco Christum praedicante coram Sultano Aegypti," *Archivum Franciscanum Historicum* 19 (1926): 559–78; Martiniano Roncaglia, O.F.M., "S. Francesco d'Assisi in Oriente," *Studi franciscani,* third series, 25 (1953): 97–106; and Grousett, pp. 214–30.

160. Some accounts embellish FA's arrival with descriptions of how he and Illuminatus were seized and beaten before they shouted, "Soldan! Soldan!" and were taken to the sultan. There is also the addition of an event in which FA offers to endure an ordeal by fire to demonstrate God's protection of Christians. Linguistic textual analysis of these passages suggests, however, that these were later insertions composed to provide Francis with at least an ersatz martyrdom, since evidently he and his companion escaped death. Given the unanimous agreement of the sources on the kindness and civility of al-Kamil, it hardly seems likely that he would have risked causing his guests agony and even death.

162. On FA preaching as much to the Christians as to the Muslims, see, e.g., Mayer, p. 212.

164. On the conundrum that FA's way of life was resented by Church and society, see, e.g., Giovanni Miccoli (trans. Paul Barrett, O.F.M. Cap.), "Gospel and Institution," *GR* 11, no. 2 (1997): 113–41, and Joseph Roddy, "The Hippie Saint," in Cunnngham, pp. 3–9.

165. For *A Letter to Brother Anthony of Padua* (1223), see *FA:ED* I, p. 107. See also Hermann Schalück, O.F.M., et al., "Anthony: Man of the Gospel," *GR* 9, no. 2 (1995): 97–124.

166. "From the time he was returning": *MP*-91; see *FA:ED* III, p. 339. See also *AC*-77; *FA:ED* II, p. 180.

167. For the report by Henry of Avranches, see *FA:ED* I, pp. 510–11.

167. On FA's trachoma, see esp. Octavian Schmucki, O.F.M. Cap. (trans. Sergius Wroblewski, O.F.M.), "The Illnesses of St. Francis of Assisi Before His Stigmatization," *GR* 4, no. 3 (1990): 31–61, and "The Illnesses of Francis During the Last Years of His Life," *GR* 13, no. 1 (1999): 21–59.

167. On the incidence of trachoma in Egypt, see A. Santoni, p. 264: "The frequency seems associated with the dry and dusty climate, and is evidenced by the greater number of sick who come to the outpatient clinic during the warm months." See also Robert Mackey, "Salient Facts: Ten Diseases On the Way Out," *New York Times Magazine,* May 6, 2001, p. 36. For their assistance in understanding the medical and ophthalmological details concerning trachoma, I am indebted to John M. Hofbauer, M.D., and Laura E. Fox, M.D.

CHAPTER THIRTEEN

170. On the crisis within the fraternity, see, e.g., Julio Micò (trans. Paul Barrett, O.F.M.), "The Spirituality of St. Francis: Brothers to All," *GR* 8, no. 2 (1994): 141–75; Engelbert, pp. 242–57; Straub, pp. 238–43.

172. "We who were with him": *AC*-11; see *FA:ED* II, p. 126; see also Raoul Manselli (trans. Edward Hagman, O.F.M. Cap.), "We Who Were With Him: A Contribution to the Franciscan Question," *GR* 14, supplement (2000): 43.

173. "You didn't go down": O'Sullivan, p. 29.

173. "From now on": 2C-143; see *FA:ED* II, p. 340.

174. "After I resigned the office": *AC*-112; see *FA:ED* II, p. 219–20.

174. "I could not visit": *Later Admonition and Exhortation to the Brothers and Sisters of Penance* (1220); see *FA:ED* I, pp. 45–51.

174. "Have we anything": 2C-91 and *AC*-93; see *FA:ED* II, pp. 306 and 196.

175. "Strip the Virgin's altar": 2C-67; see *FA:ED* II, pp. 291–92.

175. "the least Franciscan": Engelbert, p. 248.

175. "the Earlier Rule" is published in *FA:ED* I, pp. 63–86.

176. "Let any brother": Ibid., p. 74.

177. "Who are these": 2C-188; see *FA:ED* II, p. 367.

178. "What do these brothers": *AC*-17; see *FA:ED* II, p. 131.

178. "acted just like": Julio Micò, O.F.M. Cap. (trans. Paul Barrett, O.F.M. Cap.), "The Spirituality of St. Francis: Minority," *GR* 9, no. 2 (1995): 138.

179. On the new forms of Franciscan life, see Julio Micó, "The Spirituality of St. Francis: The Gospel Life" *GR* 7, no. 3 (1993): 271–99.

179. Ugolino, as Pope Gregory IX, later issued the decree *Quo elongati* in 1230, in which (using the papal plural), he wrote, "As a result of the long-standing friendship between [FA] and ourselves, we know his mind more fully. Furthermore, while we held a lesser rank [that is, while Ugolino was a cardinal], we stood by him both as he composed the aforesaid Rule and obtained its confirmation from [Rome]." See *FA:ED* I, p. 571.

179. "When the brothers go through": *Earlier Rule* (1221), 14; see *FA:ED* I, p. 73.

180. "The brother ministers think": *MP*-3; *FA:ED* III, p. 257.

181. "The brothers have": *AC*-112; see *FA:ED* II, p. 220.

182. "This unlettered man's": Thomas of Split, *Historia salonitana*, cited in *FA: ED* II, p. 808. The event is also cited in a sermon of 1265 by Federico Visconti, archbishop of Pisa; see Michael Bihl, "E sermonibus Friderici de Vicecomitibus, archiepiscopus Pisani, de S. Francisco," *Archivum Franciscanum Historicum* 1 (1908): 652–55.

182. "violent lust": 2C-116; see *FA:ED* II, p. 325.

182. "Here, this large one": Ibid.

CHAPTER FOURTEEN

183. "filled with anguish": 2C-115; see *FA:ED* II, p. 324.

184. "is like a corpse": 2C-152; see *FA:ED* II, p. 345.

184. "A time is coming": *AC*-2; *FA:ED* II, p. 118. See also *MP*-70; *FA:ED* III, p. 315.

184. "By You": 2C-156–157; *FA:ED* III, p. 348.

184. "Suppose they all come": *MP*-64; see *FA:ED* III, p. 308.

185. "Oh, I do": 2C-188; see *FA:ED* II, p. 366; also *AC*-44, *FA:ED* II, p. 146.

185. For the paraphrasing and spiritual summary of chapter 23 of the *Earlier Rule*, I have drawn on the splendid scholarship of Leonard Lehmann, O.F.M. Cap., " 'We Thank You': The Structure and Content of Chapter 23 of the *Earlier Rule*," *GR* 5, no. 1 (1991): 53–54.

186. For the story of the first Christmas pageant at Greccio, see 1C-84 to 87; *FA:ED* I, pp. 254–57. A commentary has been written by Leonard Lehmann, O.F.M. Cap. (trans. Paul Barrett, O.F.M. Cap.), "The 'Nativity Psalm,' " *GR* 12, no. 3 (1998): 241–53. On the anti-Cathar element of the event, see Lambert, p. 145.

187. Except for Leo, there is no certainty about FA's companions at La Verna; Bonaventure and Thomas of Eccleston mention Illuminatus and Rufino, while later sources add Angelo and Masseo.

188. "longed to know": 1C-91; see *FA:ED* I, p. 261.

188. "You are the holy Lord": The *Praises of God*, with the blessing of Brother Leo on the reverse, is an authentic (and meticulously authenticated) autograph manuscript by FA; it is preserved in the Basilica of Saint Francis in Assisi. Francis wrote the blessing in the Latin Vulgate translation from the Hebrew of Numbers 6, 24–27: *Benedicat tibi Dominus et custodiat te, ostendat faciem suam tibi et misereatur tui. Convertat vultum suum ad te et det tibi pacem.—Dominus benedicat, F[rater] Leo, te.* Before he bequeathed it to the Church, Leo added years later at the bottom of the parchment: "Blessed Francis wrote with his own hand this blessing for me, Brother Leo. He also made with his own hand this sign Tau on a forehead." See *FA:ED* I, pp. 108–12. On the deciphering of FA's signature, the tau and the forehead, see Octavian Schmucki, O.F.M. Cap. (trans. Ignatius McCormick, O.F.M. Cap.), "The Passion of Christ in the Life of St. Francis of Assisi," *GR* 4, supplement (1990): 18–21. AF and Schmucki provide a critical lexicon and bibliography up to 1959.

189. "Brother Leo: health and peace": The letter is preserved in the cathedral of Spoleto; see *FA:ED* I, p. 122. The authenticity is beyond dispute; see Attilio Bartoli Langeli, "Gli scritti da Francesco: L'autografo di un 'illiteratus,'" in *Frate Francesco d'Assisi*, pp. 101–59.

190. "Among many other": *LP*-93 and *AC*-118; see Habig, p. 1070, and *FA:ED* II, p. 227. 1C-95, although it comes from 1229, is not as early as the oral tradition reflected in *LP* and *AC*. Celano enlarged on the Old Testament images of the winged seraphs in Ezekiel 1, 1 and 8, 1 and in Isaiah 6, 2 when he wrote: "He saw in this vision of God a man having six wings like a seraph [an angel], standing over him, arms extended and feet joined, affixed to a cross. Two of his wings were raised up, two were stretched out over his head as if for flight, and two covered his whole body." Francis, Celano added, was "filled with the greatest awe but could not decide what this vision meant for him. But he was much delighted by the kind and gracious look he saw the seraph give him. His beauty was beyond comprehension, but the fact that he was fixed to the cross thoroughly frightened [Francis]."

190. "I have been crucified": Galatians 2, 19–20.

191. "If any want to become": Mark 8, 34; see Matthew 16, 24–28 and Luke 9, 23–27.

191. "I carry the marks": Galatians 6, 17.

191. "great endurance": 2 Corinthians 6, 4–10.

192. On the matter of the stigmata, see Schmucki; Frugoni; and André Vauchez (trans. Edward Hagman, O.F.M.), "The Stigmata of St. Francis and Its Medieval Detractors," *GR* 13, no. 1 (1999): 61–89.

193. "Not long before his death": "A Letter on the Passing of Saint Francis Attributed to Elias of Assisi," *FA:ED* II, p. 490.

193. On the fact that the Middle Ages would have regarded as nearly blasphemous any comparison of FA with Christ, see Stanislao da Compagnola, "L'angelo
del sesto sigilio e l'alter Christus: Genesi e sviluppo di due temi francescani nei secoli
XIII–XIV," *Studi e ricerche* 1 (1971): 142. On the letter of Elias, see Felice Accrocca
(trans. Robert Stewart, O.F.M.), "Is the 'Encyclical Letter of Brother Elias on the
Transitus of St. Francis' Apocryphal?" *GR* 13, supplement (1999): 19–64.

194. "formed by his own flesh": 1C-113; see *FA:ED* I, p. 280.

194. "No early source worthy": Schmucki, p. 324.

195. On the likelihood that FA's stigmata were in fact wounds caused by the
advance of his leprosy, see J. Schatzlein, O.S.F., and D. P. Sulmasy, O.F.M., "The
Diagnosis of St. Francis: Evidence for Leprosy," *Franciscan Studies* 47 (1987):
181–217. The authors arrived at their conclusions based on meticulous historico-
critical methods, which suggest "a type of leprosy, clinically important, called 'bor-
derline' or 'tuberculoid,' [and] he may have died from complications related to this
underlying infirmity."

195. "What is this": 2C-135; see *FA:ED* II, p. 335.

195. "Whose blood stained": 2C-136; *FA:ED* II, p. 335.

195. On medieval Christ piety, I must express my admiration and gratitude for
the opportunity to have studied, many years ago, under the late Robert E. McNally,
S.J., a first-rate ecclesiastical historian. See esp. McNally, pp. 148–86.

196. On the exceptional signs of piety—voices, visions and such—the classic
work remains that of Underhill; see esp. pp. 266–97.

197. "I am a useless man": *A Letter to the Entire Order* (1225); see *FA:ED* I,
pp. 120 and 119.

198. "Let us begin": 1C-103; see *FA:ED* I, p. 273.

CHAPTER FIFTEEN

199. "Only skin clung": 1C-107; see *FA:ED* I, p. 275–76.

199. "he stayed inside": *AC*-83 and *LP*-43; see *FA:ED* II, p. 185.

199. "My dearest brothers": *AC*-86 and *LP*-47; *FA:ED* II, p. 190.

200. "I want to write": *MP*-100; see *FA:ED* III, p. 347.

200. The original Umbrian text of the "Canticle" has been published by AF,
pp. 566–67; the English is that of the editors of *FA:ED* I, pp. 113–14. The canticle
appears in slightly different form in *MP*-120 (*FA:ED* III, pp. 367–68).

202. "We are minstrels": *AC*-83; *FA:ED* II, p. 186.

202. For "Jubilemus Omnes," see Guéranger, p. 237 (French edition).

202. "So pleases me": From *The Litany of Love* by Vidal of Toulouse; see Smith,
p. 25.

203. On *per* in the "Canticle," see, e.g., Susanna Peters Coy, "The Problem of
'Per' in the *Cantico di Frate Sole* of Saint Francis," *Modern Language Notes* 91 (1976):
1–11.

204. The cauterization of FA's eyes and ears was recorded in *AC*-86 (*FA:ED* II, p. 190); 1C-101 (*FA:ED* I, p. 271); *LP*-48 (Habig, pp. 1026–27); 2C-166 and 3C-14 (*FA:ED* II, pp. 354–55 and 408–9); and *MP*-115 (*FA:ED* III, pp. 363–64). On the mixture poured into the eyes, see Octavian Schmucki, O.F.M. Cap. (trans. Edward Hagman, O.F.M. Cap.), "The Illnesses of Francis During the Last Years of His Life," *GR* 13, no. 1 (1999): 38–39.

206. "and then the swelling": 1C-105; see *FA:ED* I, p. 274. At least one scholar believes Francis ultimately succumbed to liver cancer; see J. R. Passalacqua, "Sobre las causas de la muerte de san Francisco de Asís," *Estudios franciscanos* 90 (1989): 135–41.

206. "I do not wish": *MP*-107; see *FA:ED* III, p. 356.

206. "There was a savage": *LP*-44; see Habig, pp. 1022–23.

207. The verses added by FA to the "Canticle" are published in AF, p. 577, and translated in *FA:ED* I, p. 114.

207. "Lord, just as I believe": *AC*-5; see *FA:ED* II, p. 120.

207. "Go and tell Lady Clare": *MP*-108; see *FA:ED* III, p. 357.

208. "He ate only": The visit of Jacoba is described in *AC*-8; see *FA:ED* II, pp. 122–23.

208. "They are birds": 3C-32; see *FA:ED* II, p. 415.

209. "dearly loved": *LP*-110; see Habig, p. 1087.

209. "Tell me": *AC*-100; see *FA:ED* II, p. 203.

209. The last verse of the "Canticle" has been printed in AF, pp. 602–3, and translated in *FA:ED* I, p. 114. The "second death" refers to his own death; the first death was Christ's.

211. "All things are yours": 1 Corinthians 3, 21. 23.

211. "mysticism comes into the open air": Underhill, *Mysticism*, pp. 460–61.

214. "I am not ashamed": 2 Timothy 1, 12.

214. "Goodbye": 1C-108; see *FA:ED* I, pp. 276–77.

215. "When you see": 2C-217; see *FA:ED* II, p. 388.

215. "I have done": 2C-214; *FA:ED* II, p. 386.

215. "Many birds": *AC*-14; see *FA:ED* II, p. 129.

Bibliography

Allen, Paul M., and Joan de Ris Allen. *Francis of Assisi's Canticle of the Creatures.* New York: Continuum, 1997.

Armstrong, Regis J., O.F.M. Cap. *Saint Francis of Assisi: Writings for a Gospel Life.* New York: Crossroad, 1994.

Armstrong, Regis J., O.F.M. Cap., and Ignatius C. Brady, trans. *Francis and Clare: The Complete Works.* Ramsey, N.J.: Paulist Press, 1982.

Armstrong, Regis J., O.F.M. Cap.; J. A. Wayne Hellmann, O.F.M. Conv.; and William J. Short, O.F.M., eds. *Francis of Assisi: Early Documents.* Vol. 1, *The Saint.* Vol. 2, *The Founder.* Vol. 3, *The Prophet.* New York, London and Manila: New City Press, 1999–2001.

Bartoli, Marco. *Clare of Assisi.* London: Darton, Longman and Todd, 1993.

Basetti-Sani, Giacomo. *Mohammed.* Florence: Volta, 1941.

Bishop, Morris. *The Horizon Book of the Middle Ages.* New York: American Heritage, 1968.

Blaise, Clark. *Time Lord: Sir Sanford Fleming and the Creation of Standard Time.* New York: Pantheon, 2001.

Bodo, Murray. *Francis: The Journey and the Dream.* Chicago: St. Anthony Messenger Press, 1972 and 1988.

————. *The Way of St. Francis.* Garden City, N.Y.: Doubleday, 1984.

Bodo, Murray, and Susan Saint Sing. *A Retreat with Francis and Clare of Assisi.* Cincinnati: St. Anthony Messenger Press, 1996.

Boff, Leonardo. *The Prayer of Saint Francis.* New York: Orbis, 2001.

Bonazzi, Luigi. *Storia di Perugia dalle origini al 1860.* 2 vols. Perugia: Boncompagni, 1875–79.

Brady, Ignatius. *The Legend and Writings of Saint Clare of Assisi.* St. Bonaventure, N.Y.: Franciscan Institute, 1953.

Brooke, Rosalind B. *The Coming of the Friars.* Vol. 24 of *Historical Problems: Studies and Documents,* edited by G. R. Elton. London: Allen & Unwin, 1975.

Brooke, Rosalind, and Christopher Brooke. *Popular Religion in the Middle Ages: Western Europe 1000–1300.* London: Thames and Hudson, 1984.

Brown, Raphael [Beverly H. Brown]. *Franciscan Mystic: The Life of Blessed Brother Giles of Assisi, Companion of St. Francis*. Garden City, N.Y.: Hanover House, 1962.

———. *The Roots of St. Francis*. Chicago: Franciscan Herald Press, 1982.

Brunette, Pierre, O.F.M. (trans. Paul Lachance, O.F.M., and Kathryn Krug). *Francis of Assisi and His Conversions*. Quincy, Ill.: Franciscan Press, 1997.

Butler's Lives of the Saints. 12 vols. London: Burns and Oates; Collegeville, Minn.: The Liturgical Press, 1996–2000.

Byrne, Lavinia. *The Life and Wisdom of Francis of Assisi*. New York: Alba House, 1998.

Carney, Margaret, O.S.F. *The First Franciscan Woman: Clare of Assisi and Her Form of Life*. Quincy, Ill.: Franciscan Press, 1993.

Chesterton, G. K. *Saint Francis of Assisi*. London: Hodder and Stoughton, 1923; New York: Doubleday Image, 1990.

Cook, William R. *Francis of Assisi: The Way of Poverty and Humility*. Vol. 1, *The Way of the Christian Mystics*. Collegeville, Minn.: Michael Glazier/The Liturgical Press, 1989.

Cook, William R., and Ronald B. Herzman. *The Medieval World View: An Introduction*. New York and Oxford: Oxford University Press, 1983.

Cunningham, Lawrence S., ed. *Brother Francis—An Anthology of Writings By and About St. Francis of Assisi*. New York: Harper and Row, 1972.

Daniélou, Jean. *Sacramentum futuri: Études sur les origines de la typologie biblique*. Paris: Beauchesne, 1950.

Dawson, Christopher. *The Formation of Christendom*. New York: Sheed and Ward, 1967.

De Beer, Francis, O.F.M. *François, que disait-on de toi?* Paris: Éditions du Seuil, 1977.

Deiss, Lucien (trans. Benet Weatherhead). *Early Sources of the Liturgy*. Collegeville, Minn.: Liturgical Press, 1967.

de la Bedoyere, Michael. *Francis: A Biography of the Saint of Assisi*. New York: Harper and Row, 1962.

de Robeck, Nesta. *Saint Clare of Assisi*. Chicago: Franciscan Herald Press, 1980.

———. *St. Francis of Assisi, His Holy Life and Love of Poverty*. Chicago: Franciscan Herald Press, 1964.

Downey, Michael, ed. *The New Dictionary of Catholic Spirituality*. Collegeville, Minn.: Michael Glazier/The Liturgical Press, 1993.

Eccleston, Thomas of. *Fratris Thomae vulgo dicti de Eccleston Tractatus de Adventu Fratrum Minorum in Angliam*. Edited by A. G. Little. Manchester, Eng.: The University Press, 1951.

Engelbert, Omer (trans. Eve Marie Cooper). *Saint Francis of Assisi—A Biography*. 2nd English ed. Revised and augmented by Ignatius Brady, O.F.M., and Raphael Brown. Chicago: Franciscan Herald Press, 1965.

Esser, Cajetan, O.F.M. (trans. Aedan Daly, O.F.M., and Dr. Irina Lynch). *Origins of the Franciscan Order*. Chicago: Franciscan Herald Press, 1970.

Fortini, Arnaldo (trans. Helen Moak). *Francis of Assisi*. New York: Crossroad, 1981 and 1992; orig. *Nova Vita di San Francesco*. Assisi: Tipografia Porziuncola, 1959.

Freedman, David Noel, ed. *The Anchor Bible Dictionary*. 6 vols. New York: Doubleday, 1992.

Frugoni, Chiara. *Franceso e l'invenzione delle stimmate: Una storia per parole e immagini fino a Bonaventura e Giotto*. Turin: Einaudi, 1993.

———(trans. John Bowden). *Francis of Assisi: A Life*. New York: Continuum, 1999.

Giandomenico, R. P. Nicola. *Art and History: Assisi*. Florence: Editrice Bonechi, 2001.

Golubovich, Girolamo. *Biblioteca bio-bibliografica della Terra Santa e dell'Oriente francescano*. 24 vols. Quaracchi: Ad Claras Aquas, 1906–1927.

Green, Julien (trans. Peter Heinegg). *God's Fool: The Life and Times of Francis of Assisi*. New York: Harper and Row, 1985. Translation of *Frère François* (Paris: Éditions du Seuil, 1983).

Grousett, René. *Histoire des croisades et du royaume de Jérusalem*. 3 vols. Paris, 1941.

Guéranger, Dom Prosper. *L'Année Liturgique: L'Avent*. Paris: Oudin, 1876. Translated as *The Liturgical Year: Advent* (London: Stanbrooke, 1895; New York: Benziger, 1910).

Habig, Marion A., ed. *St. Francis of Assisi, Writings and Early Biographies: English Omnibus of the Sources for the Life of St. Francis*. 2 vols. Quincy, Ill.: Franciscan Press, 1991.

Hazard, David. *A Day in Your Presence*. Minneapolis: Bethany House, 1992.

Hermann, Placid, O.F.M., trans. *XIIIth Century Chronicles: Jordan of Giano, Thomas of Eccleston and Salimbene degli Adami*. Chicago: Franciscan Herald Press, 1961.

Heywood, William. *A History of Perugia*. New York: G. P. Putnam's Sons, 1910.

Huizinga, Johan. *The Waning of the Middle Ages*. Mineola, N.Y.: Dover, 1999. (Republication of the 1924 English translation by F. Hopman of the Dutch original, published in 1919.)

Huygens, R. B. C. *Lettres de Jacques de Vitry*. Leiden: Brill, 1960.

Iriarte, Lázaro. *Franciscan History*. Chicago: Franciscan Herald Press, 1982.

Jewett, Sophie. *God's Troubadour: The Story of Saint Francis of Assisi*. New York: Thomas Y. Crowell, 1910.

Jörgensen, Johannes (trans. T. O'Conor Sloane). *Saint Francis of Assisi: A Biography*. Garden City, N.Y.: Doubleday Image, 1955. (Original Danish publication, 1912.)

Kirvan, John, ed. *Peace of Heart*. Notre Dame: Ave Maria Press, 1995.

Klepec, Sister Elizabeth Marie, O.S.F. *Daily Readings with St. Francis of Assisi*. Springfield, Ill.: Templegate, 1988.

Komonchak, Joseph A., Mary Collins, and Dermot A. Lane, eds. *The New Dictionary of Theology*. Wilmington, Del.: Michael Glazier, 1987.

Küng, Hans (trans. John Bowden). *The Catholic Church—A Short History*. New York: Modern Library, 2001.

Lackner, Bede Karl, and Kenneth Roy Philp. *Essays on Medieval Civilization*. Walter Prescott Webb Memorial Lectures. Austin: University of Texas Press, 1978.

Lambert, Malcolm. *Medieval Heresy: Popular Movements from the Gregorian Reform to the Reformation*. 2nd ed. Oxford: Blackwell, 1992.

Langeli, Attilio Bartoli. *Frate Francesco d'Assisi*. Spoleto: Centro Italiano di Studi sull'Alto Medievo, 1994.

Leclercq, Jean (trans. Catherine Misrahi). *The Love of Learning and the Desire for God: A Study of Monastic Culture*. New York: Fordham University Press, 1957.

Lunghi, Elvio. *The Basilica of St. Francis in Assisi*. New York: Riverside, 1996.

Mayer, Hans Eberhard (trans. John Gillingham). *The Crusades*. Oxford: Oxford University Press, 1972.

McBrien, Richard P. *Lives of the Popes*. San Francisco: HarperSanFrancisco, 1997.

—————, ed. *The HarperCollins Encyclopedia of Catholicism*. San Francisco: HarperSanFrancisco, 1995.

McKenzie, John L., S.J. *Dictionary of the Bible*. Milwaukee: Bruce Publishing Co., 1965.

McNally, Robert E., S.J. *The Unreformed Church*. New York: Sheed and Ward, 1965.

Moorman, John. *A History of the Franciscan Order from Its Origins to the Year 1517*. Oxford: Clarendon, 1968.

Murray, Alexander. *Reason and Society in the Middle Ages*. Oxford: Oxford University Press, 1978.

O'Sullivan, Ivo, O.F.M., trans. *Golden Words: The Sayings of Brother Giles of Assisi*. Chicago: Franciscan Herald Press, 1990.

Peterson, Ingrid, O.S.F. *Clare of Assisi*. Quincy, Ill.: Franciscan Press, 1993.

Powell, James M. *Anatomy of a Crusade: 1213–1221*. Philadelphia: University of Pennsylvania Press, 1986.

Rahner, Karl, ed. *Encyclopedia of Theology: The Concise* Sacramentum Mundi. New York: Crossroad, 1986.

Ryan, John K., trans. *The Confessions of St. Augustine*. Garden City, N.Y.: Doubleday Image, 1960.

Ryan, William Granger, trans. *The Golden Legend of Jacobus de Voragine*. 2 vols. Princeton: Princeton University Press, 1993.

Sabatier, Paul. *La Vie de Saint François d'Assise*. Paris: Fischbacher, 1894. ET: *The Life of Saint Francis of Assisi* (trans. Louise Seymour Houghton). New York: Charles Scribner's Sons, 1899.

Santoni, A. *Oculistica*. Milano: Ulrico Hoepli, 1968.

Schmucki, Octavian, O.F.M. Cap. (trans. Canisius F. Connors, O.F.M.). *The Stigmata of St. Francis of Assisi: A Critical Investigation in the Light of Thirteenth-Century Sources*. St. Bonaventure, N.Y.: Franciscan Institute Publications, 1991.

Setton, Kenneth M., ed. *A History of the Crusades*. Vol. 11, *The Later Crusades, 1189–1311*, edited by Robert Lee Wolff and Harry W. Hazard. Madison: University of Wisconsin Press, 1969.

Short, William. *The Franciscans*. Wilmington, Del.: Michael Glazier, 1989.

Smith, Huston. *Why Religion Matters: The Fate of the Human Spirit in an Age of Disbelief.* San Francisco: HarperSanFrancisco, 2001.

Smith, John Holland. *Francis of Assisi.* New York: Charles Scribner's Sons, 1972.

Spoto, Donald. *The Hidden Jesus: A New Life.* New York: St. Martin's Press, 1998.

Straub, Gerard Thomas. *The Sun and Moon over Assisi: A Personal Encounter with Francis and Clare.* Cincinnati: St. Anthony Messenger Press, 2000.

Trexler, Richard C. *Naked Before the Father: The Renunciation of Francis of Assisi.* Humana Civilitas, vol. 9. New York: Peter Lang, 1989.

Underhill, Evelyn. *Mysticism.* 1911. Reprint, New York: Doubleday Image, 1990.

Veblen, Thorstein. *The Theory of the Leisure Class.* Boston: Houghton Mifflin, 1899.

Vitry, Jacques de. *Epistolae.* Fribourg: Fragnière, 1903.

von Galli, Mario, S.J. *Living Our Future: Francis of Assisi and the Church of Tomorrow.* Chicago: Franciscan Herald Press, 1972.

Vorreux, Damien (trans. Marilyn Archer and Paul Lachance). *A Franciscan Symbol: The Tau.* Chicago: Franciscan Herald Press, 1977.

Winston, Clara, and Richard Winston. *The Horizon Book of Daily Life in the Middle Ages.* New York: American Heritage/McGraw-Hill, 1975.

Index

About the Author

Reluctant Saint: The Life of Francis of Assisi is Donald Spoto's 19th published book.

The author earned a B.A. degree summa cum laude in Greek and Latin from Iona College. He then received his M.A. and Ph.D. degrees in theology at Fordham University, where he concentrated in New Testament Studies.

He taught theology and religion on the university level for many years before turning to full-time writing. He has written internationally best-selling biographies of, for example, Alfred Hitchcock, Tennessee Williams, Laurence Olivier, Ingrid Bergman and Jacqueline Kennedy Onassis—all of them published in many languages worldwide.

Of his book *The Hidden Jesus: A New Life, Publishers Weekly* said, "Spoto cannily weaves literary criticism, historical research and theological scholarship into his story of the life and work of history's most enduring figure, and he writes with impressive clarity and pace." The *Toronto Star* summed up the critical consensus about this book, calling it "easily the finest life of Christ to come along in years."

Donald Spoto is a member of the board of directors of Human Rights Watch, of Death Penalty Focus and of the Youth Law Center. He resides in Los Angeles.

FOR THE BEST IN PAPERBACKS, LOOK FOR THE Ⓟ

In every corner of the world, on every subject under the sun, Penguin represents quality and variety—the very best in publishing today.

For complete information about books available from Penguin—including Penguin Classics, Penguin Compass, and Puffins—and how to order them, write to us at the appropriate address below. Please note that for copyright reasons the selection of books varies from country to country.

In the United States: Please write to *Penguin Group (USA), P.O. Box 12289 Dept. B, Newark, New Jersey 07101-5289* or call 1-800-788-6262.

In the United Kingdom: Please write to *Dept. EP, Penguin Books Ltd, Bath Road, Harmondsworth, West Drayton, Middlesex UB7 0DA.*

In Canada: Please write to *Penguin Books Canada Ltd, 10 Alcorn Avenue, Suite 300, Toronto, Ontario M4V 3B2.*

In Australia: Please write to *Penguin Books Australia Ltd, P.O. Box 257, Ringwood, Victoria 3134.*

In New Zealand: Please write to *Penguin Books (NZ) Ltd, Private Bag 102902, North Shore Mail Centre, Auckland 10.*

In India: Please write to *Penguin Books India Pvt Ltd, 11 Panchsheel Shopping Centre, Panchsheel Park, New Delhi 110 017.*

In the Netherlands: Please write to *Penguin Books Netherlands bv, Postbus 3507, NL-1001 AH Amsterdam.*

In Germany: Please write to *Penguin Books Deutschland GmbH, Metzlerstrasse 26, 60594 Frankfurt am Main.*

In Spain: Please write to *Penguin Books S. A., Bravo Murillo 19, 1° B, 28015 Madrid.*

In Italy: Please write to *Penguin Italia s.r.l., Via Benedetto Croce 2, 20094 Corsico, Milano.*

In France: Please write to *Penguin France, Le Carré Wilson, 62 rue Benjamin Baillaud, 31500 Toulouse.*

In Japan: Please write to *Penguin Books Japan Ltd, Kaneko Building, 2-3-25 Koraku, Bunkyo-Ku, Tokyo 112.*

In South Africa: Please write to *Penguin Books South Africa (Pty) Ltd, Private Bag X14, Parkview, 2122 Johannesburg.*